Praise for *Endless Referrals*

"If you're serious about your sales career, whether you are selling a product, service, or yourself, master the contents of this book and you will practically guarantee your future success."
—Tom Hopkins, author of *How to Master the Art of Selling*

"Bob Burg opens the floodgates to Fort Knox with this book. I like the simple, easy to understand, practical way he outlines the exact way to find endless referrals. A treasure."
—Dottie Walters, author of *Speak & Grow Rich*

"Bob Burg has long been the authority on connecting with clients and building win-win relationships. Endless Referrals *should be required reading for sales professionals and entrepreneurs everywhere."*
—Gary Keller, Founder and Chairman of the Board of Keller Williams Realty Intl. and *New York Times* best-selling author of *The Millionaire Real Estate Investor* and *The Millionaire Real Estate Agent*

"A no-nonsense approach to building your business through relationships."
—Jane Applegate, syndicated *Los Angeles Times* columnist

"Bob Burg's masterful understanding of how to leverage professional and personal relationships will challenge your most basic assumptions about selling, and transform the way you think about building your business. Endless Referrals *is a rare gem, and essential reading for anyone who wants to generate a stream of high-quality prospects and referrals."*
—Miriam Lawrence, Director, Horsesmouth LLC (an online publication serving financial advisors) and author of *Automatic Referrals: How to Instill Discipline in Your Referral Strategy and Guide Your Clients to Deliver Perfect Prospects Every Time*

"As a former vice president for the Long-Term Care division of a Fortune 100 company, I brought Bob in to help our agent staff increase business and market share. We asked him to help us change our marketing approach to include a Referral Mindset. It isn't easy to make that adjustment for an agent staff used to working exclusively with direct mail leads and existing clients.

"Through Bob's personal involvement and techniques, we had Great Success immediately! Business volume to our new targeted market increased by 300% in just 3 MONTHS! Bob's program continued to be so successful, we brought him in to speak to our entire national sales force, and took his program company-wide! Bob really helped us change how we were doing business!"
—Dave Brandt, Principal, Financial Visions, LLC

"Burg is known by those in the personal development business as the master of networking and referral-based marketing and for good reason; his information works, and works big! This revised version is his best effort yet. Buy this book, follow what he says and you will profit greatly."
—David Riklan, Founder, SelfGrowth.com and Author of *Self Improvement: The Top 101 Experts Who Help Us Improve Our Lives*

"Bob Burg has an uncommon gift for turning everyday contacts into a wealth of resources. Bob's journey and personal track record make him a trusted guide and friend to anyone who aspires to become well-known in any industry. Take it from one who knows. I read the original version of this book many years ago so that I too, could grow my business. I followed his suggestions word-for-word and today have very three successful businesses because I put the principles shared in Endless Referrals *into practice. I am very excited about this newest version. Inside the pages you will find cutting-edge advice interwoven with the thoughts and quotes of some of society's most successful leaders.*

Bob Burg gives the reader an honest look at what networking and building your referral base is all about. He is able to share his life experiences as well as those of countless others, and within those stories, find common nuggets we all relate to. Endless Referrals *is practical, well thought out and easy-to-apply. While comprehensive in scope, it is easy to read and most importantly, easy to implement. It is a must-read for anyone with a passion to grow a successful business."*
—Heidi Richards, Author, Business Coach, Inventor, "Helping Small Business Bloom"

"With more than forty years in the financial services industry, I truly believe that referrals are the most profitable and persistent source of clients. In his latest edition of Endless Referrals *Bob Burg has hit a home run! Whether new to our business, or a veteran needing an uplift, this is a 'must read' to show you step-by-step how to have a continual prospect flow."*
—Rick Denton, CLU, ChFC
Baystate Financial Services

"The world of selling is changing so improved methods and approaches are necessary to succeed. If you want to succeed in any kind of sales, you had better learn how to increase your number of quality prospects. Bob's book is the standard for networking for success and creating an endless supply of referrals. This newest version of Endless Referrals *is just what anyone in the business of helping other people get what they want, needs in order to get to the next level of sales success.*
—Harry Crosby, Regional Sales Manager for Genworth Financial and author of *Long-Term Care Insurance: The Complete Guide.* (Former Number One Producer in the U.S. of Long-Term Care Insurance Policies)

"I loved this book. I have read many books on Networking and this is clear, concise and very easy to read! The '10 Networking Questions' are right on the nose! This book will help you with your career and every relationship you have."
     —Rick Frishman co-author, *Networking Magic* and *Guerrilla Publicity*

"Reading Endless Referrals *was worth the price of a Harvard MBA. What a great way to have new business beating a path to your door! Free advertising, free pre-sold prospects, free business! A true breakthrough in real world prospecting."*
     —Tom "Big Al" Schreiter, author of *Big Al Tells All*

"Bob Burg has a knack for connecting with people. In Endless Referrals *he lays out his techniques in a simple, easy-to-follow format so that you too can develop a knack in connecting with people. This book is well written, well researched, and absolutely practical. I highly recommend it."*
     —Jim Cathcart, author of *Relationship Selling* and *The Acorn Principle*

"Bob Burg has just taken away all the excuses for not finding clients by showing you step-by-step how to find 'diamonds' in your 'acres.'"
     —Danny Cox, author of *Leadership When the Heat's On*

"Bob Burg knows what he's talking about, and shares that knowledge clearly and generously with the reader."
     —Rabbi Harold Kushner, author of *When Bad Things Happen to Good People*

"Networking is more than a buzzword for Bob Burg. In his book, he shows how to build and train a networking team that makes prospecting more effective and profitable for everyone."
     —Homer Smith, Editor, *Master Salesmanship*

"Bob Burg is the greatest teacher of networking in the world."
     —John Milton Fogg, author of *The Greatest Networker in the World*

"Bob Burg's book is a masterpiece! A must for anyone in sales and for anyone wanting to expand their financial and relationship resources."
     —Anne Boe, author of *Is Your Net-Working?*

"I find Bob Burg's networking principles an essential and useful system in an age where soft touch must match high tech."
     —Robert Rosenberg, CEO, Dunkin' Donuts

Endless Referrals

Network Your Everyday Contacts into Sales

Third Edition

Bob Burg

McGraw-Hill
New York   Chicago   San Francisco   Lisbon   London
Madrid   Mexico City   Milan   New Delhi   San Juan
Seoul   Singapore   Sydney   Toronto

This publication is designed to provide accurate and authoritative information in regard to the subject matter covered. It is sold with the understanding that neither the author nor the publisher is engaged in rendering legal, accounting, or other professional service. If legal advice or other expert assistance is required, the services of a competent professional person should be sought.

—From a Declaration of Principles jointly adopted by Committee of the American Bar Association and a Committee of Publishers.

McGraw-Hill books are available at special quantity discounts to use as premiums and sales promotions, or for use in corporate training programs. For more information, please write to the Director of Special Sales, McGraw-Hill Professional, Two Penn Plaza, New York, NY 10121-2298. Or contact your local bookstore.

Gender Usage

The author feels very strongly regarding the utilization of gender equality in his writing. The pronouns his and her, he and she, etc., have been used interchangeably and randomly throughout the text.

This book is printed on acid-free paper.

Contents

Preface

From the on-the-street salesperson to the attorney, from the entrepreneur to the accountant, endless referrals are important. From the financial advisor to the architect, from the automotive sales professional to the Realtor®, endless referrals are crucial. From the home-based business owner to the insurance agent, and from the network marketer to the software consultant, endless referrals are the cornerstone of business. Without being solidly based on endless referrals from our customers, clients, and everyday contacts, the fate of any business becomes a nerve-wracking mystery, dependent on the whims of current economic conditions and buying moods.

In this book, I show you a system for putting together the marketing aspect of your business in such a way that you'll never again have to ask yourself that age-old question feared by salespeople and entrepreneurs everywhere, "Who do I speak to next, now that my original list of names has run out?"

Why is this so crucial? Because without a list of names of people to contact and offer your products or services, *you have no business*.

I call this names list your "inventory." Most people think of their *business inventory* as the excellent products or services they sell. That is certainly a legitimate definition of inventory, but it's not what I'm talking about here. In fact, I'd rather refer to the actual products and services you and I sell as "commodities."

The purpose of this book is not to discuss your particular commodity. Of course, the commodity itself should be excellent, and you want to be able to stand behind it and fully guarantee it. That goes without question. But when I say *inventory*, I'm talking about *the number of quality names on your list*—names of people to whom you have easy access precisely because you've formed the types of relationships we'll be discussing in this book.

Every business person knows that no matter what your business, without inventory, you're *out of* business. And this most certainly holds true for this definition of the term. Having quality names on your list is the lifeblood of your business—and having an *endless* supply of quality names makes for a vibrant, healthy business!

One reason this is so important is for the impact it has on your confidence level. Without a strong list of names, every time someone tells you, "No, I'm not interested," you panic a little and lose just a bit of your "posture."

What is posture? I define posture as "when you care…but not that much!" In other words, while you would certainly prefer that the person be interested in doing business with you, you're not emotionally attached to the results. If he's interested, great. If he's not interested, that's okay, too. You're prepared to end the conversation in a very polite and gracious manner and move on to your next prospect. That's posture.

Prospects respond positively when a salesperson has posture, because they assume that if you value yourself enough to act in that manner, your product or service must also be of value.

What is the best way to develop true posture? Simply by having such a large list of quality names that you never, ever have to be concerned by someone not being interested in doing business with you. You'll always remain polite, but again, you won't be emotionally attached to the results. You'll know that making your product or service available and presenting in the right way is your job; the decision as to whether or not to purchase is your prospect's job.

Please remember this key statement:

The amount of posture you have and the amount of posture you display is directly proportional to the number of quality names on your list—your inventory.

There is practically nothing worse for your business than constantly worrying about how to find that next person to whom you can present your product or service. Yet that is usually exactly what happens when you have no system for acquiring new prospects.

A business without a steady flow (or even better, a flood!) of referrals always keeps you on the defensive, knowing that it's up to you to come up with new people to talk to. On the other hand, a business based on endless referrals fills you with peace of mind. Having a system for acquiring endless referrals means going to sleep at night knowing you'll have new business waiting for you the next day, and the next, and the next—for as long as you desire.

"So if we're talking about endless referrals, are we talking about endless prospecting?"

No. Prospecting is certainly one element in generating endless referrals, and always will be; but these days, the rules of the game are changing. Standard prospecting techniques no longer work the way they once did. The average consumer today is more knowledgeable, is less trusting, and wants to have a *know you, like you, trust you* relationship with her salesperson. Nowadays, in order to build that business based on endless referrals, we do it another way. We *network!*

Unfortunately, the term "network" is often misunderstood. Does it mean handing out business cards? Or aggressively shaking hands with everyone who comes within three feet? Do we tell people we are networking? Where can we do it? Exactly what is networking, anyway?

In essence, networking is the mutual give and take that results in a winning situation for everyone involved.

The idea of networking has always existed in some form, as in the "old boys' network," for instance, or "the grapevine." It came into prominence as a business strategy only during the 1980s and has since been finely honed as an art and science. Yet most people are not aware of this development.

I realized this as I listened to the great humorist Roger Masquelier tell a story about networking at a National Speakers Association convention. "Of course," Roger added after bringing up the term, "in the old days, we just called it *talking*." This brought laughter from the audience, and thousands of heads nodded in agreement.

At that moment, I realized that this is what most people actually believe. That networking is merely "talking," jabbering incessantly to anyone who will listen why they should be doing business with you, along with indiscriminately handing out business cards.

It isn't.

As misunderstood as networking is, there is a real need for individuals and companies in modern business to use it effectively.

Why? Because in today's tough business climate, where competition is so incredibly fierce and many markets are already saturated, people are realizing that it's vital to be able to cultivate new business without spending a lot of money doing it.

Here is how I define networking:

Networking is the cultivating of mutually beneficial, give-and-take, win-win relationships.

One result of this process, and the one that directly concerns us in this book, can be the development of a large and diverse group of people who gladly and continually refer a lot of business to us, while we do the same for them.

Throughout this book you will have the opportunity to meet and learn from people who have successfully developed businesses based on referrals by using the principles and methods described. Do each use all of them? Not at all. Certain people find that some ideas are more applicable than others to their particular profession or method of operation.

Endless Referrals, in other words, is based not on theory or on ideas that just look good on paper. It is based on a system of time-tested, proven principles and ideas that have worked for many, many people.

As you read through these pages, you may find yourself saying at times, "That particular idea wouldn't work for me," or, "I could never see myself doing that," or, "It won't work in this part of the country or with my particular customers." If that occurs, you have two choices. One is to not even try it. The other, more profitable choice is to mold the principle involved to your particular business style and type of work. Don't let the particulars get in your way: The system I'll be describing is based on foundational principles—and they *work*.

If you follow this system with a ready, willing, able, and open mind, you too will soon find yourself cultivating a network of endless referrals!

Bob Burg

Note on the Revised Edition

Well, here it is, 2005, six years since I last revised this book (the original was published in 1994, the revised edition in 1999), and people have been suggesting that it's time for another revision. I agree. Why? Because in the past six years, business and the various methods for acquiring more of it have continued to evolve.

Please, don't get me wrong: the principles haven't changed. Not a bit. The essence of selling and of the Endless Referrals System® remains the same:

All things being equal, people will do business with, and refer business to, those people they know, like, and trust.

But as technology continues to evolve at lightning speed, strategies also continue to change, and more and more people continue to fight for what appears to be an ever-shrinking piece of the same business pie. (Actually, my own belief is that we live in an abundant, limitless universe where lack never need appear—but for now, this is the way of the world and we need to know how to work effectively within those parameters.)

For the 1999 rewrite of *Endless Referrals*, I wrote (with the help of experts in the field) an entire chapter on using the Internet, explaining much of the basics involved in this technology, which had just reached its "tipping point." Today, of course, we've learned a good deal more about the Internet, and its use in business has reached the stage where its importance is self-evident: practically everyone reading this book either has an Internet presence already or is at least using e-mail to a significant degree. In this new edition, therefore, while I have again included a chapter on "Using the Internet to Help Build Your Network," the influence of the online world has spread throughout the book.

We also provide examples from businesses not mentioned in the previous two editions. As I've grown in my own speaking, writing, and consulting practice, I've had more experiences myself and wish to share these with you.

We will look in some detail at the mindset of the salesperson as it relates to referrals—a topic I didn't discuss in either of the first two versions, and which in this edition attained such importance that it grew into two chapters (Chapters 11 and 12). In working with several companies who wanted to move from a dependency on company-generated leads to a "referral mindset," I discovered that the most difficult part of the whole process was just that: the mindset of the salesperson. The methodology is simple; repositioning the salesperson's thought process turned out to be crucial. Happily, the results were often spectacular, and it seemed too valuable a tool not to share with you. So, why is it that so many salespeople don't ask for referrals? We'll find out why, and what to do about it.

How to network effectively to find a new job or career, another topic that was not in the previous two editions, is something we'll discuss in Chapter 16. I can't tell you how often I'm asked about this, and because it seems more and more relevant with each passing year, it seemed a worthwhile subject to provide some guidance in here. Along with my own observations, I also share advice from a couple of the top people in that field.

In this edition we also look more at what is known as "Attraction Marketing." In past editions, I've taught readers how to "go out and get the business" (by building mutually beneficial, give-and-take, win-win relationships). Now we'll also explore another tack that's worked for me and many others, by providing a method for prospects to "identify" themselves as such so that you can then build the relationship from there. This will save you a lot of time while ensuring that you always have good, qualified prospects waiting to fill your "sales funnel" or "profit funnel." Be sure to check this out in Chapter 14.

Even in this chapter, however, we are in no way abandoning the Endless Referrals System®. No way, no how. The basic premise of *know you, like you, trust you* applies just as much in this aspect of marketing and selling as in any other. We are simply providing more options and allowing for a richer mix of really good methods for developing new prospects, customers, and clients.

After all, the name of the game is to continually develop more and more business, and to have a lot of fun while doing it. My goal with this revised edition of *Endless Referrals* is for you to be able to use this information more than ever as a foundation to help you reach your personal and business goals and achieve your dream of financial freedom.

Acknowledgments

There are so many people I need to thank that it would take a separate book just to list them. Instead, let me thank several groups of people and apologize in advance for the many, many friends and teachers along the way that I'm not able to acknowledge here only because of limitations in my allotted space.

One is the National Speakers Association, which has more than 3500 of the nicest, most supportive, sharing and caring people in the world.

Also, my fellow speakers, authors, and salespeople who were so willing to lend their ideas and success stories to this book for the benefit of my readers. Thank you so much.

Those who gave me moral and written support when it was needed (which was always). Lloyd Jones, a wonderful agent and entrepreneur and a true salesperson, and Donya Dickerson at McGraw-Hill: your knowledge of the publishing business, encouragement, and professionalism were a guiding light. And you were incredibly great to work with, as well.

I must thank my office staff, who throughout the years have helped make my speaking habit possible by keeping me on the road constantly. (Come to think of it, that's probably where they like me best!) Thank you for your loyalty, love, and support.

Thank you to Thom Scott, who worked hard to make the chapter on Attraction Marketing the chapter it is (and it's a *good* one!). It's mainly his expertise that is featured there.

John David Mann, my editor on several projects now and co-author on another: thank you, my friend, for helping to polish this edition and make it shine. You write my stuff better than *I* do.

Thank you to my clients, without whom I would not have an audience nor the pleasure of being involved in such a wonderful, rewarding career.

And, of course, my thanks to you, the reader, for your participation, feedback, and help in making this book a best-seller.

To each and every one of you, I wish you the best of success—
and great networking!

Dedication

To Mom and Dad—Your love, support and encouragement have kept me going for 47 years. Words will never be able to describe how much I love you and what you mean to me.

To Samantha and Mark, my beautiful niece/goddaughter and handsome nephew. I love you!

CHAPTER 1

Networking: What It Is and What It Does for You!

The late Og Mandino was an extremely successful man. A renowned speaker and storyteller, he is probably best known as author of the classic best-seller, *The Greatest Salesman in the World*, a book that has sold more than 30 million copies. Yes, that's 30 *million* copies! And that was only one book. His others—many of them classics in their own right and all with powerful, life-changing lessons—also continue to sell extremely well.

Earlier in my career, and just a few years before Og passed away, I had the honor on several occasions of presenting just before he did at large public events. At one of these events, I told him it was one of my biggest thrills to be his "opening act"; he just laughed and said the honor was his. He was a very kind and humble man.

A year or two earlier, in July 1992, Og was the keynote speaker at the annual National Speakers Association convention. For about 45 minutes he talked about the fact that nobody who is truly successful ever does it alone. He talked about his wife, his family, his associates and friends—all the people who had helped him through the rough times and over the hurdles. And, if you're familiar with Og's story and personal transformation, you know those rough times and hurdles were many.

But What Does That Have to Do with Networking?

Let's go back to the definition of networking from the Preface: the cultivating of mutually beneficial, give-and-take, win-win relationships.

Now let's take a look at how Webster's dictionary defines the term *network:* 1. Any arrangement of fabric or parallel wires, threads, etc., crossed at regular intervals by others fastened to them so as to leave open space; netting; mesh. 2. A thing resembling this in some way.

Now, for the purpose of this book, let's leave out the words and thoughts in both definitions (mine and Webster's) that don't apply and keep those that do. Oh, and let's substitute the word *people* for the words *fabric, parallel wires,* and *threads* in Webster's. Here is what we get:

> *Network: An arrangement of people crossed at regular intervals by other people, all of whom are cultivating mutually beneficial, give-and-take, win-win relationships with each other.*

The Basic Setup

Let's look at the first part of what we have.

```
•     •     •     •     •     •     •

•     •     •     •     •     •     •

•     •     •     •     •     •     •

•     •     •    YOU    •     •     •

•     •     •     •     •     •     •

•     •     •     •     •     •     •

•     •     •     •     •     •     •
```

Just as we are each positioned at the center of our own particular universe, each of us is also positioned at the center of our network. We realize, of course, that all the other people are positioned at the centers of their networks, and that is as it should be.

Each of the people in any given network serves as a source of support (referrals, help, information, etc.) for everyone else in that network.

Those who know how to use the tremendous strength of a network realize this very important fact:

> We are not dependent *on* each other; nor are we independent *of* each other; we are all interdependent *with* each other.

The true strength really comes through realizing that all the people in our network are also part of other people's networks that we ourselves don't personally know. And that, indirectly, makes each of *those* people part of our network, too.

Sphere of Influence

Are you familiar with the term *sphere of influence*? Sphere of influence simply refers to the people you know—people who are somehow, in some way a part of your life, directly or indirectly (and sometimes even *very* indirectly).

Your sphere of influence includes everyone from immediate family members to distant relatives, close friends to casual acquaintances, the person who delivers the mail, the plumber, the tailor, the person who cuts your hair—practically anybody who in some way touches your life and whose life you touch.

Have you ever heard of Joe Girard? Based out of a Chevrolet dealership in Detroit, Michigan, Joe Girard was one of the world's most successful car salespeople. Actually, he was officially the *most* successful car salesperson in the world—for 14 consecutive years! That's how long he was listed in the *Guinness Book of World Records* for selling the most cars in a year's time. And not fleet sales either, but individual new car sales. Joe Girard sold oodles and oodles of cars. My feeling, and I hope it's yours too, is that anyone with that kind of record has wisdom we should be willing to listen to, if he's willing to share it.

Happily, he is. In his book, *How to Sell Anything to Anybody*, Girard explains what he calls Girard's Law of 250, which states that each of us has a personal sphere of influence of about 250 people. According to Girard, about 250 people will attend your wedding and your funeral. Here's how he arrived at that number. He once asked the funeral director at a funeral he was attending, "About how many people usually come to pay their respects?" "On average? About 250," was the response. Soon after this, Joe attended a wedding where he and asked the caterer the same question, only this time, about wedding receptions. The answer? About 250 from the bride's side and another 250 from the groom's side.

In other words, according to Girard's Law of 250, everyone knows about 250 people in his or her life important enough to invite to their wedding and have show up at their funeral. Now, even if that figure seems high (and given that not everyone in our sphere of influence will necessarily be invited to our wedding or attend our funeral), the numbers do work out, and quite well.

Here's an exercise you can do to prove this to yourself. As you're doing this, don't prejudge, prequalify or for any other reason leave someone off the list. We're doing this only to make a point. You'll understand in a moment how it ties in. By the way, the following is not meant to limit you in any way; it's just a suggestion to help get you started.

First, take a pencil and paper and write down the names of those people you know who immediately come to mind. Everybody! Don't worry about whether they qualify to purchase your product or service; that's not important for right now. Write down as many of these names as you can think of. If you're like most of us, you'll find that not many people readily come to mind. You'll learn why that is in the segment, "How to Ask for Referrals (So That You Actually Get Them)" in Chapter 6.

After you've exhausted this list, then turn to your local Yellow Pages telephone directory. Go to the letter "A" and notice all the job classifications that begin with A. Go through these one by one and write down the names of anyone and everyone you know who works in those industries or professions. Now do the same with B, then C, D, E and all the way through to Z. Examples from each would be, "Who do you know who is an A—Actuary, B—Banker, C—Chiropractor, D—Dentist…?" and so on. Write them all down. Again, no qualifying. Just write them down.

Now go to the White Pages directory to look at people's last names, beginning again with A. Who do you know with the last name, Aaron? How about Abbot, Acheson, Adair, Atkinson? And then B: Baluk, Bass, Brenner, Burns, Byers and so on. And yes, do the same with C, D, E and so on, all the way through Z.

Next go through first names. There are just over 50 male and female first names; actually there are probably many more, depending on how fancy you want to get, but even going just with the most common names: Who do you know by the name of George, Debra, Tom, Tammi, Steve, Barbara and so forth?

Now think about associations and religious, political, and business organizations in which you might be involved and write down the names of those within that framework who come to mind. If you actually have a directory, use that.

Keep writing down the names of *everyone* you can think of. Yes, your list is now growing and growing. When finished, you'll discover that the number of people you know will at least come close to 250, and that's before knowing how to effectively network. Without even trying, most of us have a sphere of influence of about 250 people.

And more importantly, so do most *other people*.

Why is that "more important"? Because, although not everyone on your initial list is a qualified prospect for whatever it is you sell, there's a good chance that those on your list know of other people who are. And those people will know of still others who are, too. Sure, there will be some crossover, that is, people whom both of you know, but that's not a problem.

And this is only the beginning. Again, this is without doing any sort of proactive networking wherein you'll meet new people and form new relationships. And many of those people, people you've never met before, know 250 or more other people you'd have no other way of ever knowing, or who would have no other way of knowing of you.

Hang on: this is about to get truly exciting.

You see, this is where, for most of us, our most lucrative sphere of influence comes into play—the one developed via the Endless Referrals System®.

Why? Because even if the new people you meet are themselves only "average" (meaning, of only mild potential value to your business), they each probably know at least 250 other people well enough that those people will attend *their* wedding and funeral, 250 people they know in some way or other. And by utilizing the Endless Referrals System®, you'll learn how to successfully meet the "above-average" contacts—those people who themselves have *very* valuable spheres of influence to which they can eventually introduce you.

Now let's tie this all together. Keeping in mind that every time you successfully go through the process of making a new person a part of your network—just one new person—you actually increase your personal sphere of influence by a potential 250 people. And since each of those 250 people also has a sphere of influence of another 250 people, adding this one new person to your network has indirectly put you into potential contact with 62,500 people! It's not hard to see how you can quickly amass an enormous sphere of influence that can soar to incredible heights.

(Of course, again, there will be some crossover and overlap, so cut that number in half, and just to be safe, cut it in half again. Come to think of it, let's cut it in half one more time. At more than 7800 people, the numbers still look pretty good, don't they? And again, that's just from one person!)

This Network Will Increase Our Sales

These days, buyers are different than they used to be. They are educated, trained, and skeptical. They are backed by consumer protection laws, as it should be. The adage *caveat emptor*, "let the buyer beware," is no longer apropos.

Probably the biggest change of all is that today's buyers are much more relationship-oriented. People want to buy from people they know, like, and trust.

That's where our network comes into play, but in a different way than you might imagine. You might be thinking, "Those people in our network already know us, like us, and trust us. They are our buyers."

No! You'll recall that not everyone on that list is a potential buyer. However, they may well be *potential referral sources*. And they are only the tip of the iceberg. All things being equal, the people who know us, like us, and trust us will tend to buy from us or refer us. But if we stop there, we are walking away from a lot of potential business.

Remember, those people are at the center of their own individual networks. They themselves can connect you to a potential 250 or more other people. Keep in mind, those 250 have their own 250. Knowing that, and knowing how to work the situation, will result in a ton of new business.

The Golden Rule

The following statement is the central premise, the foundation, of the entire Endless Referrals System®. I certainly didn't make this saying up; it's as old as the hills. And for good reason: it's an immutable law. Here it is:

> *All things being equal, people will do business with,* and refer business to, *those people they know, like, and trust.*

This is the bronze, silver, golden, and even platinum rule of networking. In other words, if two people both have similar or equal products, price, know-how, or any other determining factor that could possibly come into play, *it's the man or woman who has personally won over the prospect or referral source who will earn that sale or referral.*

The intent and theme of this entire book is to show you how to get people to know, like, and trust you.

Let's take this one step further. We also want these people to *want* to see you succeed and *want* to help you find new business. You might say, we want these people to be your Personal Walking Ambassadors. And that goal isn't particularly difficult to accomplish.

In today's high-tech world, successful, long-term selling is relationship-oriented; the more high-tech our world continues to become, the more important the relationship will grow. People want and choose to do business that way. You might say, the more high-tech, the more soft-touch, that is, the more *personal* touch matters. Relationships now rule the selling process.

Yes, now more than ever: all things being equal, people will do business with, *and refer business to*, those people they know, like, and trust.

Things Aren't Always Equal

By the same token, if all things are *not* equal, and a person cannot provide the quality, price, or whatever else is necessary, it doesn't matter how the other person feels about them, they won't get the business or referrals.

No matter how well people know us, like us, and trust us as a person, we have to be able to come through for them when they give us their business or referrals. If we can't or don't, we'll be in danger of losing not only their direct business but that of their 250-person sphere of influence as well. As Tim Sanders points out in his terrific book, *Love is the Killer App*, "Once you earn their business your performance still must be able to scale." In other words, the relationship might get you in, but then it's up to you to deliver the goods.

For instance, there is a dry cleaning company in my town. The owners and employees are lovely people who I believe *try* to do a good job. However, it just doesn't seem to work. Personally, I can honestly say I know them, like them and trust them. Trust them, that is, to do practically anything in the world for me—except clean my suits.

Now, the fact that they happen to be dry cleaners doesn't work out particularly well for them. They nearly ruined three of my best suits. They seemed to have trouble following instructions, as well. I would tell them I wanted very light starch on my shirts, but when I'd arrive to pick up my clothes, my shirts would be practically standing at attention waiting for me. (In fact, I thought I saw one of them actually walking toward the door to greet me.)

Despite my positive personal feelings about these people, it just didn't work out. After a while, I could no longer justify doing business with them directly—or giving them any referrals, either. Now, if they were delivering service at a level anywhere close to their competition, they would to this day continue to have my direct business and quite a bit of my referral business as well—and who knows how many of my referrals would in turn refer others? But they are not, so they don't.

Again, *all things being equal*, people will do business with, and refer business to, those people they know, like, and trust.

It Isn't Just What or Who You Know

Sure, we've all heard the axiom, "It isn't what you know, it's who you know." Chances are you had that saying related to you by a crusty old macho businessman type, as he sagely nodded, pleased and proud to share his eternal wisdom.

Of course, what you know is also important. Let's face it: if we want to be successful in business, we have to know what we're doing and what we're talking about. We must be able to provide proper guidance to our prospects, customers, and clients. And if we can't provide excellent (or at least adequate) service after the sale, we can rest assured we won't be doing business with that person ever again.

We will also lose out on the business of those in their 250-person sphere of influence. Why? Because nothing gets around faster than negative comments. You can also bet those comments will somehow make their way back to the original person who used his or her influence with that other person to get you the referral in the first place. That original person will then, of course, have to be removed from your "who you know" list.

But back to the "sage advice": it's true—to an extent. Certainly, in today's world of sales and business, to get the opportunity to do business with someone in the first place, who you know is often vitally important. But that's not all there is to it.

> *It isn't just what you know, and it isn't just who you know. It's also* who knows you *and what you do for a living...*

That is, when that person, or someone that person knows, needs your products, goods, or services. And:

> ...providing that first person knows you, likes you, and trusts you.

Again, your goal is to have as many new people as possible feel that they *know you, like you, and trust you*; to feel that they *want* to see you succeed and *want* to help you find new business. Do you remember I said that goal isn't particularly difficult to accomplish? Well, it isn't. How do we accomplish it? By networking.

What Networking Isn't

Since we've been discussing the basics of what networking is, let's talk a bit about what it isn't. Networking really became quite the buzzword in the late 1980s and early 1990s, and continues to be today. Everyone seems to use the word, yet many people don't really know what it is and isn't.

The term *networking* is most often thought of as what happens when someone hands his business card to everyone with whom he comes into contact. The often aggressive shoving of said business card in said contact's face is many times followed by, "Gimme a call—I'll cut you a deal," or "If you ever need to buy a whichamahoozee, I'm the one to call."

That is not networking. That is hard-selling, which is the antithesis of networking. For now, I want you to forget about business cards. Well, don't forget about them altogether—they do serve a purpose, albeit a minor one. As far as I'm concerned, business cards have three main benefits.

1. You Could Win Something

The first benefit is quite tangible, though not to be taken too seriously: you might win a free lunch at a local restaurant by dropping your business card into a fish bowl. Have you ever done that? Won a free lunch? Paid for your business cards, right? (Maybe there is such a thing as a free lunch after all.)

You can also win a door prize at an association meeting, again, by dropping your business card into a fish bowl. You could even win a free book or CD program at a seminar via the same means.

2. You Could Get a Lead

This second benefit is a more significant one, depending on your profession (although it is absolutely *not* networking): you can include your business card with your bill payments or with a tip after your meal.

We all have bills that go out each and every month—electric bill, cable TV, water, telephone, mortgage payment, and more. Doesn't it make sense that there must be someone at the other end opening the envelope?

Depending on the type of product or service you represent, if it can potentially fit anybody's needs and you will probably never get to meet that person anyway, you might as well include your business card with your bill payment. You never know what might happen. That person, or someone in her 250-person sphere of influence, might need to buy what you have to sell.

Tom Hopkins, an internationally known speaker and author of the book, *How to Master the Art of Selling*, talks about this method. When he was getting his start in real estate, he used to include his business cards with his bill payments. One day Tom got a call from a woman who said, "Mr. Hopkins, you don't know me, but my husband and I want to buy a bigger home and would like to talk to you about it." After agreeing that he'd be delighted to do just that, he asked her how she got his name. She replied, "I handle your account at the Gas Company, and I've got about two dozen of your cards in the top drawer of my desk." Apparently, she didn't know who else to call. I'm sure the fee Mr. Hopkins earned by helping that woman and her husband acquire their new home more than paid for his business cards for the rest of his life.

Granted, that's probably not going to happen very often. But if it happens even once in your selling career, that's great—you made out on it. The fact is, business cards are so inexpensive that you might as well include them any time you have the chance; you have nothing to lose.

Another thought along the same line: you can also leave your business card with your tip at the end of a restaurant meal. You never know. Your waiter or waitress, or someone in his or her 250-person sphere of influence, might need to buy what you have to sell. But when you do that, you need to make sure you leave a big enough tip; otherwise you will be remembered, but it will be for something else.

3. You Can Get Others' Cards

The third benefit is the one that matters: you can use your business card to get the other person's business card. As far as I'm concerned, this is the one truly valuable benefit of business cards, and it's so important, we'll look at in some detail in the next chapter.

Although I make light of business cards, and generally find they are not worth much more than the paper stock on which they are printed, they can have some genuine value when used correctly. Obviously, successful sales-people such as Tom Hopkins, Joe Girard, and many others who believe in them are living proof of their use as an effective business tool.

What I'm trying to point out here is that business cards *by themselves* are not about to make you, me, or anyone else successful. They are simply an extension of ourselves and what we are doing right.

What you'll find throughout this book is that networking involves giving to others and helping them succeed in their lives and careers. It's caring about the other person and his wants, needs, and desires. When going about this in a pragmatic and organized fashion—in other words, when following a specific road map or *system*—you'll find that you get back tenfold what you put out, both personally and professionally.

And that's exactly what we'll look at in the next chapter.

The System Is the Solution

Since we've seen the word, "system" several times now, this is a good time to ask the question, "What is a system, anyway, and how will it benefit you?"

One definition of a system (Webster's again) is "a set or arrangement of things so related or connected as to form a unity or organic whole." Here is another: "a set of facts, principles, rules, etc. classified or arranged in a regular, orderly form so as to show a *logical plan* linking the various parts." And yet another, which takes the concept to the next step and ties it together very nicely: "a regular, orderly way of doing something, that results in a *predictable outcome*." That word "predictable" is the crucial element: a solid, proven system takes you out of the realm of chance and random trial-and-error, and puts you on a path to reliable results.

In any area in which one might desire to succeed, whether it's building a business, losing weight, improving a relationship, or lowering a golf score, the key to success is to find a system that has been proven to work in that particular area, and then simply applying that system to your own efforts.

In fact, this idea is so crucial to our success in any endeavor, I've written a short booklet focusing purely on this idea, called *The Success Formula*. You can read it for free at www.TheSuccessFormula.com.

For our purposes, let's define a system this way:

A system is the process of predictably achieving a goal, based on a logical and specific set of how-to principles.

What a system can do *for you* is incredibly exciting. Here's how Michael Gerber, noted business consultant and author of *The E-Myth* and *The E-Myth Revisited*, explains the benefits of using a system (I'm paraphrasing here):

Systems permit ordinary people to achieve extraordinary results, predictably.

Without a system, however, even extraordinary people find it difficult to predictably achieve even ordinary results.

None of this, of course, is meant to imply that you or anyone else are "ordinary." What it does say is that if we should happen to be ordinary in terms of our ability to network, prospect, or obtain referrals, a system can help us achieve extraordinary results.

And that's what the Endless Referrals System® can do for *you*, if you simply learn it and follow it.

Key Points

- Networking is the cultivating of mutually beneficial, give-and-take, win-win relationships.
- We are not dependent *on* each other; nor are we independent *of* each other; we are all interdependent *with* each other.
- Each of us has a personal sphere of influence of about 250 people. And so does every person we meet.
- All things being equal, people will do business with, *and refer business to*, those people they know, like, and trust.
- It isn't just what you know, and it isn't just who you know. It's also *who knows you* and what you do for a living—when that person, or someone that person knows, needs your products, goods, or services. Providing that first person knows you, likes you, and trusts you.
- Business cards are not a big deal. We need them mainly to get the other person's card.
- A system is the process of predictably achieving a goal, based on a logical and specific set of how-to principles.
- A system permits ordinary people to achieve extraordinary results, predictably.

CHAPTER 2

Questions Are the Successful Networker's Most Valuable Ammunition

The great sales trainer J. Douglas Edwards was famous for uttering the phrase, "Questions are the answers." What exactly did he mean by that? Simply this: In sales, the person who asks the questions controls the conversation.

One might ask, "But wouldn't the person doing the talking control the conversation?" It would seem that way, wouldn't it? However, when we ask the right questions, we lead the other person exactly in the direction we want him to take. That's why great salespeople aren't pushy. Great salespeople *never* push. They lead!

In fact, Mr. Edwards had another statement that's right on the mark here:

The only reason for making a statement is to set up another question.

Of course, he was speaking in the context of a sales presentation. Ask questions—the right questions—that will ultimately lead a person to the right decision: buying that salesperson's product or services.

It's Just As Valuable in the Networking Process

The same principle applies equally well in networking.

Recall a point we learned in Chapter 1: Coming on strong—handing your business card to people and asking for their business or referrals right off the bat—is ineffective. Not only that, it's downright counterproductive.

What we need to do is make an impression at the first meeting that will simply elicit the *know you*, *like you*, *trust you* feelings that are necessary for a mutually beneficial, win-win relationship. We do this by asking questions—

the right questions. (And we'll discuss what the "right" questions are in a moment.)

When and Where Can We Network?

Networking opportunities occur almost every day, practically anywhere and at any time. We might expect to network at business functions, at Chamber of Commerce functions, on the golf course, in association meetings, or in organized networking or lead and referral exchange groups.

But that's only the beginning. Opportunities to meet new networking contacts and prospects also occur in places and at times when we may not realize they're there, or in situations that we may not realize are appropriate for networking.

What are some examples? At a PTA meeting, racquetball court, or night school class; in the shopping mall, on an airplane, in a casual introduction by a third party—the list goes on and on. How many times have you found yourself in one of these places, feeling certain there were some potential business contacts waiting to be discovered? But you also felt that networking would be frowned upon, that it would be considered...well, *tacky* by some? Maybe even, by yourself? Please keep this in mind:

> *If you are networking correctly, the other person will never notice you are networking.*

This is *not* because you are doing anything sneaky or manipulative. It's simply that the other person will be enjoying the conversation even more than *you* will. And if that's the case, would she feel you were in any way out of line? Not at all. And as you'll see, you'll add so much value to that person's life from the very get-go that a conversation with you—and an eventual networking relationship with you—will be quite welcome indeed.

The first thing you do is simply introduce yourself to a person you want to meet. Of course, you don't do this in an aggressive, intimidating, turn-off fashion. You don't walk over with your arm stretched out and business card extended. That's important to keep in mind when meeting this person for the first time.

You tell him your name and offer a firm but nonaggressive handshake. He will respond reflexively by telling you his name. Then ask what he does for a living. He'll tell you and ask you the same question. You tell him briefly, but go right back to showing interest in *his* business.

The next step is very important.

After the introduction, invest 99.9 percent of the conversation asking the other person questions about himself and his business. Do *not* talk about yourself and your business.

Why? Because at this point, he doesn't care about you or your business. Let's face facts: your business and my business are probably two of the things in this world that person cares least about. That's just the way it is. He wants to talk about himself and his business. Let him! This is known as being you-oriented. Most people, of course, are I-oriented.

Will this get you off to a good start with your networking prospect? Let me answer that question by asking you a question: Have you ever been in a conversation with someone who let you do practically *all* the talking? If so, did you say to yourself afterward, "Wow! What a fascinating conversationalist!" Sure, we've all done that. Isn't it true that the people we find most interesting are the people who seem most interested in us? You bet!

Warning!

There's a danger that you need to be aware of at this point. Let's pretend the person just asked what you do for a living, and that when you answer, it just happens to be something that person really needs.

For instance, let's say you are a financial advisor. You respond not by saying, "I'm a financial advisor," but instead by giving a short benefit statement, such as "I help people create and manage wealth."

Now the person looks at you and says, "What a coincidence. My spouse and I were just talking about the fact that we are very weak in that area and need to do something about it. After all, we're working hard, but we have no financial future, nothing put away for the later years. We know we definitely need to talk to a person such as yourself right away."

At this point, everything inside you wants to do a bent-elbow fist-pump and go *Yesssss!!* That, unfortunately, would not be the correct response.

Tempting as it might be to try to set up an appointment with this person and his spouse right on the spot, a seasoned networker will realize that this person is just not ready yet. The *know you, like you, trust you* feelings have not yet been established.

Bombarding this person right now with all the many ways you can help him (what my prospecting mentor, Rick Hill, calls "firehosing") will most likely result in just the opposite of what you want to accomplish. Instead, simply go right back to asking questions about him and his business.

The type of questions we need to ask in a situation like this are what I call *open-ended, Feel-Good Questions®*. Let's look at both these terms.

If you've read any books on sales or taken any kind of sales training, you may already be familiar with the idea of "open-ended" questions. These are simply questions that cannot be answered with a simple "yes" or "no," but require a longer response—consequently, they invite further dialogue.

I first learned about open-ended questions when I was a television news anchor for an ABC affiliate in Oklahoma. Management decided that we should have more live interviews, each lasting about three minutes, during our newscasts. Now, three minutes doesn't seem like a particularly long time to most people. On live television, three minutes can be an eternity! Especially when it came to some of my guests. And truth be told, I was not exactly a network-quality interviewer at this point in my career. What a combination!

I blame myself much more than I do my guests. After all, they were not necessarily used to being interviewed on television. In some cases, they were brilliant people, but not especially charismatic or eloquent. For instance, during the oil crisis of the early 1980s, I was interviewing Mr. Johnson from the local bank:

> ME: So, Mr. Johnson, how do you feel the current oil prob-
> lems will affect the local banks and local residents?
> MR. JOHNSON: Uh…it's gonna be tough.
> ME: Okay, it's gonna be tough. Can you elaborate on that
> point?
> MR. JOHNSON: It's gonna be *really* tough.

Right about this point I started thinking, *This would be a fantastic time to take a commercial break.* But then I heard the director through the earphones screaming, "Stretch! Stretch! You still have two minutes and forty-five seconds left!"

That was tough—or as Mr. Johnson might have said, *really* tough! But it taught me that if I was going to survive these three-minute live interviews, I needed to learn how to ask questions that would get my guests talking and keep them talking.

What I did—and my suggestion to you is to do likewise—was to watch some of the top network television interviewers, people such as Diane Sawyer, Larry King, or Barbara Walters. Whether or not you personally enjoy watching these outstanding professionals, the fact is, they know how to ask questions that get people talking *and keep them talking*.

Barbara Walters, of course, asks questions that get people *crying*. That's not good for our purposes. We want to accomplish just the opposite. We want to ask questions that make people feel good about being in a conversation with us—that's the whole point of the Feel-Good Question®.

Feel-Good Questions® are simply questions that, by their very nature, make the other person feel good; about themselves, about the conversation, and about us—even though we've just met them and they hardly know us.

Ten Networking Questions That Work Every Time

I have 10 Feel-Good Questions® in my personal arsenal. They are absolutely *not* designed to be probing or sales-oriented in any way. You'll notice that they are all friendly and fun to answer, and each will elicit answers that will tell you something about the way that person thinks.

You'll never have the time to ask all 10 during any one conversation, nor will you need to. In fact, if you did ask all 10, it would most likely come off as intrusive. Most likely, just two or three will do fine. Still, you should internalize all 10, and know them well enough so that you are easily able to pick and choose those you deem most appropriate for the particular conversation and time frame.

Here are the 10 questions.

1. How did you get your start in the widget business?

   People like to be the Movie of the Week in someone else's mind. "I worked my way through college, then started in the mail room, then blah, blah, blah, and finally began the fascinating career of selling widgets." Let them share their story with you while you actively listen.

2. What do you enjoy most about your profession?

Again, it's a question that elicits a good, positive feeling. And it should get you the positive response you're seeking. By this time you've got him on a roll.

3. What separates you and your company from the competition?

I call this the *permission-to-brag* question. All our lives we're taught not to brag about ourselves and our accomplishments, yet you've just given this person carte blanche to let it all hang out.

4. What advice would you give someone just starting in the widget business?

This is my *mentor* question. Don't we all like to feel like a mentor— to feel that our answer matters? Give your new networking prospect a chance to feel like a mentor by asking this question.

5. What one thing would you do with your business if you knew you could not fail?

This is a paraphrase of a question from noted theologian and author Dr. Robert Schuller, who asks, "What one thing would you do with your *life* if you knew you could not fail?" We all have a dream, don't we? What is this person's dream? The question gives her a chance to fantasize. She'll appreciate the fact that you cared enough to ask. And you'll notice that people always take a few moments to really ponder this one before they answer.

6. What significant changes have you seen take place in your profession through the years?

Asking people who are a little bit more mature in years can be perfect because they love answering this question. They've gone through the takeover of fax machines, the advent of PCs and then the Internet, and the transition from a time when service really seemed to matter.

7. What do you see as the coming trends in the widget business?

I call this the *speculator* question. Aren't people who are asked to speculate usually important, hot-shot types on television? You are therefore giving this person a chance to speculate and share his knowledge with you—to be an expert! You're making him feel good about himself.

8. Describe the strangest or funniest incident you've experienced in your business.

Give people the opportunity to share their war stories. After all, isn't that something practically everyone likes to do? Don't we all have stories we like to share from when we began in business? Something very embarrassing happened that certainly wasn't funny then but is now. The problem is, most people rarely or never get the chance to share these stories. And here you are, actually *volunteering* to be this person's audience!

9. What ways have you found to be the most effective for promoting your business?

Again, you are accentuating the positive in this person's mind, while finding out something about the way he thinks. However, if you happen to be in the advertising field, absolutely *do not* ask this question. Why? Because right now, it would be a probing question, and would be perceived as such by your networking prospect. Eventually you will get to ask that question, but not now.

10. What one sentence would you like people to use in describing the way you do business?

Almost always, the person will stop and think really hard before answering this question. What a compliment you've paid her. You've asked a question that, quite possibly, the people who are closest to her have never thought to ask.

It's *How* You Ask

You may be wondering whether or not some people might feel you are being nosey asking these questions during a first meeting. The answer is no.

Remember, during your initial conversation, you won't get to ask more than two or three of these questions anyway. But more importantly, these are questions people *enjoy* answering! If you ask them the way I have worded them here, you will not come off like Mike Wallace conducting an interrogation for *60 Minutes*. That's not the impact you want! These questions are simply meant to feel good and establish an initial rapport.

There are also *extender* questions that can be utilized effectively when the person's answer needs lengthening. (These are the ones I most needed to know about back on the live TV news!) For instance, the words, "Really? Tell me more." The person will usually be only too happy to accommodate you.

Then there is the *echo* technique, taught to me by my friend and fellow speaker Jeff Slutsky, author of *How to Get Clients* and many other excellent books. According to Jeff, you need only repeat back the last few words of a networking prospect's sentence in order to keep her talking. For instance:

> NP (NETWORKING PROSPECT):...and so we decided to
> expand."
> YOU: "Decided to expand?"
> NP: "Yes, we thought the increase in our revenue would jus-
> tify the cost."
> YOU: "Justify the cost?"
> NP: "Yes, you see, if the amount of..."

Jeff also warns, though, that we must every so often adjust the phrasing of our echo, or eventually the person is going to look at us and say, "What are you, anyway—an echo?"

The One Key Question That Separates the Pros from the Amateurs

This next question is key to the process of getting this person to feel he knows you, likes you and trusts you. It must be asked smoothly and sincerely, and only after some initial rapport has been established. The question is this:

How can I know if someone I'm speaking to is a good prospect for you?

Let's discuss why this question is so powerful. First of all, just by asking the question, you have separated yourself from the rest of the pack. It is the first indication that you are someone special. You are probably the only person he has ever met who asked him this question, and certainly the only one who ever asked it during a first conversation together.

During my live seminars, where I often address audiences numbering in the thousands, I'll ask for a show of hands from those who have ever been asked that question (or one even remotely similar) by anyone they had just met. Seldom do more than a few hands go up. Often, none!

You have also just informed this person that you are concerned with *his* welfare and wish to contribute to *his* success. Most people would already be trying to sell their own product or service, but not you. You are wondering out loud how you can help the other guy.

And you can be sure that your prospect will have an answer.

I remember once talking with a person named Gary who sold copying machines, and I asked him this question. He suggested that the next time I walk by a copying machine in an office, I take a look at its accompanying wastepaper basket. "If that basket is overflowing with tons of crumpled-up pieces of paper," he said, "that's a good sign the copying machine is breaking down a lot. That's a good prospect for me."

Don't we all have ways of knowing when someone would be a good prospect that the general public does not know? People you meet from now on will be glad to share their knowledge in that area with you. And don't you think they'll appreciate your sincere interest? You bet they will!

Again, that question will be the first indication that you are somebody special and different—a person worthy of doing business with, either directly or by way of referrals. My advice is to learn that question word for word until it becomes part of you and you could ask it, as the saying goes, "in your sleep."

One important point to keep in mind is to *not* ask that question too early in the conversation. First establish a rapport—and your sincerity—by asking your first few open-ended, Feel-Good Questions®.

In the many years since the first edition of this book was published, I've been told by an enormous number of people, whether through the mail, e-mail, or live at my seminars, that this one question has transformed their business lives. They've seen the look of disbelief in their new friends' eyes, astounded that they'd been asked such a question. And from that point on, a very profitable relationship has begun.

In my opinion, there are two simple reasons for this.

For one thing, you've given to this person the feeling and knowledge that her success is going to increase simply by associating with you. That right there, of course, makes you more "attractive" to that person, who then feels a vested personal interest in cultivating an association with you—which includes giving back to you.

The other reason is that it actually causes *you* to think of ways you can help others, thus taking the focus off yourself. As Stuart Wilde writes in his book, *The Trick to Money Is Having Some*, "The secret to success is to subjugate your ego and serve others."

There is an extraordinary equation, sometimes called "The Law of Compensation," that says:

> *In a free-enterprise based economy, the amount of money you make is directly proportional to the number of people you serve.*

And often before you serve them (or their referrals) directly, through your products or services, you will have occasion to serve them indirectly, through other sources such as the referrals *you* give to *them*.

No doubt about it: the "One Key Question" will serve you profitably throughout your life and career.

Loring "Snag" Holmes, an insurance sales professional, found that out right after he attended one of my seminars. About a week after the program, he was introduced to a prospect through a mutual friend. Here's what Snag says about the encounter:

> *When he found out I sell insurance, he immediately became defensive—not the first time I've experienced that response. Before learning these principles, I would've tried to keep selling this person on an appointment. Instead, what I did was focus on him and his business. He seemed to loosen up a little. It turned out that he sold office products. After I asked, "How can I know if someone I'm speaking to is a good prospect for you?" his attitude shifted 180 degrees! I should've been asking these questions for the last 30 years.*

Alison Oliver, an account executive for a billboard company, was nervous about her brief luncheon appointment with a corporate buyer. The man had been difficult on the phone, and Alison was not looking forward to a battle over soup and salad. As Alison reports:

> *We ended up meeting for a good hour and fifteen minutes, even though it was obvious he had planned on a much shorter meeting. All I did was talk about his favorite subject—him! Within a week I made the sale, and he personally called my boss to commend me on my selling skills.*

These are two incidents that resulted in almost immediate sales—and that isn't even the purpose of this questioning technique. All we're looking to do here is establish a positive relationship, which will result in direct business and a lot of referral business *down the road*. But these principles are so powerful that often, they *will* result in immediate sales.

What do we do then? Maintain the relationship and go on to work that person's 250-person sphere of influence.

An unexpected (and certainly unconventional) confirmation of the power of you-oriented questioning came from a good friend of mine in the National Speakers Association, Sydney Biddle Barrows. Sydney gained both acclaim and notoriety after her book *Mayflower Madam* hit the best-seller list. It was the true story about the rise and fall of the escort service Sydney had owned—the most successful in New York City, in fact.

Understandably, because of the nature of her business, Sydney was less than anxious for her friends to know what she did for a living. When people asked her, she would simply ask them something about themselves. According to Sydney, keeping her little secret from her friends was one of the easiest things for her to do.

Countless times, via you-oriented questioning, I've been able to establish excellent contacts on airplane trips. On one occasion, I kept a person talking about himself for the final hour and 45 minutes of the flight. (This took some concentration on my part!) As we landed I said, "If I can ever refer business your way, I definitely will." He replied, "Me too," and I could tell he meant it. Then, with an embarrassed smile, he asked, "By the way, what do you do?" Amazing! Just by my focusing on him, he was totally sold on me without even knowing anything about me.

Another time I sat next to a syndicated columnist on a flight from Chicago to San Francisco. I asked all about her and her career as a journalist. The result? A feature story on me and my program that ran in all the papers that syndicate her column. This process works!

Always in Good F-O-R-M

There's one concern you might have that I'd like to address before we move on: "What if the person I'm speaking with is either not directly in sales, or just wouldn't have prospects?"

For instance, what if you're talking with a person who's in the financial end or technical end of a business, or a stay-at-home dad or mom? Do the type of questions we're asking here become irrelevant in such a situation?

Actually, the *type* of questions—Feel Good Questions®—are just as relevant regardless of what the person does, although some of the questions could now be changed to address either their line of work or some other part of their life.

For example, the famous F-O-R-M method now comes into play. F-O-R-M is simply an acronym for:

F—Family
O—Occupation
R—Recreation
M—Message (what they deem important)

Let's begin with F, family. Regardless of what this person does for a living, you can ask about his "family" and he'll most likely be happy to talk for as long as you'd like. Most people are overjoyed to tell you about their star soccer-playing or straight-A-getting high schooler, or their talented spouse. Or their grandson or granddaughter. By the way, it's crucial to remember that you never want to one-up someone who's bragging on his children. If he tells you that Pat got all A's and one B on her last report card, and your child happened to score all A's, keep that particular piece of information to yourself for the moment!

O or occupation we already discussed.

R, recreation. Let me ask you this: do people enjoy talking about their recreation? Absolutely! They love their recreation! Softball, tennis, snow-skiing, mountain climbing, bridge, stamp collecting…whatever it is, they do it because they love to do it. People are often passionate about their recreational activities. You can ask them most of the Feel Good Questions® about it, such as "How did you get started?" or "What do you enjoy most about it?" or "What changes have you seen take place?" and so forth. You'll feel the rapport happening faster than you could ever imagine.

And M, which stands for message: this means, what's important to this person? What does she stand for? What is it she values? Is she heavily involved in a charitable cause? Is she involved in a religious or political cause? By the way, people often say you should never discuss religion or politics with people. I disagree: you can *discuss* it—just don't *argue* with people about it! Be supportive and listen to what they have to say. You don't have to agree. But they'll love to tell you all about it, and they'll feel good about themselves, about the conversation and about *you*, while they do.

If you're wondering about the One Key Question, in this context it might look like this:

How can I know if someone I'm speaking to is someone you'd like to meet?

Again, same principle, with a slight adjustment based on your own unique circumstances when speaking with your new prospect.

I was speaking once with a prospect who told me that his daughter Beth had just graduated from college and was looking to break into the advertising field. I asked him how I could know if someone I was speaking with would be a good prospect for Beth. He told me. I did some research, and through my network I found someone who knew someone in the field and was able to make the introduction. I ended up with a huge account. Why? Because I showed my prospect I cared enough to be concerned with his challenges— and more, with the challenges of another human being whom he loves deeply. It's no surprise that he took an interest in me, and all things being equal, the business was mine.

Back to Your Prospect

All right: your conversation with your new networking prospect has now concluded, and you've hardly mentioned yourself or what you do for a living. That's okay—as long as you have *his* business card.

So, ask him for it. (As we learned earlier, the main reason for having your business card is not to give it to someone else but *to get the other person's card*.) He'll be glad to give it to you. If he asks you for yours, by all means give it to him; just keep in mind that your card will most likely disappear at his earliest convenience, either by actually being directly tossed or forever lost in his Rolodex®, card file, or contact management software program.

And that's completely okay. It's nothing personal. He probably receives lots of cards in the course of the normal week, and even though he already thinks pretty highly of you and is glad you're interested in referring business to him, unless he's an expert networker himself, he's going to let it end there.

What's important is that *you have his card*. You'll see why later on, when we look at how to successfully and profitably follow up with this person.

Key Points

- Networking opportunities occur constantly, anywhere and at any time.
- If you are networking correctly, the other person will never notice that you are networking.
- After the introduction, invest 99.9 percent of the conversation asking that person questions about himself and his business. Do not talk about yourself and your business.
- Even if what you do interests the other person right away, turn the conversation back to that person and his business.
- Ask several of the 10 open-ended, Feel-Good Questions® to find out more about your networking prospect. Remember, these questions are not intended to be probing in nature, but simply to establish a rapport.
- The one key question is, "How can I know if someone I'm speaking to is a good prospect for you?"
- You can also ask "F-O-R-M" questions when the person is not in a "sales" type of business.

CHAPTER 3

How to Work Any Crowd

Mention the term *networking* to many business owners or salespeople, and images of their local Chamber of Commerce will immediately spring to mind. Why? Because across North America and throughout the world, Chambers of Commerce have instituted monthly events known as Business before Hours, Business after Hours, Networking Functions, or Card Exchanges.

Regardless of what they're called, the concept is that Chamber of Commerce members attend these get-togethers with plenty of business cards in tow, ready to exchange them with each other. If all goes according to plan, when one of the members eventually needs a particular product or service, she will simply have to check her business card file and *voila!* She will know who to go to.

The purpose of this exercise, according to Chamber of Commerce executives, is, and I quote, "Chamber members doing business with other Chamber members." In other words, creating a self-sufficient business environment within the membership.

A Good Thought, But...

It's a great concept! There's only one minor problem—it doesn't work. Why not? Because no matter how loyal people may be to their Chamber of Commerce, they will most likely only do business with someone for the reason we've already explored in depth: *All things being equal, people will do business with, and refer business to, those people they know, like, and trust.*

Pressing the flesh and handing out an endless number of business cards will not convince people to feel any of these things about you. And most people simply don't know how to work a Chamber of Commerce audience in such a way as to elicit those feelings. And in this scenario, every time you *don't* get somebody's direct business, you also *don't* get the business of his 250-person sphere of influence.

Let's take a look at the proven methods that will allow you to take advantage of a wonderful situation, where you may have a ton of good prospects right in front of you for as much as two straight hours.

First, Let's View the Situation

Picture in your mind's eye the typical Chamber of Commerce card exchange scenario (and you can apply the same principles to any type of gathering, be it a charity event, social party, other business-social event, etc.). Let's say this is an after-hours event, running from 5:00 to 7:00 p.m.

What happens during these two hours? The majority of attendees sit at the bar or hang around the hors d'oeuvres table. They have a few drinks, something to eat, talk with each other, flirt with members of the opposite sex, and get absolutely nothing done in the way of business. It's basically a party, and maybe even a darn good party at that, but it isn't networking.

Many people rationalize (to tell oneself "rational lies") that they are indeed networking. They're doing business, because hey, they're at this event, right? And it's after normal business hours. But the truth is, about the most productive thing anyone's doing here is every once in a while meeting somebody they don't know and exchanging business cards. Now, no disrespect meant, but *big deal!*

Oh, and occasionally, by way of sheer luck, some business will take place. Person A might just happen to need what Person B is selling, or vice versa. But the chances of this happening are small, and the odds for success are certainly not being played to their full advantage.

The First Thing to Do Is Join

Let me ask you this: If you currently belong to your local Chamber of Commerce, do you attend these events? If your answer is yes, have you gotten a ton of business from them? No? Would you like to get a ton of business from them? You can!

The first thing I suggest you do, if you're not already a member of your local Chamber of Commerce, is to join today, for two reasons. One, it's a nice way of supporting your local business community. And two, and even more importantly, it gives you an opportunity to use the Endless Referrals System® during those card exchange events as a genuine networking, selling, and referral-gathering tool.

How do we make these usually social functions become genuine networking events and actually work for us? It begins by knowing why you are there in the first place: You're not just after these people's business; you're also after the business of each of their 250-person spheres of influence. I'm going to give you seven steps to help you accomplish that goal; here are the first three:

1. *Adjust your attitude.* By this I mean understand that the only reason you are at this particular function is to *work*: to build your inventory of quality prospects for your names list. That you're there to work doesn't mean it can't be fun. Networking *is* fun. Establishing mutually beneficial, give-and-take, win-win relationships with people is fun. Making more money is fun. But we are here at this card exchange, networking function, or whatever we want to term the occasion, to work.

2. *Work the crowd.* By this I mean, be a "sincere politician"—be sincere but with an air of confidence about you. Be open, but don't come off like a sharp hustler. Be nice. Have a smile on your face. Very simple, right? Okay. That's a start.

3. *Introduce yourself to someone new.* If possible, introduce yourself to someone who is what's known as a *Center of Influence.* These are people who have a very large and important sphere of influence themselves. Typically, Centers of Influence have been in the community for a long time. People are familiar with them, and what's more, they know them, like them, and trust them. Centers of Influence may or may not be particularly successful in business— though usually they are—but regardless, they know a lot of other people whom you want to know. And they have the ability to connect you with these people.

But How Do We Find Them?

My friend, fellow speaker, and author Rick Hill, one of the very best prospectors I've ever met, has a great method for locating a function's Centers of Influence. He notes that people usually break up into groups of four, five, or six. According to Rick, each group usually has a dominant person or unofficial group leader, that one man or woman who seems to control the conversation or around whom the conversation seems to revolve.

He's right. Next time you're at a Chamber of Commerce function or any kind of social gathering, notice how easy it is to find that one person in every group. When someone makes a point, all heads turn to the unofficial leader for her response. When she speaks, everyone hangs onto her every word. The group laughs when she laughs, and everyone tends to agree with whatever she says.

Remember, these people probably know a lot of people. Make a point of meeting, one-on-one, the Centers of Influence you notice.

But how do we do that, if they are always around other people who are hanging onto their every word? Basically, as you're walking around the room, bottled water in hand, simply keep your eyes on the few Centers of Influence you see. Eventually, one of them is going to leave his or her present group.

It's the Manner in Which You Introduce Yourself That's Important

Just wait for your opportunity, then walk up and introduce yourself to that person. Perfectly acceptable behavior! That's what both of you are there for.

If you're at all embarrassed about introducing yourself cold to somebody, that's understandable. We all have those feelings at times; I know I do. But realize that if you simply approach that person politely and nonaggressively (without a business card in his face and ready to pounce), 99 times out of 100 he will be quite receptive.

Again, such people know that pretty much everyone present (including themselves) is there for the purpose of networking, regardless of whether or not they know how to go about doing it successfully. More than likely, the Center of Influence is just as anxious to make another contact in you, as you are in him.

Now the Process Begins

After you have exchanged names, ask your Center of Influence what line of business she is in. She'll tell you and ask you the same.

That's a start. Respond *briefly* with your benefit statement, then quickly move on to the next step, which is step 4:

4. *Talk about her.* After your introduction, invest 99.9 percent of the conversation asking the other person questions about herself and *her* business. Do not talk about yourself and your business.

From the last chapter, you already know why this is so: Your networking prospects don't yet care about you and your business. They want to talk about themselves and their business. Let them. Now is the time to ask several of the 10 open-ended, Feel-Good Questions® we discussed in Chapter 2. If you don't remember what they are, go back and review them before you attend your next business function. And *memorize* them: They are the tools you'll need here.

The Question That Separates the Pros from the Amateurs

Remember the most important question in Chapter 2? Now's the time to ask it.

How can I know if someone I'm speaking to is a good prospect for you?

We've already discussed why this question is so important. And here's something else: I guarantee that you will be the *only* one at this event who is asking this question (unless somebody else in the room has already taken my course or read this book). In any case, that person will be more than happy to tell you what to look for in a prospective customer. He will be impressed with you and your concern for him. Believe me—and everyone else who has found this question to be so beneficial to their careers—this works!

At this point, you might be asking, "If everybody knew about the Feel-Good Questions® and the One Key Question, wouldn't that take away my advantage?"

Here's my answer: These principles are intended to result in a mutually beneficial, win-win situation for everyone involved in the process. That being the case, doesn't it figure that the more people who know these principles, the better for everyone involved?

The main thing is to learn this important networking principle, internalize it, and apply it consistently. Those who do so will be far more likely to attain great success. The fact is, though, most people won't. I sincerely hope you are one of the small percentage who will.

As you end your productive conversation (with you doing 99.9 percent of the listening), it's time for Step 5:

5. *Ask for your new contact's business card.* If she asks for yours, by all means give it to her, but realize that the key is to get *her* card. (We'll see why in detail in the next chapter.)

Next, go find and introduce yourself to another Center of Influence whom you observed earlier, or one you happen to observe now, and run through the exact same process as you did with this last person. And note: Just because someone doesn't *appear* to be a Center of Influence doesn't mean they're not—or that they won't be six months or a year from now. And one more suggestion: When you see someone who simply looks like he could use a smile or a kind word, go out of your way to give it.

Two reasons: First, it's just the right thing to do. That person might have really had to motivate himself and move past some personal fears just to attend this function. A "hello" and a kind word from you may well give him a jolt of confidence and feeling of acceptance, and really make a difference in his life.

Secondly, you never know who you're talking to, who that person might really be—or who he knows. Here's a quick example that illustrates both of these points.

When I was attending a meeting of an association to which I belong, I noticed a person standing around named Jim who looked like a lost soul. I engaged Jim in conversation and introduced him around to some of the other members. About a year later, I received a call from someone I didn't know, wanting to do business with me. I asked how he had heard of me, and he mentioned Jim.

I called Jim to thank him and asked him what made him think of referring me, since we had met only that one time and he had really no way of knowing whether or not I was even qualified to serve the person to whom he referred me. He explained that at the function where we had met, I was the only person present who went out of his way to make him feel comfortable, and he had always wanted to do something for me in return. Wow!

Naturally, I believe I was in fact qualified to do the job that Jim had referred me to do, but the point is, that didn't really matter to Jim: I received the referral because I had taken the time to make someone in an uncomfortable position feel more comfortable.

Please know I share this story with you not to impress you, but to impress *upon* you two things: one, it's simply nice to be nice to people; and two, you never know who it is that you're being nice to. I know you understand this and that you would do it for the *first* reason alone—but if it also happens to come back to you in a good way, such as new business or a nice referral, that's okay too.

Back to our event: Remember the first person you talked with, your first Center of Influence? You've got her business card, but you're not complete with her yet: now comes step 6.

6. *Go back and use her name.* Later on, pop back by and call your networking prospect by name.

Let's say it's half an hour since you met, briefly conversed, and went separate ways. You're now back at the hors d'oeuvres table by this recently met Center of Influence. You very pleasantly say, "Hi, Ms. Gregory. Are you enjoying yourself?" That's going to make an impression on her, especially because by this time she has more than likely forgotten your name. I guarantee you that at this point, she will make a point of noticing your name—and she'll *remember* your name.

If remembering people's names is not something you feel particularly good at, no problem. There are some excellent books you can purchase on this topic, including *The Memory Book*, by Harry Lorayne and Jerry Lucas. I have also written a book that covers this subject, entitled *The Memory System*. With a little bit of practice, you will surprise yourself at how adept you become at mastering this very important networking skill.

Connect Others (or, "Matchmaker, Matchmaker, Make Me a Match")

Over the course of a single event such as this, you should be able to make at least several good contacts; why not introduce these people to each other?

It's the hallmark of networking mastery, and it happens to be the last step in this process, step 7:

7. *If you have the opportunity, introduce people you have met to others.*
   Ideally, the best introductions to make are those between people who can be of mutual benefit to one another.

I call this "creative matchmaking." Position *yourself* as a Center of Influence: the one who knows the movers and shakers. People will respond to that, and you'll soon become what you project.

Give each person a nice introduction and explain what the other does. Suggest ways they can look for referrals for each other. Remember the critically important step we talked about earlier: asking that person how you can know if a person you're speaking to can be a good prospect for them. Tell Gary how to know what would be the sign of a good prospect for Anne, and tell Anne the same about Gary. Wow! Will they be impressed!

For example: "Anne, Gary was telling me that if you're ever in an office and notice a copying machine with a wastepaper basket next to it, and that wastepaper basket is filled to the rim, overflowing with crumpled up pieces of paper, that's a good sign that copying machine has been malfunctioning lately and that would be an excellent prospect for him."

And then you might say to Gary, "And Anne sells telephone equipment to small companies who need to expand what they now use. She was mentioning that if you happen to be in an office and see two people talking to each other through Dixie® cups with a string attached, that's a good sign they might need to update their telephone equipment." (That Anne, she's such a kidder.)

Your two new contacts are going to be reminded that you cared enough about them to really listen and remember. It will show sincere interest on your part, and that will make these people more interested in helping you.

All this time you're just beginning to give them a hint of the fact that you are an ace, someone to do business with or refer to others.

Here's one more thing you can do that will deepen the impression: sometime during the conversation, politely excuse yourself and leave the two of them speaking with each other. Guess what, or who, they'll talk about? Most likely, the one common element in their lives up to this point—you! And what an impression you've made on them both. They most likely still don't even have much of an idea of just what it is you even do, and that's okay. There'll be plenty of time for that.

Decide in Advance Who Your Networking Prospects Are

Another way you can ensure meeting people with whom you can have mutually beneficial networking relationships is to introduce yourself to people involved in *professions complementary to yours.*

For example, a mortgage broker should try to meet Realtors®, who can refer plenty of business their way. Why? Because Realtors® are always working with people who need to borrow money to purchase a home.

Another method is name tags. You might have spotted a real estate company name on someone's name tag as you passed by each other. Or you might have overheard part of a conversation indicating that the person is a Realtor®. You'll find a way to know, if you want to know badly enough.

If you sell financial growth instruments and your niche market is teachers, who would be a good person to meet at one of these events? The superintendent of the school system would be ideal. But what if he or she isn't there? In that case, how about someone whose job or social activities puts her in a position where she is in contact with the superintendent or one of the individual school principals?

Or, let's say you sell supplemental insurance with a focus on corporate employees: in this case, meeting a human resources director, manager, or someone in a similar position could prove very worthwhile.

If you create computer software programs or are a computer troubleshooter, then meeting a person who sells computer hardware would certainly be a positive step in the right networking direction, wouldn't it? A sign shop owner should try to meet those who either buy signs or, more importantly, people who are in a position to talk to others who buy signs.

In any case, regardless of how you meet your best contacts, your next step will be to cultivate them successfully.

How else can you determine in advance of the function who would be some good people for you to meet? Be creative. With a little reconnaissance work, you can discover beforehand who will be there and exactly who you'd like to meet. Whether it's a Chamber of Commerce business networking function, a charity event, or an association meeting, a list of attendees and information on them is typically available. Just do the research. There might be directories, either hard copy or online, or a friendly administrator at the organization's office might be willing to answer any questions you have in this regard.

You can check your organization's directory beforehand and find out who does what. Ask others who might know who the Centers of Influence are. You can even call the Chamber, let them know what you do and tell them you'd like to know who some of the people are you should meet. If he or she asks why you're interested, just tactfully and honestly share the fact that you'd like to have an idea going in who some of the people are you might be meeting or would like to meet. Typically, if it's not a big deal to you, it won't be a big deal to the person you're speaking with and you'll most likely find that person will be very accommodating.

By asking, you can also discover who the shakers and movers are. At one event, a woman I had never met before approached me with a business idea. When I asked how she knew of me, she told me she simply asked around at a couple of meetings, inquiring who some of the better-known networkers in town were, and my name came up.

If you call up your local Chamber of Commerce or any other organization before their next event, tell them you're in the process of expanding your network and want to meet some of the shakers and movers within the organization, they'll give you some good suggestions on who you should meet.

If you're not comfortable doing something like that right now, don't. Do just what we've been discussing and you'll be fine. Once you get a little more confidence in your abilities as a communicator, and in the process itself, you'll know that you have a lot of viable options you can successfully utilize whenever you choose to do so.

Now your business function has come to an end. Hopefully, you've met about five or six good contacts. Even one or two would not be bad—that's all you need. One or two good contacts are much better than just handing out a bunch of business cards to people with whom you will never end up doing business. That's what everyone else was doing. You've taken a different, more personal approach. The scenario is now set for the follow-up.

Build on Your Small Successes

At this point, you probably feel a lot more confident when it comes to working a room full of strangers (or even a room *mostly* full of strangers) than you did before. You've seen that doing this effectively has very little to do with having the "gift of gab" and much more to do with having the skill of listening to others and making them feel good about themselves.

Still, since this concept might be new to you, you can take practice steps to build your networking muscles and build your networking skills level in a way that will serve you and your prospects very well.

Every so often, people ask me how they can overcome their shyness or lack of confidence to meet new people and proceed through the entire process we've just covered. The answer is five words: *Build on your small successes.*

There is nothing unusual about having fear in this area. If you feel out of your comfort zone, if you are shy or feel uncomfortable about starting a conversation with someone new, begin by committing yourself to go to this event and simply say hello in passing to a few people. Success!

Next event, commit to saying hello, shaking hands with a few people, and, with a gentle smile on your face, exchanging names. Success! The next time, set yourself to say hello, exchange names with a few people, and ask what line of work they are in. If you're up to it, ask one or two of the open-ended, Feel-Good Questions®. Success! As you begin to feel more and more comfortable (and you will!), you'll stay in the conversation longer, and before you know it, the process will become completely natural. You'll become a master at working a crowd.

I am a big believer in building on your small successes. One success inevitably leads to another, and once you've had a couple of good experiences with positive results, you'll find you are a lot more likely to continue the process. I'm not saying you necessarily *need* to do what I've just laid out; in fact, you'll most likely find that the seven-step process we looked at in this chapter is incredibly easy to apply. Still, know that the option of starting small and building on your small successes is there for you, should you feel the need to start with one toe in the water.

In the next chapter, we'll look at some methods of profitable follow-up. Simple in their application, they are designed to ensure that when the time comes and your prospect needs your products, goods, or services (or knows someone else who does), you will be the only one who could possibly spring to mind.

Key Points

- Chamber of Commerce functions (as well as other business and social events) are excellent sources of networking, if used correctly. Otherwise, they are practically worthless.

- There are seven steps that will ensure your success at business functions:
  1. Adjust your attitude. Realize that the purpose of attending this function is to work and build your network.
  2. Work the crowd. Be pleasant and approachable.
  3. Introduce yourself to someone new. If possible, have that person be a Center of Influence.
  4. After the introduction, invest 99.9 percent of the conversation in asking that person questions about herself and her business. Do not talk about yourself and your business.
  5. Ask for your networking prospect's business card.
  6. Later on, pop back by and call that person by name.
  7. Introduce people you have met to others and help them find ways to benefit one another.
- You can predetermine people with whom you wish to network based on complementary professions.
- You have the option to start small and build on your small successes.

CHAPTER 4

Profitable Follow-Up

U p to this point, we've done well in finding and meeting our networking prospects. Maybe we've done this by way of chance meetings or non-business occasions, or possibly during an organized Chamber of Commerce function or other formal event. We've made a great, positive impression on those we've met. What's next?

Now comes the follow-up. By systematically and consistently implementing the following methods, we will separate ourselves, the successful networkers, from the "wannabes."

Perhaps you're thinking, follow-up is a royal pain. It can be—but only if you do a lot of unnecessary, time-consuming tasks that don't get results! What I'm going to show you is a methodology that, once you internalize it as a set of good habits, will not seem like a hardship at all.

What it *will* do is help you build a powerful network that results in a lot of referral business.

"Hit" Them Right Away

First, once you've met your new contacts, *send each one a personalized thank-you note*. Sure, we've all been taught that. Basic Sales Training 101, wasn't it? However, very few people actually do it.

People simply don't realize what an important step they're missing out on. They don't understand what powerful results they would get from implementing this simple step without fail. How can I be so sure people don't understand this? Because if they knew, they'd do it!

People who send notes get remembered for two reasons:

1. They stand out from the competition, because they are one of the few.
2. The recipient will actually see who it is sending them that note. (We'll explain how in a moment.)

In most communities you can mail a letter before midnight and it will arrive at its intended location the very next day—assuming, of course, that the destination is local. A letter that shows up at the person's desk or home the day after you meet is a nice touch.

This note should be a nonpushy, simple, brief note, written in blue ink (research indicates blue ink is more effective, in both business and personal correspondence). It should say something like, "Hi Dave (or Mary, or even Mr. or Ms., depending upon the particular situation), Thank you. It was a pleasure meeting you. If I can ever refer business your way, I certainly will."

The Impression This Makes

Let's look at what you've done. You have shown (again) that you have a lot of class, and (again) that you are conscientious. You've shown (again) that you are a person worthy of doing business with directly or having business referred to.

And just as important, here's what you *didn't* do: You didn't come on strong or try to do a hard sell. You simply thanked the person for the meeting. We all like to be thanked, don't we? And you also let this person know (once again) that you have *her* best interests in mind with the promise to make an effort to send business her way.

You might be tempted to add something about keeping you in mind if she, or someone she knows, ever needs your products or services. I strongly suggest that you don't do that. The person understands why you sent her the note, and you've already made your impression.

Sometimes, the more we understate our case, the more dramatic an impact we'll make. Besides, you're going to give this person plenty of opportunities to be thinking of you in the very near future.

Let me share with you the type of stationery I use for these notes. I send mine on an individually designed note card that measures 8 by 3½ inches. In the top right-hand corner is my company name and logo. Beneath that is my picture. Just beneath the picture is my name, and below that is my company address and telephone number. All this is on the right-hand side of the note card, leaving plenty of room for writing the note. Of course, if you're part of a company in which set-up might be a compliance issue, please check with that department. In my experience with this type of clientele, typically there is no problem, other than perhaps a request to slightly alter the wording you may have chosen.

Picture This

The picture is very important. You want them to know without question who sent this note; without your picture, they might not. People today meet many other people during the course of a day. As impressed as they were with you during the meeting, as the saying goes, "Out of sight, out of mind." What we're doing is giving them a quick reminder right off the bat.

Although this is only the first step toward having them see your face whenever they or someone they know needs your products or services, it is an important one. For maximum effectiveness, you must put your picture on your individually designed note card.

Ask your local printer to typeset and print these for you. If you are particularly "computer-abled" (as opposed to "computer-disabled" like many of us!), you might even design your own. In any case, the expense is minimal, and the payback is well worth it. I highly recommend your investing in this type of note card. See Figure 4-1, page 42.

First Class All the Way

Now, back to how to send your note. Although it could be sent as a postcard, I advise against it and suggest enclosing it in a regular number 10 envelope. Address the envelope by hand (again, in blue ink) as opposed to typing it. Do not put a mailing label on it—or on anything else you ever send to this person, for that matter. I'm not a big believer in using mailing labels because I

BURG COMMUNICATIONS, INC.

www.burg.com
www.TheSuccessFormula.com

BOB BURG

P.O. BOX 7002
JUPITER, FL 33468-7002
561-575-2114 • 1-800-726-3667
FAX: 561-575-2304
e-mail: bob@burg.com

Author: **THE SUCCESS FORMULA** (Samark)
ENDLESS REFERRALS: Network Your Everyday Contacts Into Sales (McGraw-Hill)
WINNING WITHOUT INTIMIDATION: How To Master the Art of Positive Persuasion (Samark)

Figure 4.1 Actual size is 8 x 3½ inches. Notice there is lots of space in which to write your note. (And, of course, in place of my book titles, you'll have your own benefit statement.)

want the person receiving the information to *know* I really care. Hand-stamp the envelope (as opposed to using a postage meter). An even nicer touch is to use a large, commemorative stamp.

In other words, personalize it. Make it special in your networking prospect's mind's eye. You want this envelope to be opened and the message actually read. If it looks like junk mail, it may well be thrown out without even being opened. A hand-addressed, hand-stamped envelope will grab people's attention more effectively than one with an impersonal mailing label and postage meter.

Since we've done it the right way, let's take a look at our networking prospect's probable response. She sees the envelope on her desk the next morning. Because it appears to be (and actually *is*) a personal letter, she opens it. Chances are she still won't even associate you with the company name on the envelope at this point. (Remember, out of sight...!) Now, as your networking prospect pulls out your note card and sees your picture, she remembers the good feelings associated with you. You are the one who asked all those questions yesterday at that event, the one who made her feel important. You asked how you could help her, and even introduced her to others.

But uh-oh, your prospect may now be thinking, *here comes the solicitation.* "If I can ever sell you, or someone you know, a whichamahoozee, let me know."

But you didn't do that, right? Far from it!

All you did was to thank her for the meeting and let her know you'll try to refer business to her. She will certainly appreciate you for thinking that highly of her, and will remember the effort.

Make the Time

If by any chance you have had the thought, "I'm too busy, I don't have time to write a thank-you note to every new networking prospect I meet," then my answer is, "Yes, you do!"

The pros, the champions, the ones who are determined to succeed (and you're one of them), do the little things right, consistently. That includes writing and sending the notes.

I say this because through the years, I've noticed that successful people share similar traits. One is that they are avid note-writers; successful people write thank-you notes all the time. George Bush did this from early on in his career, and he networked his way up to the position of chief executive of the United States.

There are those who get the cart before the horse and say, it's because these people are successful that now they have the time to write those notes. We all know that's not true. They were doing the little things right, such as writing notes, *before* they were successful, and now it's simply something called "habit." It's the same in practically every profession: Show me an avid note-writer and, nine times out of ten, I'll show you a success.

It's ironic that such a simple habit like writing thank-you notes would seem to separate those who are successful from those who are not. One reason for this is that they're consistently touching people in a way that most others don't. Perhaps another reason is that as successful people, they've simply gotten into the habit of doing the little things right, and consistently writing thank you notes is just one example among many of those "little things."

From Negotiating to Horse Races

Dr. Jim Hennig is an authority on the art of win-win negotiating. Dr. Hennig points out that in negotiating, "It's often the little differences that make the big differences." He goes on to say, "Doing the little things right can often be the difference between the successful and the unsuccessful negotiation."

That's so true, isn't it? And it applies to just about everything else in life, too. After all, don't they say, "Baseball is a game of inches." In boxing, a split decision is often what makes the difference between the champion and the person whose name we forget two weeks later. Maybe even the next day. An average of just a few strokes makes the difference between the top PGA or LPGA money winners and those who barely survive the tour.

My brother Rich, a big horse-racing buff, once gave me a superb analogy of how the little things mean a lot. Typically, in a $200,000 purse, the horse that finishes first brings in $120,000 for its owner. The second horse, who might have lost by just a nose in a photo finish, brings in $40,000. The third horse, who lost by just a neck, brings in about $12,000. And the fifth horse, who lost by just a length—one-fifth of a second—earns its owner the whopping sum of $3000. In this case, one-fifth of a second made a $117,000 difference

As Dr. Hennig says, little differences make the big differences!

Back to our thank-you notes. Those of us who are committed to realizing the benefits of effective networking write them even when we don't want to. Let me share with you a shortcut that will make the process a bit easier.

During some downtime, take 25 or 30 of your personalized note cards. Leave room at the top for the salutation, and below this space write, "Thank you. It was a pleasure meeting you. If I can ever refer business your way, I certainly will." Then sign your name.

Put an elastic band around these prewritten note cards and place them neatly in a shoe box inside the trunk of your car, along with an equal number of already hand-stamped envelopes.

From now on, whenever you meet a new networking prospect, simply go to your car immediately afterward, write his name at the top of a note, handwrite the name and address on the envelope (that's why you took his business card) and drop it in the nearest mailbox.

Sure, it's still a little bit of extra work—a *very* little bit: but as speaker and best-selling author Zig Ziglar says, "You don't pay the price for success; you enjoy the *benefits* of success."

Keep in mind that sending this note is simply a way of establishing yourself and your credibility with this person. It will not typically get immediate results. That's not to say it will *never* happen, just not usually.

The Incredible, Amazing Note Card

After the One Key Question, probably the single idea that has garnered the greatest amount of feedback from those who've attended my programs, read previous editions of this book, or listened to my CDs is the amazing results people have achieved, over time, by using these note cards. What's also interesting is the number of times they actually have seen immediate results, either in the form of direct business or as encouragement to keep in touch with the person to whom they sent it. (This doesn't surprise me, because it's happened to me, as well.)

Immediately upon attending one of my seminars for financial advisors, Tom Stevens had his note cards made and began using them every time he met someone with whom he felt it would be worthwhile to stay in touch. Shortly after doing this, he met a local businessman named George at a Chamber of Commerce function (you know, those things that "don't work"). That night he followed up with his note card.

Two days later he received a typewritten note back from George, which read as follows:

Hi Tom,

Thank you for dropping me that nice note! I really liked your neat note card.

Enjoyed talking with you at the hobnob. Of course our discussion was the most enjoyable of the night for me, but I am sure it was because you allowed me to talk mostly about myself

I've enclosed some literature about my company. I hope this helps when referring anyone to me.

I appreciate your help, but more than anything, I hope we can somehow stay in touch.

Sincerely,

George

From George's letter, we can see that Tom was following to a tee the advice from Chapter 3 on how to work a crowd. As you can note in the second and third paragraphs, Tom let George do practically all the talking and must have asked how he could know if someone he was speaking to would be a good prospect for George.

As you can see, this is a very holistic system: the more you follow it from the beginning to the end, the more impact each of the elements involved will have.

Here's another example:

Dennis Ederer, a financial advisor who attended a program I did for his company at their annual convention, wrote me the following:

Good morning Bob.

I just received my thank-you note cards from the printer and have already applied them in my business. I believe that this was the smartest advertising investment I have made thus far.

I met briefly with a woman who is interested in doing business with me, but her husband wants to continue doing business with their current advisor. Well, I mailed a thank-you note the same day and she received it the next day. She told me that she showed my note card to her husband and stated that this was the person they were going to work with in the future. Her husband replied, "I guess you have made up your mind."

I will also use my thank-you note card to communicate general information, such as, "Please endorse the enclosed form and return it to me in the enclosed stamped envelope." No more yellow sticky notes. My business name, my benefit statement and my picture are presented each time I communicate.

Sincerely yours,

Dennis

Great job by Dennis. In this case, while the fee might not have been immediate, the *process* was, and that's ultimately what counts. I know of others who, immediately after sending their note cards, were invited to meetings set up by the people to whom they sent their notes in order to meet those people's contacts.

And these work regardless of your profession. Cal Faber, a former automotive sales professional and now successful business owner from Vancouver, British Columbia, began sending out thank-you note cards immediately after reading the 1999 edition of this book. He began sending his note cards to those he met at Chamber of Commerce functions, social events, chance one-on-one introductions, and so forth. He also sent these to people who visited his dealership and bought, people who visited and didn't buy, and people who referred business to him.

According to Cal, applying this suggestion along with the other principles he learned in the book, "I was able to go from zero to over a $100,000 in my first year of automotive sales—without ever having been in sales or the automotive business before."

Cal stayed with the fundamentals and his business continued to improve; in his second and third years, his income climbed over 30 percent—while at the same time, he was able to reduce his work week to less than 25 hours!

Cal was kind enough to e-mail me the newspaper advertisements from his dealership that announced him as consistently being the number-one salesman in the dealership. Cal attributes the personalized note cards to being a huge part of his success.

Doesn't this just make sense? After all, how many salespeople in any business send note cards such as this? Not many, right? Okay, now: how many *automobile salespeople* send notes like this? The reason for Cal's success is self-evident. He sticks to the fundamentals and does the little things right, consistently sending out his note cards and using them to build relationships and profits.

My initial experience using these notes was on a local level, but I had such great success that I soon began using them in my speaking business, too, which is national in scope. (In other words, I rarely meet my prospects in person until they have already become my clients.) Didn't matter: worked just as well. They helped me develop referral-based relationships with other speakers, too, as well as with my direct prospects. So, if many of your prospects are long-distance, use these note cards, as well. And remember, put your picture on it; that's what gives you the edge.

In my own business, because of the diversity of topics, other speakers are often a tremendous source of referral business for me. On one occasion I was in the audience while a fellow speaker I hadn't yet met gave a wonderful presentation. We talked briefly afterwards, and later I sent him a note.

He, also being an active networker, responded with a note of his own. He also gave me a referral, which turned into a booking. Naturally, I immediately wrote him a note to thank him for the referral and to assure him that the prospective client to whom he referred me would receive the highest professional courtesy and so forth. He then wrote me back a very nice note thanking me for the thank-you note for the referral. In his note he wrote, "It's obvious, Bob, that you are a true professional, and I'm happy to give you referrals."

Remember, at this point he had never actually seen or heard me speak!

Since then the two of us have become great friends, and I've had the opportunity to refer him to many clients, and vice versa. A true win-win.

Again, the purpose of these note-card notes is not the sort of immediate results or instant gratification as in the examples we just saw. It usually doesn't happen that quickly, nor is that what the process is designed to accomplish. It is designed to set the stage for future follow-up on your part. And every so often, you will see a quick payoff for your consistent effort.

So don't forget, a simple note or two (or three) can do wonders when it comes to networking. Don't you enjoy receiving thank-you notes? I do. And I remember those who send them.

Before moving on, let's answer a question you might have been asking yourself throughout this segment: "Bob, why not just send an e-mail? That's what everyone else does these days."

Ahhh, Grasshopper (are you old enough to remember the old "Kung Fu" television show?), *how often the answer is contained within the question.*

The fact that *everyone else* sends e-mail is one reason sending these personalized note cards is even more effective than ever. Talk about standing out from the crowd! And the truth is, even before the advent of e-mail, most people didn't send thank-you notes, so it was effective way back in those "ancient days," too. What's more, even those people who did send thank-you notes rarely had their pictures on their stationery. And finally, the rare person who does send a thank-you note in a networking context usually includes within it a solicitation—which takes away the positive effect of the note anyway!

Little wonder that following this practice, as we've looked at it here, will distinguish you as a truly rare and valuable contact.

Getting back to the question. I believe e-mail is a wonderful, very beneficial communication tool. Once you've sent this initial handwritten note, by all means, keep in touch via e-mail as well. I'm just saying that the impression you'll make with that handwritten note absolutely blows e-mail right out of the water.

E-mail is so easy to send, it's perceived as being almost effortless. Not that this is a bad thing. But when you've taken the time to write a brief, handwritten, personal note; addressed and stamped it by hand and mailed it—now *that* took some thought, effort and time, and all of that will be greatly appreciated by the recipient, your new networking contact.

Relatively little effort: *huge* potential payoff.

Keep Them in Your Thoughts

Be sure to send your networking prospects any articles, newspaper or magazine clippings, or other pieces of information that relate to them or their businesses. If you hear of something that may be helpful to them, send it on your personalized note card.

For example, let's say a networking prospect sells temporary services to businesses.

You hear a rumor that a large company is about to open in a certain building. That would make an excellent and much appreciated informational note, wouldn't it? You could simply call the person, but I would drop a note as well. Dropping that note is so effective and will work to your advantage.

A sample might be:

> *Mary, just a quick note to let you know Amalgamated International is about to open in XYZ building. I did some checking and found out the building owner's name is Joan Garrett; her number is 555-1234. Thought this would be a good prospective lead. Good luck.*

Then sign your name. Can't you see how the person on the receiving end of that note would appreciate your thoughtful gesture?

Sending newspaper or magazine articles affecting our networking prospects is a very valuable idea. I know, it's another point we all learned in Basic Sales 101, but how many people actually do it consistently?

One challenge people might create for themselves is limiting their horizons. You might be thinking, "Well, how often does someone in my network actually get his name or picture in the newspaper? Maybe the special Monday business section, if they got promoted or something, but how often does that happen?"

Here's a suggestion: As you look through the newspaper, *scour* it to see what bits and pieces of news or information might somehow, in some way, affect those in your network. If something you read has anything to do with them, their profession, personal interests, hobbies, whatever, send it along with a short note.

Let me cite a firsthand example.

When I was in local sales, I had a prospect who owned a local franchise. He was definitely a Center of Influence whose business and referrals I very much desired.

One morning in the newspaper, I saw a rather uncomplimentary article about the headquarters of that franchise. This can be a rather touchy situation, because we don't want to send our people bad news. Nonetheless, I cut the article out of the paper and wrote a note on my note card, saying, "Although I don't agree with the article, I thought it would still be of interest." I enclosed the article and note in an envelope and sent it.

He called the very next day to thank me for my consideration. He hadn't seen the article and was glad I cared enough to send it. In fact, he planned to write a rebuttal letter to the editor as a result, which he did.

Now: did I get his business that day? No. But I did two months later, when he was ready. In other words, when he needed the products or services that I handled, I was the only one who came naturally to his mind. The founder of the National Speakers Association, the late Cavett Robert, said it best (and by the way, actually said it first): "People don't care how much you know until they know how much you care—about them and *their* problems." After knowing how much I cared, he was more than willing to find out how much I knew. Over time, I also received numerous referrals from him, and I am quite sure I would continue to do so to this day if I were still in any type of local business.

Going back to e-mail for a moment: it's entirely appropriate to send these, as well. While you don't want to be someone who sends all sorts of annoying tidbits to everyone you know, information of genuine interest to another person will certainly be much appreciated.

Small Investment—Big Payback

Next, *send your networking prospects a note pad every few months or so to keep you on their mind.* This note pad should contain your company name, logo, your picture and, as on your note cards, your name directly beneath the picture. (Again, if appropriate, check with company compliance to make sure the formatting meets their requirements.)

Your address and telephone number should also be included. Make sure to keep all the information about you on the top quarter of the page, to give people plenty of room to write their notes. Otherwise, they'll simply throw it out.

Practically everyone sitting at a desk uses scratch pads or note pads, often kept right beside their telephones. When people constantly see your picture as they jot their notes, you become familiar to them. As Rick Hill puts it, "People buy from and refer to those who are familiar to them." Your networking prospects are going to have your face right in front of them a lot of the time, and both your visibility and credibility will automatically increase in their minds. And unless you're in real estate sales, I can practically guarantee that you'll be the only one in your profession whose scratch pad is sitting on your prospects' desks.

You see, what you really want is for your networking prospects to think of you *and only you* whenever anything comes up concerning your business.

If you're a Realtor®, you want them thinking of you whenever they think of buying or selling a home—and even more importantly, whenever they hear anybody else talk about buying or selling a home. In fact, whenever they think "home," you want them to think of you!

If you're an insurance agent, you want them to think of you whenever "insurance" comes up in a conversation. If you're a copy machine salesperson, you want them to think of you whenever "copying machine" comes up.

One time, my director of marketing called a prospect on the other side of the country because she knew it was planning time for the prospect's company's annual convention. The moment my name was mentioned, the meeting planner said, "Oh yes, I have his note pad right here on my desk. How's he doing?" Bear in mind, I had never spoken with this woman—yet she felt she knew me, by virtue of seeing my picture every single working day, and her first impulse was to ask how I was doing!

The result was that we got the booking. I'm positive the decision to have me present a program at their convention was not based solely on the note pad—but I'm also certain that it opened the door, kept me in the ball game, and kept the benefits of my program on that person's mind.

BURG COMMUNICATIONS, INC.

Author:
THE SUCCESS FORMULA
(Samark)

ENDLESS REFERRALS:
Network Your Everyday Contacts Into Sales
(McGraw-Hill)

WINNING <u>WITHOUT</u> INTIMIDATION:
How To Master The Art Of Positive Persuasion
(Samark)

BOB BURG
www.burg.com
www.TheSuccessFormula.com

MEMBER

NATIONAL
SPEAKERS
ASSOCIATION

P.O. BOX 7002 • JUPITER, FL 33468-7002
561-575-2114 • 1-800-726-3667 • FAX: 561-575-2304
bob@burg.com

Figure 4.2 Notice there is lots of room for your prospect, current client, or referral source to write. (And of course, in place of my book titles, you'll have your own benefit statement.)

The Opposite Is Also True

Ethel is a Realtor® and a member of a large office. She has lived in her community all her life and is well liked and respected. One day she ran into a woman with whom she had been friends for years. The woman said excitedly, "Ethel, you're going to be very happy to know I just listed my home for sale with one of the salespeople in your office."

Ethel, for reasons easy to understand, was less than delighted with this news. She asked the woman, nicely but with disappointment in her voice, "But we've known each other for years! Why didn't you list it with me?" The woman, now realizing her faux pas, replied, "Ethel, I'm so sorry. I just didn't think of you at the time."

What that shows is that people generally don't care about our success as much as we do. That isn't surprising. People are concerned with their own success, their own desires and their own problems. Even if they really like us, they usually are not thinking of us. As a result, if we are not somehow in front of them at the very time of a buying decision (whether they are buying directly or in a position to refer business), there's a chance they might not think of us until it's too late.

Another case in point occurred many years ago, but the principle involved is certainly just as relevant today. A person in my town had been trying for two years to sell me a cellular phone. This was when cellular phones were first becoming popular and, as usual, I was lagging somewhat behind the times and still didn't want one (or didn't know I wanted one). Every so often I'd get a call from him and he'd ask me if I was ready to buy. I'd always decline.

I simply didn't feel I needed one, so I was in no particular hurry. As far as the idea of one day possibly doing business with him, that wasn't a problem. He certainly fit into the "knowing, liking, and trusting" category. I always figured that when I was ready to invest in a cellular phone, he'd get a call.

But something happened to change that. My parents, who live very close to me, used to travel two hours to Miami every couple of weeks to visit my sister, her husband and *especially* their two grandchildren. (Fortunately, Robyn, Steve, and the kids live a lot closer now, so it's not nearly as long a trip.) There was one stretch on the Florida Turnpike that was fairly deserted. This always had me concerned. What if Mom and Dad's car broke down in the middle of nowhere where they wouldn't be able to contact anyone for help?

We have a rule in our family. Whenever any one of us takes a trip of any substance, whether by car or plane, we always call to say we've arrived safely. On one occasion, when they had gone to Miami for a visit, the time when they should have arrived came and went, still without a call. I was getting more worried by the minute.

When Dad finally called, he told me what had happened: their car *had* broken down on a deserted section of road—in fact, in that very stretch I'd worried about. Fortunately, a tow truck happened to be in the area and everything turned out fine. Thank goodness, that kind of luck is typical with my Dad and Mom. Nonetheless, the incident was enough to motivate me (or more accurately, to *panic* me) into purchasing a cellular phone for them. (They *still* didn't want one.)

What did I do? I immediately reached for the Yellow Pages and began looking for cell phone companies. Later that day, a salesperson returned my call. We immediately set up an appointment. We met, I bought a car phone and gave it to my parents.

The question I ask you now is, what happened to the local cellular phone guy I knew? I'll tell you *exactly* what happened: nothing. He didn't even enter my mind. I was so emotionally wrapped up in the situation with my parents that I never thought of him, let alone considered calling him. I ended up purchasing the phone from a relative stranger, and I felt terrible about it. Explaining it to him was even worse.

Now, what if every few months I had received a note pad from this guy with his name and picture on it? Wouldn't he have more likely sprung to mind, especially in my time of panic, when I wasn't thinking logically? Wouldn't he have been the *only* person I would have thought of? Absolutely. I would have reached for his note pad far more readily than for the Yellow Pages—his name and number would have been right there on top!

We've got to keep ourselves in front of our networking prospects constantly. Of course, we must accomplish this in a very nonpushy, nonintrusive manner. The goal is to be the only one they think of when it comes time for them, or anyone in their sphere of influence, to need or want our products, goods, or services.

Why the Scratch Pad

Wouldn't other types of promotional items, such as newsletters, pens, magnets and others, do just as well?

These sorts of items are fine; often they're great! And certainly they can never hurt. Newsletters, especially, can be excellent marketing tools. But none quite accomplishes what the humble scratch pad can.

The disadvantage with these other items is either that their shelf life isn't long (as in the case of the newsletter) or they don't have your picture on them, and can't always be seen by your networking prospect anyway. A pen will eventually run out of ink and be thrown away, and there goes your name and phone number. The scratch pad will be kept and used. And while the individual scratch pad will eventually be used up as well, this only provides you with yet another reason to contact them—by sending them another scratch pad with a hello note written on it!

In a nutshell, here's why the scratch pad with your picture on it is so important:

You want them, when they *hear* your name, to know your face and what you do for a living. You want them to *see* your picture and make the connection between your name and what you do for a living. And when they, or someone they know, want or need what you have to offer, you want them to immediately *think* of your name and know your face.

Refer Business

The best way to get business and get referrals is to *give* business and *give* referrals.

Continually look for opportunities to refer business whenever you can. Position yourself as a referral source. There is simply no better way to get someone to want to do something for you, than first doing something for them. There are two reasons for this:

First, they will most likely appreciate what you did for them. Human nature being what it is, most people are genuinely nice and appreciative and will want to give you something back in return. While this is not *why* you do it (and in fact, doing something for someone for the specific purpose of getting back an immediate "repayment" is quite counterproductive, as we'll discuss in more detail in the next chapter), it is often a natural result.

Dr. Robert Cialdini (www.influenceatwork.com), an experimental social psychologist and author of the excellent books, *Influence: The Psychology of Persuasion* and *Influence: Science and Practice*, takes this a lot further. He says this tendency to want to give back has an actual name; he calls it, "The Rule of Reciprocation," and his books offer some remarkable evidence and case histories illustrating its amazing power. According to Cialdini (and I'm paraphrasing slightly), "This rule says that we as human beings *naturally* try to repay in kind what another person has provided us."

The second reason is the reverse of the first: the other person will know that if they give business back to you, you'll probably reciprocate as well, and keep giving business back to them! You obviously have the ability to do so; after all, you sent them business in the first place.

From now on, whenever, wherever, and however you happen to learn that someone needs a particular product or service, just ask yourself who is in your network who would be the best provider of that product or service. Introduce them to one another in whatever way would be most appropriate to the situation and people involved. Doing this, you'll plant so many seeds of goodwill that, between what you've done so far and what we're going to continue to discuss, you'll soon have more referrals than you can handle. (But you'll find a way.)

Thanks for the Referral

When you receive a referral (and after implementing the Endless Referrals System®, which we've only just begun, you'll receive plenty), be sure and follow up every time, immediately, with a handwritten, personalized note of thanks. I suggest using the personalized note card we discussed earlier. Again, enclose it in a number 10 envelope for that extra touch.

According to Tom Hopkins, author of *How to Master the Art of Selling*, the note should read something along these lines:

> *Dear Mary, thank you so much for your kind referral of Bob Jones. You can be assured that anyone you refer to me will be treated with the utmost caring and professionalism.*

Now, isn't that effective? Short, sweet, professional and to the point. It says it all. Not to mention that it will surely reaffirm the referrer's feeling that you were the right person for that referral.

Of course, depending on the situation, you can alter the wording of the note or even the type of thank you. I've sent people who gave me really big referrals everything from flowers to gift certificates to nice restaurants. It's certainly worth the investment, as well as a nice way of saying thank you to someone you genuinely like and to whom you feel grateful.

However you thank them, do it in such a way that separates you from the rest. Constantly show that person why *you* should be the only person in your particular line of work receiving the referrals of her 250-person sphere of influence.

Key Points

- *Send a personalized thank-you note* on an 8-x-3½–inch personalized note card that includes your picture. The note should be written in blue ink, enclosed in a number 10 envelope, hand-addressed and hand-stamped. Make the time to consistently write and send these notes.
- Send any articles, newspaper or magazine clippings, or other pieces of information that relate to your networking prospects or their business. If you hear of something that might be helpful to them, send it on a piece of your note card stationery.
- Send your networking prospects a note pad regularly to keep you on their minds. Include your company name, logo, picture, and contact information.
- Refer business to others.
- Send thank-you notes after receiving referrals.

CHAPTER 5

Understanding the Law of Successful Giving and Successful Receiving

A s you've seen in the two previous chapters, at this point in the process, you are giving a lot, giving continuously, and it might seem as though you are the only one doing any giving. Actually, it *should* seem that way—because it's probably true! Not to worry: All this giving is setting you up for an avalanche of referrals on a consistent, ongoing basis that will eventually lead to more referrals and more business than you can imagine!

This really *is* all about giving (about being a go-*giver* as opposed to a go-*getter*) and about how giving will come back to you many times over. And there's nothing "la-la" about this: It's based on universal laws and principles that have stood the test of time.

Most people are familiar with the saying, "Give and you shall receive." Many have seen this principle operating in their lives. It's simply one manifestation of the law of cause and effect.

Sometimes this law proves itself almost immediately; other times, it takes years. Sometimes the result comes directly from the cause, and other times indirectly. Some people seem to experience the results of this law more tangibly and in ways easier to understand than do others. But we all know intuitively that this law works.

Why does this law work? Why do we receive so abundantly when we give?

In his 1910 book, *The Science of Getting Rich*, Wallace D. Wattles set down certain rules that will help you become prosperous if you follow them. When he talks about being rich, he's talking specifically about financial riches, not the many other excellent interpretations, such as personal fulfillment, happiness, health, and so forth. But he also makes the point (which I heartily subscribe to) that if you become wealthy the *right way*, then those other important aspects of your life will become just as healthy as your finances.

Here is one of Mr. Wattles's rules to becoming rich:

Always give more in use value than what you take in cash value. You cannot give a person more in cash value than you take from them, but you can give them more in use value than the cash value of the thing you take from them.

What does this mean? On the surface, he's saying that when you sell a product or service, although you'd go broke if your product or service cost you more than you took in financially, you can actually provide a product or service that adds more value to those customers' lives than the cash value they paid for it, while making a profit at the same time.

He describes this in terms of his own book (which back in 1910 must have sold for a fraction of today's $12 price tag):

The paper, ink and other material in this book may not be worth the money you paid for it. But, if the ideas in this book bring you thousands of dollars, you have not been wronged by those who sold it to you. They have given you a great use value for a small cash value.

Excellent point. (Of course, I hope you feel the same way about *this* book!)

Wattles was discussing this principle in terms of a direct sale. However, we're talking about the value you give, not in selling your products or services, but simply in the *relationship* you're beginning with a new networking partner. Given that, let's take a deeper look at what Mr. Wattles wrote. Taking the passage above that says, "You cannot give a person more in cash value than you take from them, but you can give them more in use value than the cash value of the thing you take from them," let's rephrase and condense it:

Give someone more in use value than what you take from them.

This simply means, always do your best to add to *the other person's* life and success, without concern—especially at the beginning—for what you are receiving from the relationship.

There's an excellent reason why this attitude will help you accomplish much and reach great financial heights. Again, according to Mr. Wattles:

People are built with a desire for increase *in their lives.*

When carefully considered, his statement makes perfect sense. After all, human technology has advanced considerably since the beginning of recorded history. This is so because human beings desire increase, whether in their health, wealth, convenience, artistic sense, spiritual lives, or in any other way imaginable.

This is why, when you have a product, service, or skill that can help people increase an aspect of their lives, you can make a lot of money.

A few quick examples: Percy L. Spencer, the inventor of the microwave oven, satisfied the desire for more convenience. Debbi Fields, founder of Mrs. Fields Cookies, tapped into people's desire for more pleasure, as did a man by the name of Candido *Jacuzzi*. There are many, many more examples on a local level—from the person who helps people satisfy their desire for an increase in their financial security by helping them invest in the right financial growth products, to the computer troubleshooter who helps his customers satisfy their desire for increase in the work they can accomplish on their computers.

When people sense that just by being associated with you, their lives will experience significant increase, they will naturally want to advance the relationship. And they will do so by doing their best to give back to you.

To me, this passage from near the end of Mr. Wattles's book is one of the most profound statements of all time; it is also key to understanding the way of the successful networker:

> *No matter what your profession, if you can give increase of life to others and make them sensible [i.e., "aware"] of this gift, they will be attracted to you, and you will get rich.*

And this leads to one of the most important concepts of all.

The Grand Paradox: "Real-World" Giving and Receiving

Remember the Golden Rule of Networking?

> *All things being equal, people will do business with, and refer business to, those people they know, like and trust.*

When we give to (or do something for) someone, we take an important step toward causing those "know, like, and trust" feelings in that person. As mentioned before, the best way to get business and referrals is to give business and referrals. Why? Because when someone knows you care about them enough to send business their way, they feel good about you.

Actually, they feel *great* about you, which produces the natural desire to give back to you. They also know that it's in their best interests to cultivate a mutually beneficial, give and take, win/win relationship with you.

Of course, it doesn't have to be actual business that you give. It could be information that would help them in their business, personal, social, or recreational lives, or any other area of interest to them. Perhaps you suggested a book (or sent them a copy) that you knew would be of true value to them. Maybe you knew their son or daughter was looking for work at a certain company and, knowing someone there who knew the personnel director, you made a call and put in the kind word that helped ensure employment.

What's important to remember is to give, not with an emotional demand that the person to whom you're giving must repay you in kind, but purely out of the joy of adding increase to the life of another human being.

This is the grand paradox of giving and receiving: When you give purely out of the love of giving, you cannot help but receive. Yet when you give only *in order* to receive, it doesn't work out nearly as well!

One reason this is so is that people are attuned to your intent; it's human nature. When you give in order to get, it comes across as such to the other person. More often than not, they can tell. Some folks have a knack for getting away with this more than others, but eventually it will come back to haunt them.

When you give because it's something you desire to do, and do so without the expectation of direct reciprocation, you'll find that the Law of Cause and Effect works for you in ways the typical business person might never even imagine.

Thomas Powers, founder of the online network, Ecademy, and author of the book *Networking for Life*, puts it very nicely: "The energy...arises from a willing suspension of self-interest."

One reason I love that sentence is that it perfectly encapsulates the one trait common to those I call "superstar networkers." These are people who constantly ask themselves how they can add to the life and business of the other person, as opposed to what they can *get* from them.

Please understand, this does *not* mean they don't expect to prosper. In fact, they *know* they'll prosper, and in a huge way. But they are not emotionally attached to having to reap the rewards right then and there, or even ever, directly from that person. Thus, they can fully focus on the *giving* part of being a successful networker. They know that the more they give, the more they'll eventually get. Yes, it really does work that way.

Let's take a closer look at what I mean by superstar networkers.

Superstar Networkers

Superstar networkers, those whose businesses are extremely profitable and whose personal lives are filled with friends and loving relationships, share two powerful traits in common.

Number one, they are givers.
Number two, they are "connectors."

First let's discuss what I *don't* mean by givers. There are plenty of people who seem in a sense to be givers, but the way they give is so sharply limiting that it doesn't fulfill the qualities of giving we've been talking about at all—nor does it produce the same results. These fall into two broad categories.

The Quid Pro Quo Networker

This is the person who gives only in order to get something back. (Or, as the esteemed Dr. Hannibal Lecter put it so eloquently, "Quid pro quo, Clarice…quid pro quo.") This type of pseudonetworker always has an agenda when they do anything for another, and they soon gain a reputation for being that way.

While a QPQ networker can and sometimes does attain his share of business, he will never develop the kind of long-lasting, mutually beneficial, give-and-take relationships with others that the superstar networker will enjoy. He will never elicit in others those feelings of knowing, liking and trusting that is the hallmark of the genuine networker's relationships. If he *does* get anything back from the relationships he forms, it will at most be exactly what he gave in the first place and no more—and most likely, it will come grudgingly. What's more, it most likely will come back from that one source alone, and only that one time. This is not the case with our superstar networkers.

What's interesting about a QPQ giver is that he often *thinks* he is the ultimate networker. That's the belief system he comes from—that networking is a strategy for getting from others. "Hey, sometimes I might even have to give a little first, and why not, if that's what it'll take to get what I want from them." Any success this person achieves will be mere inches on the yardstick of profitable superstar networking.

The Martyr

This is the person who gives in a way that ends up hurting himself. The Martyr actually sets himself up to be taken advantage of. Why would anyone possibly want to do this? Because there's a payoff—though not the kind of payoff that yields success. It's the sort of payoff that says, "Look at me, I'm a martyr. Here I am, always doing for others, but no one does for me." In other words, it provides an excuse for not being successful.

This person is convinced that giving does not and cannot ever result in success. And he's right—for him. But on an unconscious level, he's not really seeking success; his more primary goal is to stay within a comfort zone dictated by his belief system.

These are examples of what a true giver is *not*. Now let's look at what a true giver *is*.

The Genuine Networker

The superstar, mega-successful, high-dollar-earning networker is the greatest and most active giver you know. He is constantly referring business to others. She is always on the lookout for a piece of information that will interest someone in her network of friends and prospects—regardless of whether or not it's business-related. He is always suggesting ways that someone from whom he purchases goods or services can improve his own business.

Genuine networkers give. They give actively and without expectation. They are always thinking of what they can give, how they can give, and to whom can they give.

They are who I term *superstar* networkers.

Tim Sanders, author of the bestseller, *Love Is the Killer App*, describes this as "the act of intelligently and sensibly sharing your *intangibles*." According to Sanders, our "intangibles" are our *knowledge*, our *network*, and our *compassion*.

Some superstar networkers seem to excel in one type of giving above all others and become known for this. For example, some individuals are always recommending great books, or constantly making introductions to people who can benefit one another.

Mike Litman, author of, *Conversations With Millionaires*, talks about how this creates what he calls an "asset of value." This, says Mike, is what you bring to the table in your relationships with others. And it doesn't cost you a cent! (Or perhaps the price of a book or a stamp.) The result? The other person's appreciation, which as you already know, can prove to be virtually priceless.

What's interesting is that successful, giving, profitable, superstar networkers seem to have a knack for hooking up with *other* success givers. It's not luck: they are specifically looking to identify these types of people. Why? Because they know that while average networking relationships are 50/50, the most exciting and profitable ones are 100/100. In other words, both people are trying so hard to help each other succeed, that success comes back to each of them in spades.

Connectors

I also mentioned that these people are "connectors." They are always asking themselves who they can set up with each other. They know that everyone they know or meet might be a valuable contact to someone else in their network. The fun part is introducing them and setting up the relationship.

You can probably see how the goodwill and positive feelings you elicit in others can come back to you in incredible abundance.

Again, the essence of being a Connector is the proactive drive to make the connections—not out of a calculating intent to get something in return, but out of the joy and satisfaction of seeing the positive, exciting developments that can spring out of the new associations you help form. It's something very much like the pure joy of the creative artist: the thrill of the creation itself is its own reward.

Connectors don't worry about whether they'll "get anything" in return. They *know* they'll be taken care of—and well taken care of. It's simply not an issue.

The essential point here is that being a Connector isn't a genetic fluke. You don't have to be born a Connector—you can become one!

Simply develop (through practice) a habit of giving without expectation, without concern for what you're going to "get" from the other person. Know that when you tap into the sheer joy of giving and connecting, you're going to get, and get big-time. Try not to think about it too much. Just get out there and try to give yourself away! Way before you even get close, you'll get back so much in return, you'll know you've become a superstar networker.

Some Shining Examples

My network is filled with people such as those described above. We constantly keep each other in mind, often providing suggestions, contacts, and yes, lots of referrals. This includes people such as my dear friend, the networking superstar, Terri Murphy.

Even though we don't speak that often, whenever we do, Terri immediately wants to know if there are any people or potential clients I'd like her to introduce me to. Of course, I always want to do the same for her, not out of obligation, but because I just flat-out like her so much. And you know what? Perhaps out of some obligation as well, but if so, it's an obligation I enjoy since she's been so helpful to me over the years.

In the previous editions of this book I referred to Terri as "The 14-Million-Dollar Woman," because when she was an active Realtor®, that's how much she sold every year, through good markets and bad. (And this was back when $14 million dollars was a number achieved by very, very few in that field. As Terri says, only partly joking, "That's when $14 million was a lot of money!") Terri achieved much of that on a part-time basis while she was developing her speaking and writing career. (She has since retired from active real estate sales and writes and speaks full-time.) If you knew her even for one minute, you immediately see why.

Once, while speaking near her city, I paid her a visit to see just how she did it. As I walked with her through town, it seemed as though I was with a visiting Hollywood celebrity. People loved her—they *adored* her. And why? Because she not only *seems* concerned with other people's welfare, she *is* concerned with it.

What's more, she *acts* upon it. Terri actively tries to help everyone with whom she comes into contact. She connects people with each other in a way that helps everyone benefit. As a result, people feel good about her. They know her, they like her and they trust her.

Terri (www.terrimurphy.com) has now parlayed her huge success as a local Realtor® into an equally huge (or huger) success as an international authority on real estate and communication skills. Her books include *Listing & Selling Secrets*, *E-listing & E-selling Secrets*, *Taking Charge!—Lessons in Leadership* and *The EZ Guide to Real Estate Investments*. To this day, and in her new profession, she utilizes the same basic principles of giving and connecting that brought her such outstanding success in the first place.

I met my friend and occasional joint-venture partner Sean Woodruff (www.woodruffdirect.com) through the introduction of a good mutual friend, Stephanie West Allen (www.allen-nichols.com). Stephanie is a giver in the truest sense of the word and a classic connector.

Early in our friendship, I had helped Stephanie with a project she was working on. Sean had also provided some expertise. Stephanie was grateful and connected Sean and me, thinking we might team up on some projects. I was impressed with Sean right away, as it was obvious he had that giving spirit as well. Sean later said he sensed the same thing about me.

Before long, Sean and I worked together on several profitable joint-venture projects. By the way, the friendships between Stephanie and me, Sean and Stephanie, and Sean and me, all took place via the Internet, well before any of us had ever met in person. To this day, and as of this writing, although I've now met both Stephanie and Sean in person during my travels, the two of them have yet to meet one another face to face.

In fact, they've never even spoken on the telephone.

Yes, these principles work just as well on the Internet!

Another great networking relationship, this one with Chris Widener (www.chriswidener.com), author of *The Angel Inside* and founder of "The Ultimate Success Series," began on the telephone after we were introduced through a mutual joint-venture partner, Kyle Wilson. Kyle is President of Jim Rohn International (www.jimrohn.com), and had suggested that Chris interview me for a coaching program he was running with that organization.

After the interview, while Chris and I were discussing some business goals we each had, a name came to his mind that he thought would be a terrific connection for me. Immediately, not only did he give me the person's name and contact information, but he went out of his way to call the other person to pave the way for *my* call. Although this particular contact didn't end up paying off as Chris and I had hoped, it sure told me a lot about Chris and his giving spirit. He and I continued to brainstorm, have each referred the other to several profitable contacts, and we continue to collaborate and refer each other as opportunities arise.

As my friend, Ivan Misner, Founder of BNI (Business Network International, a referral-exchange organization we'll refer to later in the book) and author of the bestseller, *Masters of Networking* says, "Givers gain." Yes, it's that simple.

I mentioned that "successful givers" look for and seem to attract other successful givers. This reminds me of something Jim Collins points out in his amazing book, *Good to Great: Why Some Companies Make the Leap...and Others Don't*.

While Collins's book focuses on major corporations (looking at why some took a giant step into a whole other category of success while others remained where they were or faltered), the lessons—each and every one of them—are just as applicable for today's smaller business person.

In Chapter 3 of his book, Collins discusses the concept of "getting the right people onto the bus" (and the wrong people off the bus). In other words, more important than the direction you want to go or the products or services that will get you there, what is imperative is that you align yourself with the right people.

In the research that led to the book's publication, the author found that as long as the right people "were on the bus," that company always prospered. When they weren't, then nothing else mattered: the company stagnated or faltered. This surprised the author and his research team, at first. But it makes a lot of sense, doesn't it?

After all, if there's one thing we're learning in this book, it is that people do business with, and refer business to, those people they know, like and trust. And, the key word is "people." Not products, not services, not directions, and not ideas. Of course, all of these must be good and worthwhile, as well. But it's the people and the relationships that are key and that make the difference in your success.

Giving First: A Personal Experience

I'd like to share with you one story from my own business that embodies this point,

Several years after I had begun speaking professionally, there was a corporate client (one with many divisions) that I was trying to land. Not only could I not seem to get a foot in the door, I couldn't even find the door to try to stick my foot in. These people seemed to be invisible.

About this time, at one of the first National Speakers Association conventions I attended, I happened to meet a man who had been speaking professionally for quite some time. I struck up a friendship with him and his family and began looking forward to seeing them at various events. During this entire time, despite the fact that I knew he was quite successful, I never asked him for anything. I did, however, help him as much as I could.

Several times, when I was unable to accept an engagement because I was already booked for that date, I would refer him to the company who had called me. Having articles published fairly often in magazines, I would refer him to the editor as a possible writer. This was appreciated by all parties, of course, and didn't take anything from me in any way. (This is one of the great things about giving: it helps everyone and hurts no one.)

A couple of years after meeting this gentleman, I discovered that the client I had been unsuccessfully seeking was a major client of his. Now, I probably could have come right out and asked him for help, but I didn't feel that would be quite right. I didn't want him to feel that because I had gone out of my way for him, he "owed" me anything. But I did feel comfortable asking for his *advice* on how I might best pursue this corporation.

I said, "I know this is a huge client of yours, and I'm not in any way asking you to make a connection for me. But I'd love to know what you think is the best way for me to go about contacting the right person, so I can at least get the opportunity to establish and develop a relationship with them."

He would have none of that. He said, "I'll have the gentleman who's my main contact call you." And he did. Over the years since, that client, together will all the spin-off engagements I've had within that company's umbrella, has accounted for several million dollars in sales.

That was not the first, and certainly not the only time, that giving first has literally paid big financial dividends. It's the way I run my business; it's the way I run my life. Giving first works.

A Prototypical Networking Superstar

My friend Bea Salabi is the absolute prototype of the successful giver. Bea, who owns a local mortgage lending company called Palm Lending, came into town as the owner of a new mortgage brokerage company that consisted of just Bea and one partner. A year later, Bea had three very profitable offices and over 30 team members. A huge success story

Bea is someone who goes out of her way for anyone and everyone she can, from sponsoring a family of eight children, to serving on her local board of directors for Habitat for Humanity, to taking over 1500 local underprivileged children to the movies in one summer. And please don't think she does this with the idea of acquiring business. She doesn't. (Although oddly enough, it always seems to happen.)

On the other hand, she also throws huge, lavish parties for her prospects and clients. From the parties, she clearly knows she'll eventually receive business, and she really goes all out in providing an abundance of delicious food, a massage therapist, entertainment, and many other goodies. Though this is part of her business public relations efforts, she's just the type of person who goes all out when she gives. It's simply part of her nature.

What I've found is that people very seldom have a successful business personality and a completely different, separate, nonbusiness personality. Bea certainly illustrates this observation: She gives in high style, whether it's for her business, charity, or friends. Come to think of it, for Bea, it's *all* "for friends"!

Here's a typical Bea story (one example out of dozens I could cite) of how giving purely for the sake of giving led to receiving many times over.

A local woman was having her house foreclosed on. A couple found out about it through their church (the same church this woman attended) and came to Bea, saying they'd like to buy the house to prevent the foreclosure. They would hang onto the home, they said, until the woman was able to buy it back from them.

Bea offered her services for free, and did not receive a single cent from the transaction. However, as a result of her giving efforts, she received numerous referrals, which in turn ended up resulting in—are you ready for this?—more than 25 closed transactions. And for these transactions, she did indeed earn commissions.

How did this all come about? Apparently, the couple turned out to be true Centers of Influence, and because they felt so strongly that Bea's efforts should not go unrewarded, they began spreading the word about her. This is what happens to successful givers.

Be like Bea, and all the other ultrasuccessful networkers who know that the way to receive in abundance is to be a giver and connector, and to do so with your principle goal being simply to help the people in your network. Do this consistently, and keep adding people to your network, and you'll become like a water pump that's been correctly and sufficiently primed—and you'll receive a steady, gushing flow of endless referrals upon endless referrals.

Key Points

- It is a universal law that when we give, we will always end up receiving, usually even more abundantly than we gave.
- One of Wallace D. Wattles's rules for becoming rich is, "Always give more in use value than what you take in cash value."
- The Grand Paradox: When you give purely out of the love of giving, you cannot help but receive. Yet when you give only *in order* to receive, it doesn't work out nearly as well!
- Superstar networkers are givers, and they are connectors.

CHAPTER **6**

Training Your Personal Walking Ambassadors and Asking for Referrals (So That You Actually Get Them)

Thus far we've learned a method for effectively meeting people and winning them over in a very nonaggressive, nonthreatening way—including everything from your initial introduction through genuinely caring follow-up.

You may even have already matched some good people with other good people and had a hand in the success of those you've chosen to include in your network. It's probably safe to say that these people feel good about you. They *know you, like you, and trust you.* They want to see you succeed, and they want to help you find new business. These people are what I call your "Personal Walking Ambassadors."

However, there is still a challenge: While these people may *want* to help you find new business, they might not know how. You may be in a profession in which your prospects seem obvious, and people may be totally familiar with what you do—but that doesn't matter. For other people to know how to network for you may be more difficult than you realize.

Help Them Help You

What you've got to do is make it easy for them. Train (a better word might actually be *teach*, or *help*) the people who want to network for you. how to do just that.

Sometimes, things we take for granted are confusing to someone else. Have you ever had a good acquaintance or close friend whose means of making a living was unknown to you?

A friend of mine named Tom is vice president of an engineering firm. When asked what he does for a living, he replies, "I'm an engineer." What does that tell me? What does that tell anyone? Absolutely nothing. I'd like to refer business to him when and if the opportunity arises, and I've asked him numerous times to explain, in layman's terms, just what it is he does and who his prospects are. Unfortunately (for me, but far more so, for Tom), I still don't get it! He hasn't yet developed a simple method of explaining what he does.

Another friend is a computer consultant. A computer consultant...what is that? It could mean anything, couldn't it? It reminds me of a scene from the movie *Father of the Bride*. When Steve Martin's soon-to-be son-in-law describes himself as an "international computer consultant," he laughs and adds, "Every time I say that, it sounds like I'm unemployed"—which is exactly what Steve had told his wife he thought it meant.

And it isn't only such broad, vague terms as "engineer" and "consultant." Even more tangible, clearly defined professions can be problematic for those who are not versed in that particular field. To solve this, we can borrow a method usually involved in a one-on-one sales presentation: the "features versus benefits" perspective.

Features versus Benefits

What's the difference between a feature and a benefit? A feature is what something *is*, whereas a benefit is what something *does*. A feature is a thing; a benefit is the solution to a problem or the fulfillment of a desire.

This distinction between features and benefits is often stressed in sales training classes because it's so important for sales professionals to realize that people buy a product or service not for its features but for the benefits they will realize by taking ownership.

Keep in mind that benefits often encompass opposite ends of the spectrum. In other words, the benefits might include the fulfillment of a desire and/or the solution to a problem.

When I was in direct sales, we would use the analogy of the elderly woman from the cold Northeast. She visited an appliance store in the middle of a freezing winter in order to purchase a heater. The salesperson, who was a glib, expert presenter, began rattling off all the heater's wonderful features.

He expertly informed the woman what type of material the heater was made of, the way it was crafted, and even the BTU output. He described the engineering and research that went into it, the bells and whistles. He even told her about where it was made and how long the manufacturer had been in business. After patiently listening to this salesperson's eloquent description of the impressive list of features, the woman asked meekly, "But will it keep an old lady warm at night?"

That's the difference between features and benefits.

Frank Maguire (www.frankmaguire.com), author of *You're The Greatest!* and a good friend, is one of the founders of Federal Express. According to Frank, "We decided early on that we were not in the 'delivery' business...but in the business of `peace of mind.' Our clients' biggest fear was late delivery."

Late delivery could ruin a business, or at the very least, ruin a good account. It was their clients' biggest perceived problem—their biggest source of pain. Frank knew his clients needed to feel assured that regardless of the situation, their package would "absolutely, positively" be there when it was supposed to be (i.e., overnight!).

Life insurance is a feature. Financial abundance, as well as protection and security for loved ones, are the benefits one derives from owning a life insurance policy. For a life insurance sales professional to say, "I sell life insurance" is merely to point out a feature. To say, "I show people how to plan for a sound financial future while protecting themselves and their loved ones for the present," is declaring the benefits to the prospective client. In the latter case, this benefit statement both satisfies a want (a sound financial future) and solves a problem (protecting the insured's loved ones).

"I sell real estate" is a feature. "I help people successfully market their home and purchase their perfect dream home" is the benefit one will derive by working with that salesperson.

"I am a dentist" is a feature. "I provide healthy teeth and smiles, with no pain" is the benefit to the prospective patient, and the referrer will easily understand that. (Note that this takes some thought and care to figure out and phrase well. "I make people sit in chairs for hours while I drill metal objects into their teeth" is just as accurate, but somehow misses the mark.)

Remember, as we network, we have to realize that it isn't only the person to whom we are speaking whose business we are after. More important is her 250-person sphere of influence. We want to state the benefits of what we do in such a vivid, crystal clear manner that the person we're talking to can not only picture it, but also remember it and repeat it—potentially as many as 250 times!

And it doesn't stop there.

Actually Tell Them *How* to Know

There's yet one more step to this process. Remember the One Key Question you asked this person during your first conversation? "How can I know if someone I'm speaking to is a good prospect for you?" Well, after you have established your *know you, like you, trust you* relationship with this person, you can also let her know, in plain and simple language, how to recognize if someone would be a good prospect *for you.*

For example: remember Gary, the copying machine salesperson? He pointed out that when walking by a copying machine, you might notice a lot of crumpled up pieces of paper overflowing from a wastepaper basket. According to Gary, that's a perfect indication that this copy machine hasn't been working well lately, which means that its owner might need a new one—and you could provide Gary with an excellent lead or referral.

You can give others exactly this type of coaching. If you are a printer, you might suggest that a person just starting a new business may be a good prospect for you. If you are a solar energy equipment salesperson, then suggesting that your fellow networkers keep their eyes and ears open for people complaining about high energy costs would serve you well.

Remember that even though *you* know what it is you need, other people most likely don't. Help them to help you.

Keep in mind that no matter how good a rapport you establish during your initial conversation with networking prospects, it's only *after you have earned their loyalty* that you can legitimately expect your benefit statement and "how-to-know" prospecting tip to carry any weight with them. That's okay. We're assuming that at present, they are quite grateful to have you in *their* network, and are only too happy to be your Personal Walking Ambassador.

Your Personal Benefit Statement

We've covered possible benefit statements for several professions. Later in this chapter, I'll list a few more suggestions. While there's not room here for me to write out a different benefit statement for every possible profession and the various niche markets to which they'd gear them, these examples will give you a sense of how it's done.

First, let's look at some guidelines that will help you come up with one of your own.

Your benefit statement should be a short, succinct, descriptive sentence, no more than seven seconds in length. It should describe what you do and how it will benefit the person using your services.

Once you've developed this benefit statement, practice it on people you know. A family member or close friend is ideal; so is a trusted associate with whom you work. Get their critiques and ask them to be totally honest. Don't worry about perfection. Don't worry about getting your feelings hurt. Your first try isn't etched in stone. You'll keep improving on it as time goes on.

In my case, when I first began teaching the principles of networking, my benefit statement was, "I show people how to network for profit." It was a fairly decent benefit statement. It was short, concise, and it included a desired benefit to the person attending my seminar, namely, profit.

Decent—but far from spectacular. So I kept working on it. I asked myself the benefit my prospects would get out of my program. Benefits that were tangible, that they could relate to, and that would tell them *how* they were going to achieve all that profit.

I knew that my prospects fit into two main categories. The first category was direct salespeople depending on referrals to accelerate their business. The second was professionals such as financial advisors, chiropractors, dentists, lawyers, and accountants—people whose business greatly depends on referrals, but who definitely do *not* consider themselves to be salespeople (even though they really are). And the people in this second group had to be very discreet in seeking out referrals from those who were not already patients or clients.

Notice that both groups wanted and needed *referrals*, so I needed to include that term in my benefit statement—and it had to be plural. They didn't need one referral. They needed continuous, *endless* referrals. Hmm...That's it! My new benefit statement became:

I show people how to cultivate a network of endless referrals.

This not only became my new benefit statement, it also inspired the title of a book—in fact, the book in your hands right now. That benefit statement has become my trademark, and it's helped me position myself as an authority in the networking field.

There is no mistaking the promised benefits. Anyone *not* interested in bringing in endless referrals for his business will walk right past it on the bookstore shelf. However, practically everyone who *is* interested in attaining what the title promises will stop, pick it up, and take a deeper look. And I know it's an effective benefit statement because of the positive comments I receive from those in the direct response industry.

These people are masters at writing headlines that grab our attention. They *have* to be. After all, they have just split seconds to get us interested enough to keep reading the message. Their "benefits-laden" headlines often make the difference between a successful advertising campaign and an unsuccessful one. When a prospective mail-order buyer sees that headline, it must immediately present enough of a benefit to get that prospect to continue reading the ad.

Let's Put It Together

A good benefit statement often begins with something like, "I show people how to..." or "I help people to...." It's generally not a good idea to begin sentences with the word "I," but in this case we almost have to. If you come up with another beginning that works as well for you, by all means, use it.

What's vital is that you show how you help some*body* do some*thing*, or how you do some*thing* for some*body*. That something can be to help them achieve a positive goal, or avoid or conquer a particular pain, or both.

One of the best benefit statements I ever heard was from a young man during a seminar in Minneapolis. I was suggesting benefit statements for people in the audience involved in different professions. Somebody asked me to suggest a benefit statement for stockbrokers, or financial planners. After I gave a few of my standard suggestions, a gentleman named Gregory Zandlo of North East Asset Management raised his hand. He had a benefit statement he'd been using which he thought was worth mentioning. It was:

We help people create and manage wealth.

Wow! That says it all, doesn't it? How much more effective could a benefit statement possibly be? It's short, sweet, and to the point. It can also fit into any conversation without sounding pushy. And it points out a desire (creating wealth) while solving a problem (managing that wealth).

Follow Gregory's lead: Take a moment right now to come up with a benefit statement in the fewest possible words. Take a separate piece of paper, and do that now. And please don't worry about perfection—just take the first step and put something in writing. You can always revise and perfect it later.

How did you do? It doesn't matter; you are on your way! Keep thinking about it and working on it. Ask those in your network to lend you their ears and provide feedback. Mold this statement. Reshape it. Then memorize it. Internalize your benefit statement so that you know it without having to think. Then experiment with it and check out responses.

Rick Hill, whom I mentioned earlier, uses what he calls the "raised eyebrow test."

According to Rick:

> *When you tell someone your benefit statement and they either yawn or start looking around the room for someone else to talk to, you probably need to continue working on it. If, however, they raise their eyebrows with interest and say, "Hmm, tell me more," or "Really—how do you do that?" you're probably on the right track.*

I think that's as good a description as you'll ever find. And Rick, whose program focuses on prospecting, has an excellent benefit statement himself. When asked what he does, he responds:

> *I teach companies large and small how to develop a never-ending chain…of new business.*

Great! And notice the pause after "never-ending chain." "That," says Rick, "is to help that person picture that never-ending chain."

A Few More Benefit Statements

The following are just a few benefit statements used by those in particular businesses. A few are repeated from earlier, but they seemed worth repeating.

CHIROPRACTOR: I help people heal themselves naturally, without drugs.

ACCOUNTANT: I give large and small companies timely and accurate financial information while legally minimizing their business and personal tax liability.

REALTOR®: I help people successfully market their home and buy their perfect dream home.

FINANCIAL ADVISOR: We help people create and manage wealth.

ADVERTISING AGENCY: We show you how to dramatically increase your company's revenues through strategic positioning in the marketplace.

LIFE INSURANCE AGENT: I help people prepare for a sound financial future while protecting themselves and their loved ones for the present.

GRAPHIC ARTIST: I show you how to present your perfect image to those with whom you want to do business.

SOLAR ENERGY SALESPERSON: We help people save energy and save money all at once through solar heating.

TRANSACTIONAL ATTORNEY: Our firm helps people successfully arrange transactions while helping them avoid costly mistakes.

LITIGATING ATTORNEY: Our firm helps people resolve disputes in various forms and avoid costly consequences.

Tell Them How to Know If Somebody *They* Are Talking to Would Be a Good Prospect for *You*

You should take this step *only* when you are sure the other person is ready. If you have already won this person over, they will *want* to network for you. You can come right out and mention to this person that you could use her help.

Because she is grateful for the business you've referred to her, she might actually say to you, "What can I do for you now that you've been such a help to me? You've thrown business at me, you've thought of me. Now what can I do to know if somebody I'm talking to would be a good prospect for you?" This is when we let them know the answer.

If you are a chiropractor, you might respond, "Anyone with neck pain or back pain is a good prospect for me." An accountant might say, "If you know of someone needing help managing the financial end of the business, that person would be a good prospect for me." A banker could suggest that, "A family that mentions adding on to their home would be an excellent prospect for me." An automotive sales professional could suggest, "If you hear someone complaining about his car or mentioning that his lease will be up soon, that's a great prospect for me."

This transaction of information can occur in either a formal or informal session. Because a win-win relationship has been established, the other person will be glad to know this information.

Aside from championing you to others, your Personal Walking Ambassadors will typically be very happy to suggest others directly to you.

One idea is to invite a Personal Walking Ambassador to lunch. Assure her that you look forward to continuing to help her find new business. At the same time, show and teach her how to refer others to you. This is where knowing how to ask for referrals correctly will make you a lot of money, while not knowing will cause you to leave a lot of it on the table.

How to Ask for Referrals (So That You Actually Get Them)

Years ago, shortly after I had joined a company's local sales force, the sales manager held a meeting one morning focusing on how to increase referrals. The question he asked was, "How do you get referrals?" One of the young salespeople who had just come over from another company was supposed to be a real dynamo. He immediately threw up his hand and said, all-knowingly, "You *ask* for them!"

To my amazement, the sales manager said, "That's right." I remember thinking to myself, "How naive!" Actually, they were both half right. You do have to ask. Where they missed the boat is this: You have to do more than just ask. You must ask in a way that elicits that person to be able to come up with quality names.

Have you ever asked someone, either after a sale, or at any other time when you really felt good about this person wanting to help you: "Kay, do you know anybody else who could benefit from my products or services?"

I'll bet Kay began to stare off into space. She was thinking about it—and thinking about it in earnest, really concentrating. After all, she wanted to help you, as well as help those she cared about whom you'd be serving via your terrific products or services. Finally, she said, "Well, I can't think of anybody right now, but when I do, I'll definitely let you know." You then probably never heard from her again regarding a referral.

It wasn't Kay's fault. She just wasn't asked in a way that would help her find the answer.

When we ask people "who they know" or if they "know anyone who…" we are giving them much too large a frame of reference. A blurry collage of 250 faces (their sphere of influence) will run through their mind, but no individuals will stand out. They might feel frustrated, like they're letting you down. After everything you've done for them, they feel bad that they can't come through for you as well. It might even make that person feel resentful toward you.

Here's the solution: find a way to funnel their world down to just a few people. We've got to give them a frame of reference that they can work with.

Have You Heard the One about the…

Let me explain it this way. Has anybody ever asked you if you knew any good jokes? Now, you probably know plenty of good jokes, but can you actually think of one when someone asks you? I can't.

Here's another example. One night I called my local golden oldies radio station and requested the song "Only in America" by Jay and the Americans. The announcer told me they no longer carry that song on their play list. "But" he asked, "do you happen to know any other oldies you'd like to hear?" I can tell you right now that I know hundreds of oldies I'd like to hear, but could I think of even one at that moment? No way!

It's the same when we ask people if they know "anybody" who could benefit from our products or services. Most likely they know plenty of people who could, or who might. Try to get them to think of even one person at that time using that methodology, however, and it's probably not going to happen.

The Solution Is to Isolate

In his classic, *How to Master the Art of Selling* (www.tomhopkins.com), Tom Hopkins suggests that instead, you provide the person with a frame of reference.

Let's take the following example. You are talking to Joe, a Center of Influence in your community. Joe really likes you. You've sent him business, provided him with some background information for one of his projects, and, who knows, maybe you even fixed him up with a blind date that worked out. You are well aware, through asking the right questions during previous conversations, that Joe happens to be a golfing enthusiast. Let's look at how we might approach this situation with Joe.

> YOU: Joe, you were telling me you're an avid golfer.
>
> JOE: Yes, I am. Been playing for over 20 years. If I ever get to retire, I'll probably play every day. Right now, though, it's only on weekends. And I mean, *every* weekend.
>
> YOU: Hmm. Is there a specific foursome you play with most of the time?
>
> JOE: Well, yeah, there's Joe Martin, Harry Browne and Nancy Goldblatt.
>
> YOU: Joe, as far as you know, would any of them happen to need...

And then you get into the benefits of what you do. Now, it might be that none of the three Joe mentioned are a good prospect at this particular time, but at least you are increasing his odds of being able to help you. You gave him three people he could *see*. Maybe one or more of them *might* need your product or service. If he tells you, "I'll ask them next time we go out," it could result in some business for you down the line.

Now let's move along to the next frame of reference.

> YOU: How long have you been involved with your local Rotary Club?
>
> JOE: About six years now. Great bunch of people.
>
> YOU: Joe, are there one or two people in your club that you tend to sit next to every meeting? [Notice you didn't ask, "Does *anyone* in your club need..." It might be a large club, thus you would be right back with the same problem of too many people for him to be able to isolate anyone.]
>
> JOE: Really just one person—Mike O'Brien. Been friends with him and his family for years.
>
> YOU: Has Mike ever mentioned possibly being in the market for a...?

Let's look at just one more frame.

Perhaps Joe is on the board of directors of his local professional association. Again, instead of asking if *anyone* in the association would fit the type of profile you're looking for, ask him how many people serve on the board with him. Suppose the answer is five. Five is a small enough number for him to handle and be able to visualize each person.

> YOU: Joe, picture those five. Do you feel any of them would
> be open to knowing about...?

Do you see where we're going with this? Somewhere within the frames of reference you're providing, one or several people will come to mind. In effect, while you're limiting the number of people in his world from whom to choose, you are actually increasing the number of people he'll be able to identify and provide as referrals. Very effective.

And understand, once you get the first couple of names, you'll start working your way out to include as many people as possible. What's interesting is that once he gives you that first person's name—and that first one is the most difficult—from there, it's a piece of cake.

Between your helping him to identify people, and then one name breaking the ice and each successive name triggering his memory of someone else he knows, all of a sudden, that trickle of names becomes a stream, which becomes a gushing fountain, and then you're literally sitting back and taking names.

Important point: While the person is giving you these names, don't worry about any additional information, such as telephone numbers, addresses, points of qualification, or anything else. There's plenty of time for that once Joe has exhausted his list of names. While he's giving them to you, just write the names down. After he's through, *then* you have the option of asking for whatever additional information you feel might be helpful.

One more thought: Depending on the product or service you sell, helping people identify people to refer might be even easier and more natural than the above examples.

For example, if you work a particular niche industry, such as educators, then you would simply help them identify educators they know. If your niche is accountants, the same principle applies. If your market is corporate buyers, same thing: realize that this person most likely knows many other corporate buyers and is perhaps even a member of a trade association catering specifically to their counterparts within other companies.

Or maybe you're working a neighborhood and you can inquire about which neighbors they have relationships with. You can also help people to identify others by simply running the "occupation alphabet" we discussed earlier, asking them who they know who is an accountant, a banker, a chiropractor, a dentist, an engineer, and so forth. The more you have this already worked out in your head *before* your actual conversation, the more confident and effective you will be.

I remember my delight in seeing that, after the original edition of this book, a young man involved in direct sales posted a review on amazon.com stating that utilizing this particular method of asking for referrals, he received 23 referrals from a Center of Influence just a week after he met him. Once you begin getting comfortable with this process, you'll be astounded by the number of high-quality referrals you get. Business becomes a good deal of fun at that point. It won't always happen as quickly as it did for this young man, but it doesn't have to happen that quickly all the time for it to still be hugely successful.

You might be wondering if this will seem pushy. The answer is no, not if this person has genuine good feelings about you and wants to see you succeed. You can also arrive at your meeting with a few names of your own for your friend to call. Nothing at all wrong with doing that. And, even if this is not the case, there's a method for being able to ask that makes it totally comfortable for both you and your referral source, which we'll discuss in detail in Chapter 12.

One thing I always do is tell the referrer, "I promise I'll call." And when I call the referred prospect, I say, "Hi, Ms. Johnson. This is Bob Burg calling. I *promised* Joe Callahan I'd call you." Sort of positions us a little better in that person's mind right off the bat, doesn't it? (Please make sure you actually did promise.)

In sales we always want to make it easy for a potential buyer to buy from us. When seeking referrals, we want to make it as easy as possible for a potential referrer to refer to us. Know the frame-of-reference questions you are going to ask *before* you ask them. If you feel comfortable with the process, they will too.

Key Points

- We need to train our Personal Walking Ambassadors to know how to network for us.
- Know the difference between features and benefits. A feature is what something *is*, whereas a benefit is what something *does* (fulfills a desire and/or solves a problem).
- Develop a benefit statement for the product or service you provide.
- Tell people how to know if someone *they* are talking to is a good prospect for *you*.
- To ask for referrals in a way that helps the other person come up with answers, isolate a specific group of people in the referrer's mind so he can "see" them.

CHAPTER 7

Prospecting for Fun and Profit

The very first question one might ask when beginning to read this chapter is, "Isn't this entire book about *prospecting?* After all, when we network, aren't we prospecting for business?"

Yes...and no. When we network, we are prospecting. When we prospect, however, we aren't necessarily networking.

Networking and prospecting are like first cousins—same family, but still different. In this chapter, we're going to look at prospecting from this angle: Prospecting is getting to the point where the networking relationships begin. Networking, in turn, becomes a vehicle for long-term, lasting results.

Here's a rule to live by:

Never stop prospecting!

Yes, even when we reach the point that all (or *nearly* all) of our business comes from referrals, we continue to prospect within our network. And it's also a good idea to continually open new doors.

Prospecting is often viewed as that process we've always heard about and most of us in sales have experienced: the endless telephone calls (i.e., "cold calls"), knocking on doors, and hearing the words, "I'm not interested."

It Doesn't Have to Be That Way

There are ways to prospect that are fun, exciting, and profitable. Sure, you'll see people face to face and prospect by telephone. (Although with the recently enacted Do Not Call laws, cold-calling is rapidly becoming a thing of the past. Increasingly, you'll find you need to secure permission to contact a new person at his home the first time, which is something we'll cover in Chapter 12. As of this writing, cold-calling people at their place of business is still not prohibited.) The difference is in the results you're after, your methods of obtaining those results, and your attitude along the way.

You must first realize that sales and prospecting has always been, and always will be, a numbers game. If you make enough calls and see enough people, you will make your share of sales—even if you do things wrong. Of course, things go a lot better if you do things right: You'll make more sales in much less time, and by calling on far fewer people.

A neat formula in practically any type of prospecting takes into account the relationship between calls and contacts, contacts and appointments, and appointments and sales.

For instance, let's say that for every 100 numbers you call (or people/businesses you call on in person), you actually get to speak or make contact with 40 decision makers. Out of those 40 contacts, you will close 10 appointments. And out of those 10 appointments, you'll make four sales.

Letting the numbers and percentages work for us, we realize that every time we call and don't make contact, make a contact but don't get an appointment, or make an appointment but don't close the sale, we're one step closer to success!

That sounds strange, doesn't it? Here's what I mean. You know the chances are four in 10 that when you call or visit, you'll contact the right person. If you miss your first one, fine! You've just increased your odds on the next call. If you miss the next, congratulate yourself—you're yet another step closer to your first contact.

Obviously, it isn't quite that simple. The numbers work over a long period of time. Nonetheless, the more calls in which you don't hit your goal (contacting the right person), the greater your odds are that the next one will be it.

How to Put a Dollar Value on Small "Failures"

Let's take those same 100 calls and the same ratios. Let's say in this scenario that each closed sale makes you $600 in commission.

If it's going to take 100 total calls to make four sales ($2400), then can't we break that down into $24 per call? That's right! Every time you pick up the phone or visit a business or knock on a door, you net $24.

If you can't make the initial contact, that's $24. If you make the initial contact but can't close the appointment, that's $24. If you make the contact, close the appointment but can't close the sale, that's $24. And when someone says, "I'm not interested!!" simply say (to yourself), "That's $24, please."

How to Prospect Yourself into a Raise

You can raise your salary one of two ways: by making more calls *or* by turning a higher percentage of initial calls into contacts, contacts into appointments, and appointments into sales. That second strategy is what we'll discuss for the remainder of this chapter. We'll look at effective ways of prospecting, both by telephone and by visiting in person.

Turn Your Telephone into $$$

The telephone can understandably be an intimidating object. After all, people can be rude, which means prospects can be rude. When we make prospecting calls, we know we are probably taking people away from something they are already doing to increase their own business. Because they don't yet know the benefits of our products or services, they might not like that. Their resentment might come across to us in a most obvious way.

If you are like me, you are naturally sensitive to rejection. Hey, I like to be liked! It isn't fun when people say they're not interested, or hang up the phone, or fib to quickly rid themselves of our pesky presence. But realizing that this is the worst-case scenario and that their rejection isn't personal (after all, they've never met us), we can now turn these calls into the beginnings of making money.

Let me point out something right now about using the telephone. Depending on your particular business, you might be using the telephone simply to get in-person appointments. That is the usual case. When I was in direct sales, we had a saying: "Never try to sell your product over the telephone." The only thing we would ever try to close on the telephone was the in-person appointment.

There are businesses, however, where the telephone is used both to prospect *and* to close the sale. As a professional speaker, my business definitely fits that description. After all, if my marketing staff or I had to visit meeting planners and decision makers all over the country in order to close a booking, we'd spend much more time in travel and money in travel-related expenses than we could ever recoup by actually speaking and marketing our books, CDs, and other resources.

Other businesses fall into that category as well, so I'll discuss this aspect of teleprospecting before talking about phone techniques for simply closing the appointment.

As I've shared at live seminars the method my staff and I use to prospect and sell by telephone, I've heard from many people selling numerous other products and services that these work for them as well. So as you read how we do it, imagine how you can bend and adapt this methodology to your own unique situation.

Please keep in mind: Because of the Do Not Call (DNC) laws, we are not talking here about cold-calling people in their homes. While not everyone registers to join the DNC list, more and more people will continue to do so, and perhaps soon, cold-calling into homes will become all but obsolete. This discussion pertains to what is known as "B to B" or "business to business" prospecting. We will, however, take a close look at obtaining permission to call someone in his home as the result of a referral (yes, even in this case you must now receive the referred prospect's permission).

Know You, Like You, Trust You Is More Important Than Ever

Probably the most difficult aspect of teleprospecting is that you are not right in front of the person during your presentation. There is less control in this situation, because you can't read the person's facial expression and body language and you don't know if she is giving the conversation her undivided attention or working on something else while you're speaking to her.

And it is certainly easier for someone to get rid of us on the telephone than it is in person. After all, what's to keep that person from saying, "Listen, something just came up and I have to go. I'll call you if I'm ever in need of your product." Sure he will—in your dreams.

Establishing a relationship with this person based on good feelings is essential right from the start. And this process begins with the secretary, especially if that person has assumed, or been asked to assume, the role of screener or gatekeeper.

Find the Person Who Can Say Yes

The first thing we need to do is make sure we are asking for the right person, the decision maker. We can do a wonderful job of getting past the secretary, make a great impression on the person to whom we are presenting, and close the sale beautifully. If, however, the person we've just sold on our product or service does not have the authority to say yes, we've wasted our time (as well as his).

In many instances, it is obvious who the decision maker is. In that situation, you already have a step up. But let's take a look at various ways to qualify a prospect before we go too far into the presentation.

First might be the receptionist. Sometimes receptionists don't know who the actual decision makers are, but usually they do, or at least they can refer you to someone who knows. When calling a corporation or association to book a seminar, I would say to the receptionist, "Good morning, my name is Bob Burg. Who's the person in charge of bringing in outside professional speakers for your annual convention?" In your case, the proper question might be, "Good morning, this is Jane McGregor. Who's the person in charge of purchasing widgets?" Or handling advertising, or purchasing office products, or whatever it is you have to offer.

That question will send me in the right direction. I'll then ask to be transferred to the decision maker's office, realizing I'll probably get her secretary. *Warning:* If the person answering the phone is the secretary or wants to know why you are calling, find a reason to politely get off the phone as soon as you've found out the information you wanted. When speaking with the person who'll decide whether or not to screen us or put us through, we need to already have that information and appear to be "in the know."

Getting Past the Gatekeeper

Let's pretend that the decision maker is Mary Jones and her secretary is Julie Smith. Julie answers the phone.

> JULIE: Good morning, Mary Jones's office. May I help you?
> ME: (informal and friendly, as though I belong) Good morn-
>   ing, this is Bob Burg. May I speak with Mary, please?
> JULIE: And where are you calling from, Mr. Burg?

She wants to know the name of our company, doesn't she? That way, she can decide if what we do will be of interest to Mary or if she should discourage us. What I'll do at this point is answer with the name of my city, and then segue right into a reflexive closing question (I'll explain that term in a moment), "What's your name?"

> JULIE: And where are you calling from, Mr. Burg?
> ME: Jupiter, Florida—I'm sorry, what's your name?
> JULIE: Julie Smith.
> ME: Oh, thank you, Julie.

Notice there was no pause between "Jupiter, Florida" and "I'm sorry, what's your name?" I didn't want to give her an opportunity to say, "No, I mean what company are you with?" Instead I went right into my reflexive closing question, "What's your name?"

A reflexive closing question is simply a question that produces an automatic response. When asked, "What is your name?" most people respond reflexively. Hopefully, she will put us through at that point. Does that work every time? No! It works some of the time.

If instead she says, "No, I mean, what company are you with?" or "What's your call in reference to?" you need to have a short statement that says just enough to raise her interest and position your call as worthwhile enough to be put through, but not enough to say what it is you actually do.

I might say, "This is regarding your upcoming convention. Mary would be in charge of profit-making programs, wouldn't she?" If you sell computer systems you might say, "I can show her how to dramatically increase your department's profitability for little cost. Julie, I'll explain to her just how to do that."

Does this work every time? No! It works some of the time. Let's say that in this case it didn't work and Julie wouldn't put you through. Or possibly, Mary isn't in. Make sure you've written down Julie's name because you will use her name as a positioning tool for credibility on your next call, which is a few days later. After all, you don't want to go through the same song and dance again.

JULIE: Good morning, Mary Jones's office. May I help you?

ME: (very friendly) Hi, Julie?

JULIE: Yes.

ME: (very friendly) Julie, hi! This is Bob Burg, how are you?

JULIE: (wondering who the heck Bob Burg is) Uh, f-fine, and you?

ME: Great. Hey, is Mary in?

Keep in mind that Julie talks to many people every single working day. She can't possibly recall every person and conversation. Also remember that, although it may be Julie's job to screen calls, it isn't her job to keep people from getting through who *should* be put through. In this scenario, I sound as though I belong. As though I've been there before. Does this technique work every time? No! It works some of the time.

There are many ways to get past the gatekeeper. I come across more and more of them every day in various books and sales newsletters and at seminars I attend. Not every idea will work for you, or for me, but some will. Let me share just a couple of methods that have consistently worked for me.

Try These—They Work!

The first is the use of Priority Mail, available from your local post office. For $3.85 (at the time of this writing) you can send a letter to the decision maker in a huge, attention-getting, red, white and blue cardboard envelope. Usually, because of the perceived value of this package (it *must* be important if it was sent Priority Mail), it will, in fact, get in front of the boss.

Inside this huge, multicolored, cardboard envelope is your letter enclosed in a regular number 10 envelope. It should be brief, businesslike and to the point. It should let the person know who you are and should also contain a short benefit statement and a request to be put through next time you call. Here's a generic example:

Dear Mr. Thomas,

Would you like to know more about a surefire way to cut down on your sales staff's wasted, nonproductive time? Gadger Gidgets.

These profit builders, designed specifically for _____ (his type of business) will show you how to increase production and profitability by up to 34 percent, and at a very affordable price.

When I've called, you've been very busy. I'm sure that's the norm for you. May I make a request? I'll call Thursday, October 17, at 2:10 p.m. If you are in, I'd appreciate your taking my call. I promise to be brief and help you determine quickly if our system might fit your needs.

If you are not in and would like to speak with me, could you have your secretary schedule a time for me to call back at your convenience?

Sincerely yours,

Steve Larkin

Notice that the time I gave was 2:10 p.m. Whenever scheduling any appointment you should suggest an odd time, as opposed to 2:00, 2:15, 2:30, or 2:45. This gives the impression of your time being clearly slotted, accounted for, and important. The same goes for percentages: 34 percent is actually much more credible than 35 percent. Why? Because it's much more specific, and it suggests documentation.

Of course, you should only say something like this if it is a fact. And if the exact percentage result was 35 percent, you're *still* better off going with 34 percent. If increased production and productivity are not at least 34 percent, absolutely *don't* state that!

Back to your letter. If Mr. Thomas is impressed with the possible benefits mentioned in your letter, he'll take your call. If not, it is up to you to decide whether to blow that one off and say "NEXT!" or try another tack. (By the way, even more impressive than Priority Mail, although considerably more expensive, is overnight delivery, such as Federal Express.)

Here's something I learned from Harvey Mackay's book *Swim with the Sharks without Being Eaten Alive.*

Mackay explains how to get to the person he calls the "tough prospect," the one who won't take your calls. Mackay's method (which I am loosely paraphrasing here) can also work as a way of getting past the screen. This has earned positive results for my staff and me on numerous occasions.

Here's how it works: Simply put a money value on the time you'll take to speak with the decision maker. The following example is a conversation I had with a secretary who had consistently denied me access to the boss for over three weeks. After reading Mr. Mackay's book, I decided to go for it.

ME: May I speak with Mr. Prospect, please?

SECRETARY: No, he's busy.

ME: May I make a telephone appointment to speak with him?

SECRETARY: No, he's too busy even for that. Just send whatever it is you have in writing! (charming individual)

ME: I'll tell you what. Please put me on hold and ask Mr. Prospect if I can take just 200 seconds of his time. Tell him that if I go even one second over, I'll donate $500 to his favorite charity.

SECRETARY: (bewildered) Hold on a moment.

COMPANY MESSAGE OVER "EASY LISTENING" BACK-GROUND MUSIC: "You'll find this to be one company that really loves people..." (The message playing was actually pretty close to that!)

SECRETARY: He'll take your call at nine tomorrow morning...and his charity is the Heart Fund.

TELEPHONE: Click!

I got to speak to the decision maker. (Nope, didn't make the sale.) And since then, I have found this approach works quite often. Most secretaries are happy to go along with it. Also, in many cases, the decision maker will come right to the phone, probably curious as to what kind of person would make that kind of statement. Again, does it work all of the time? No—but I can guarantee it will *never* work if you don't try it!

Before going on to our conversation with the decision maker, I ask you to keep this in mind: Always be pleasant to the secretaries, and realize they are just doing their job. Maybe they sometimes do it a bit overzealously, but we're certainly not going to win them over by being testy or argumentative. We have to make these "key" people our friends. We do that by being courteous, using their names, finding mutual points of interest, and establishing a rapport.

Now You've Got the Decision Maker

Okay, so now I've been put through to Mary Jones. She is the decision maker who could retain me to do a presentation on "How to Cultivate a

Network of Endless Referrals" at her company's next sales convention. (You'll have to take this example and modify it to accomplish what you want to accomplish with your product or service.)

> MARY JONES: Hi, this is Mary Jones. How can I help you?
>
> ME: Good morning, Ms. Jones (not "Mary" yet), this is Bob Burg. I understand you're the person in charge of bringing in outside professional speakers for your annual convention. Is that correct?
>
> MARY JONES: Yes, it is. What can I do for you?
>
> ME: Well I…by the way, do you have a real quick minute or have I caught you at a really awful time?

I and many others have found this exact language to be very helpful: After all, has any other salesperson shown this much empathy and consideration for their potential time constraints? Also, you've given them an "out," and typically, when you voluntarily give someone an out, they are less likely to go looking for one.

However, there are those from the "old school of sales" who will probably groan as they read the words, "do you have a real quick minute?" and, perhaps groan even louder as they read the rest of that sentence. I can almost hear them saying, "Burg, why on earth would you ask a person that question? You're just giving them an excuse to say they're busy and get rid of you!"

Here's what I've found in my nearly 20 years of teleprospecting experience. People generally will answer that question in one of three ways:

1. "No!"

    Actually, this answer will probably be more along the lines of, "No I don't have a minute. This is a really bad time. I'm between meetings, trying to make a deadline, and I especially don't have time to talk to anyone who wants to sell me anything."

    As far as I'm concerned, that answer is fine. They are letting us know in no uncertain terms that this would not be a good time. We won't have their full, or even partial, attention. Trying to share the benefits of our product or service with them now would only result in resentment on their part, destroying any chance of establishing a relationship with them. Our job right now is to get off the phone, politely and promptly. We'll try again later.

2. "Yes."

I know this one sounds good. If, however, that "Yes" is followed by, "I've got all the time in the world. I'm not doing anything anyway. What can I do for you?" then be warned: That person is probably not the decision maker!

I say this somewhat tongue in cheek—but only somewhat. There are people out there in non-power positions who like to play king for a day. They will lead you on forever, yessing you to death. Then, when it's time to take action, they have no authority. I speak from experience. It's happened to me!

3. "Yes, real quick."

Typically, the response might be more like, "I have a *real* quick minute, but that's it. I'm very busy." As negative as it might sound, this is exactly the response you want!

At this point, we'll give them a brief benefit statement. This benefit statement will, of course, explain the benefits of what they can expect by doing business with us, without telling them enough to make an instant decision to say no. When they respond positively, we are then in a position to take control of the conversation—and the way we take control is not by telling, but by asking questions. Remember, no one is going to hang up the phone on you while *they* are doing the talking.

> ME: Well I...by the way, do you have a real quick minute?
>
> MARY JONES: Real quick, I'm very busy. What can I do for you?
>
> ME: I do a program entitled "How to Cultivate a Network of Endless Referrals." It basically answers the question asked by practically all salespeople in the (her type of) profession, "Who do I talk to next, now that my original list of names has run out?" Does that sound like a program that may be of value at your next convention?

Usually, the prospects I call will answer yes. That's because, before I target a particular or "niche" market, I qualify the "need it" and "want it" aspect of that market.

There are three parts to what is known as the "marketing bridge" we all need to cross when working with prospects: 1) Do they need it? 2) Do they want it? 3) Can they afford it? Whether or not they can afford my fee will often need to be determined at that time or later. Depending on your line of work and the products or services you represent, that may or may not be the case for you.

If you are in a business where you can prequalify the wants and needs of your market, great. If not, you'll have to make a few more calls in order to qualify the same number of prospects.

If the prospect does show interest, it might be appropriate (depending on the situation, you may need to wait) to further qualify her position by asking, "Mary, along with you, who else will be in on the decision-making process?" That, of course, is much more tactful than saying, "Are you really the decision maker, or are you just pulling my leg?" Again, tongue in cheek, but understand the difference.

The first way of asking shows respect and gives our prospect an *out* without causing her embarrassment. And her answer might let you know that there are other people to whom you might have to make your presentation. If you come right out and ask your prospect if she is actually the decision maker, she might have to say yes in order to save face. By the time she finally admits she is not, three months have gone by. Again, that will only waste your time and your prospect's time.

Where the Selling Process Actually Begins

From this point on, it is a matter of making a good presentation by asking questions to determine wants and needs, being able to answer objections, and closing the sale.

After qualifying and question asking, you should have a good idea of what you need to do for the next telemeeting. If you need to send information to your prospect before speaking with her again, take the proper steps to ensure she will receive your material and actually review it before your next call.

Jeff Slutsky recommends describing to prospects in detail the type of package and envelope they will receive, including size, color, and insignias or logos. Then you must get a commitment from them that they'll review your information.

After determining with your prospect the exact day and time you will have your follow-up conversation, I suggest you say something along these lines:

ME: Mr. Dennison, many people, after reviewing the information, have questions on two key points, the whatchamacallit and the whichamahoozie. I'll look forward to discussing those points with you.

That day, send the informational package with a note on your personalized note card (as discussed in Chapter 4). Since you have your picture on it, prospects will feel more like they know you and will be more comfortable doing business with you. And, if nothing else, this will remind them that you were serious about getting back in touch and expecting them to have reviewed your material. If sending a package of information is not necessary or appropriate in this case, still send a personalized thank-you note.

Since the focus of this book is not sales presentation skills or how to close the sale, I suggest you turn to other sources on these subjects and learn the proper principles and methods that will best suit you and your prospects, customers and clients.

The two books I began with nearly 20 years ago were *Secrets of Closing the Sale* by Zig Ziglar and *How to Master the Art of Selling* by Tom Hopkins. I credit these two books with equipping me with the information I needed to become a successful professional salesman. (By the way, I believe a better term than "closing a sale" is "completing a transaction." Hopefully, a sale will never actually be *closed* but will instead stay *open*—and lead to lots and lots of referrals!)

Authors such as Brian Tracy, Jeffrey Gitomer, and a host of others continue the tradition of principle-based selling and help dispel the myth of the "born salesperson."

Contrary to popular belief, people are not born salespeople, nor are they born closers. While some may have more natural aptitude in this area, selling and closing are both developed, learned skills. Selling is an art and a science. I suggest you learn, through referrals from other salespeople, who are some of the better authors in this genre, and purchase as many books on the topic as you can. Learn the common principles involved and use the various methods that work within your mode of operation. You likely will not choose to use everything you'll learn. Sometimes you "take the Skippy® and leave the Jiff®."

Another of my personal favorites is Neil Rackham (www.neilrackham.com), author of the landmark bestseller, *SPIN Selling*. In Neil's usage, the term is not to be confused with the "spin" in politics or any type of manipulative strategy. To Rackham, SPIN is an acronym that stands for Situation – Problem – Implication – Need-Payoff. He put together his system after research involving more than 35,000 sales calls over a period of 12 years. His book is magnificent, especially for those who sell higher-ticket (i.e., more expensive) items.

There are many other excellent books listed in the resource section at www.Burg.com/Resources.html.

Selling the Appointment by Telephone

Ironically, even though most people use the telephone simply to set appointments, this section of this chapter will be brief. Here's why: The toughest part is still simply getting to the decision maker, and you've already learned how to do that! Now it's simply a matter of closing the appointment.

If you are involved with a product that must be demonstrated or explained in person, do *not* get sucked into giving your presentation over the telephone. It won't work, especially for high-ticket items.

When I was selling solar energy systems, which averaged around $10,000 per unit, I was constantly asked on the phone how much a unit cost. Can you imagine answering "$10,000" without first their knowing the benefits of what the system would do for them and how much they would actually save? Depending on the individual family, water usage, home, and available tax credits, these solar energy systems could be of enormous value. For many people, the savings involved could exceed the cost, even substantially so. But do you think a salesperson would ever have the chance to come over and explain that, once they'd blurted out a price tag of ten grand? No way!

If this is the case with your product or service, you need to have a learned, memorized response for every question or objection you will receive on the way to setting that appointment, and price will not be the only one.

If you are worried that your presentation will sound "canned," have no fear. If you practice beforehand to the point where you have internalized the information, your responses will sound completely natural. Think of stage, television, and movie actors and actresses. They would never even imagine just getting up there and winging it.

Again, when first speaking with the decision maker, you must provide her with a benefit statement (even if it's in the form of a question) that will pique her interest without giving away too much information. Then, after a brief presentation or several qualifying questions, go into closing for the appointment. If I were selling a solar energy system (and let's put Do Not Call laws aside for the moment, so we can effectively discuss the principles involved), the conversation might go as follows:

> ME: Hi, Ms. Prospect, this is Bob Burg. Do you have a real quick minute or have I caught you at a really awful time?
>
> PROSPECT: It depends. What do you need?
>
> ME: I'm with Sunstrong Solar Energy Company. May I ask you just a very few questions regarding the rising cost of your monthly hot water bills?

If rising hot water bills are a concern for that prospect, the answer will probably be, "Yes." After a few more questions enhancing the prospect's interest, it is time to set the in-home appointment. This might not go, however, without a couple of questions or objections from them.

> PROSPECT: Before we waste each other's time, how much does your system cost?
>
> ME: Good question, and very important. It really depends on several things. Every home and family is different, and has its own individual needs. The nice thing is that it's my job to see that *your* needs will be met.

Now go into closing for the appointment. The classic teaching here is that it's best to do this by giving the prospect a choice of two yeses, as opposed to a yes or a no.

In other words, if we ask, "Would Tuesday evening at eight be good for you?" the prospect might say, "No." Now we have to guess on another convenient date and time. "How about Wednesday at seven?" to which the prospect responds, "Naw, that's no good either. I'll tell you what, let me think about it for a while, and if I'm interested I'll get back to you." At that point you've probably lost your prospect.

Instead, we give them a choice of two yeses.

> ME: Would tomorrow evening at 7:15 be good, or would Wednesday evening at 7:45 be more convenient for you?
>
> PROSPECT: Tomorrow's no good. I guess we can do it Wednesday.

This is called the "alternate of choice." It's very effective—but we need to be very careful when utilizing it, for two reasons.

First, people have become more educated about sales techniques, and this one has been around for a while. Second, if you phrase the alternate of choice the same way too many times, it *sounds* salesy and manipulative.

The best solution, as is so often the case, is to be authentic. Let it flow with genuine concern about your prospect's convenience.

A very helpful method of setting the appointment is to ask your prospect if he has an appointment book. If so, then ask him to please look at Tuesday evening at 7:15 and Wednesday evening at 8:15. "Which of these two times is preferable for you? ... Tuesday at 7:15? Excellent, if you'll just write it in there, I'll see you then." If he fires another question or objection at you, simply respond and go back into another alternate-of-choice question or specific date and time in order to set the appointment.

Listening Is the Key

Whether using the telephone as a complete sales tool or simply to get appointments, the key to success is having a game plan, following it religiously, and listening to your prospect.

Jim Meisenheimer (www.meisenheimer.com), who specializes in what he calls "No-Brainer Selling Skills and Sales Training Programs" and is author of the CD album, *The 12 Best Questions to Ask Customers*, and numerous books, recommends the following 10 tips for telephone success:

1. *Prepare in advance.* Prepare your questions and responses in advance. Know your product or service well, and your mind will be free to listen to the customer and focus on his or her needs.
2. *Limit your own talking.* You can't talk and listen at the same time. Jim makes an excellent point: If *we* are doing the talking, nothing's being sold.
3. *Focus.* Concentrate on your conversation and the customer's needs. This means temporarily shutting out your personal problems and worries. Difficult at times, but possible—and definitely necessary.
4. *Put yourself in your prospects' shoes.* Understand their needs and concerns by thinking like them. Take their point of view in order to help them solve their problems.
5. *Ask questions.* We know the importance of asking questions during a

presentation. Asking questions will also help clear up any points or prospect concerns you are not sure you completely understand. Paraphrasing your prospects' concerns back to them in the form of a question, followed by, "Do I understand you correctly?" or, "Is that what you're saying?" will keep you on the right track.

6. *Don't interrupt.* Nothing will turn prospects off quicker than interrupting them. The same goes for finishing their sentences for them. Don't assume you know what they are going to say (even if you have to bite your lip to keep from doing it). Jim also suggests that just because the person pauses, he or she is not necessarily through talking.

7. *Listen for the whole idea or complete picture.* Words alone do not necessarily convey what your prospect fears or desires.

8. *Respond (as opposed to react) to the ideas—not to the person.* Don't allow yourself to become irritated or insulted. Objections and questions are not personal. Also, don't let a prospect's mannerisms, such as an accent, distract you.

9. *Listen between the lines.* Often, what is *not* said by the prospect is just as important as what *is* said. Listen for overtones, doubts, concerns.

10. *Use interjections.* Show the customer you are listening by occasionally saying, "Uh-huh," "I understand what you're saying," "I see what you mean," or other fillers. But don't overdo it, or let these brief responses become interruptions.

Effective Intonation: A Key to Your Tele-Success

When building relationships over the telephone, one critically important skill is effective voice intonation. This is a relatively simple concept; however, like many of the simple things in life, it's not always easy.

Effective voice intonation goes beyond just using voice inflection so as not to sound monotone. We already know that boring a prospect to death is *not* good. What we're talking about here is being aware of the overall sound of your voice, and varying it in order to correctly and respectfully respond to the other person.

For instance, although we usually want to be positive and upbeat over the telephone, there are times when, based on the other person's challenges or situation, we need to sound more subdued. If they speak softly, we want to tone down our own volume a bit. If your prospect or client is especially relationship-oriented, then adjusting your tone from more businesslike mode to one that is more personal and sympathetic is definitely a good idea.

Effective voice intonation is a skill worth cultivating into a habit, as is every aspect of telephone communication. It's worth it to invest in books, audios, newsletters, and seminars on telephone skills in order to learn more about this vital business tool and to continually "sharpen your axe" in this area.

You may want to subscribe to Art Sobczak's (www.artsobczak.com) "Telephone Prospecting and Selling Report," an excellent newsletter dealing with all aspects of this topic. Art also puts out an excellent e-zine on this topic.

By the way, as with any effective tool, the telephone is meant to work hand in hand with other principles of networking, not to replace any of them. Make sure your picture appears on any correspondence you send. If your prospect or client knows you only by voice, it's imperative that he see your face as much as possible, in a natural way such as on note cards and scratch pads as discussed earlier (Chapter 4).

Three Quick Telephone Tips

Use a mirror to check your attitude.

Every telemarketing authority I know suggests hanging a mirror on the wall in front of you so you can see yourself as you converse. Why? Because your mood and attitude absolutely *will* come across to your prospect. If the reflection in the mirror is up and smiling, that's how you'll come across on the telephone. The opposite is also true.

Be careful with the hold button.

If you must put a person on hold, do so for as short a time as possible—15 to 30 seconds, no more. If you leave prospects on hold for any longer than that, you'll notice a change in *their* attitude, and it won't be for the better.

To better understand why, notice what happens when you are the one stuck on hold for any length of time. It's frustrating and definitely not fun.

In fact, try this experiment. Glance at your watch and notice the second hand. Then sit there doing nothing, without looking at your watch, until it seems about two minutes have elapsed. Now glance back at your watch. Your "two minutes" probably won't even come close to actually being two minutes. Time really d–r–a–g–s when your life is on hold!

Hang up last.

It is a fact of life that none of us likes that cold, impersonal sound of the "click" in our ear. When you hear that awful sound, don't you sometimes feel discarded, as though the other person was in a hurry to get rid of you and go on to whatever he or she was doing next?

That's how your prospect might feel as well. Let her hang up first.

Finding Prospects from Conventional and Unconventional Sources

The key to effective prospecting is to work smarter, not harder—to get yourself in front of qualified people with the least amount of time and effort. These are just a few methods for accomplishing that goal.

Physically Position Yourself in Front of the Right People

Rick Hill says, "If you're going to go fishing, go where the fish are." Makes sense, doesn't it? The same could be said about prospecting for gold, meeting members of the opposite sex, and prospecting for new business.

Back when Rick was setting records as a radio advertising sales representative, he used to leave his office at 2:00 p.m. every Friday. When his sales manager would ask where he was going, Rick would give him the name of a local watering hole. When the manager questioned him as to why he was doing this before the workday ended, Rick would reply, "How are my sales this month?" At that, the manager would stop his questioning.

Actually, Rick was going to the local club, where advertising agency representatives liked to hang out on Friday afternoons. Rick couldn't have put his prospects in front of him any better if he had sprung for an elaborate party.

Ask yourself where your prospects hang out. Are there certain clubs, organizations or associations you could join that would give you continuous access to these people? If so, invest some time and money and join. The dividends will more than justify the expense.

Find the Orphans

When you begin with a new company, or even if you have been there for some time, realize that every time a salesperson leaves the company, he or she leaves behind a number of customers and clients who are no longer being serviced. They are your orphans.

If your product is one that can be purchased again or upgraded—a car, a computer system, or a copying machine—contact that customer and establish a relationship. I have heard of one copying machine salesperson who was referred to as "Mr. Upgrade." That's because as soon as he joined the company, he began calling orphans and talking to them about upgrading their present system. What an excellent way to provide additional value to a customer. From what I understand, he did extremely well.

When I joined the solar energy company, I utilized orphans as referral sources because their systems should last for life (i.e., no resales), and upgrades were seldom a factor. I would introduce myself and ask how happy they were with their system. Because the product was great, I could generally count on an ecstatic answer. I would then, utilizing the methodology discussed in Chapter 6, ask for referrals of those they knew who might also be able to benefit from a similar system. Did it work all of the time? No, but it worked a lot of the time.

Use your imagination; constantly ask yourself how you might assist other people in meeting *their* needs. As Zig Ziglar's famous "signature statement" goes, "You can get everything in life you want if you just help enough other people get what they want."

What's the Itch Cycle?

I first learned about this great idea from Tom Hopkins. Statistics will show that, depending on the product, there is an average time expectancy between purchases. In other words, there is a typical length of time before a customer itches to buy again.

For instance, the average homeowner will move every five years. The average new car buyer will buy (or lease) every three years. Of course, the actual "itch" to take action is often months before that time. You'll want to know what it is for the product or service you work with so you can contact that person while he is in the "interest" phase.

Go back to the orphans. How long has it been since they last purchased? What is the average itch cycle for that product? Have they purchased more than once? If so, what was their time frame, or itch cycle, between purchases?

Look in Local Newspapers

It was mentioned earlier in the book that we should always scour the newspaper for information of interest to those in our network. That way, we let them know we care and that they are on our mind. Very effective.

The newspaper can also be an excellent prospecting tool. For instance, if you are a life insurance or health insurance sales professional and read about someone receiving a big promotion, don't you think her insurance needs will also increase? What about people who have a new baby? Check out those birth announcements! Find out where they live and send them a congratulatory note. Maybe they have an insurance person already—but then again, maybe they don't. Or possibly their insurance agent doesn't pay attention to those things and you do. A nice congratulations note and follow-up phone call could work wonders, couldn't it?

Ahh, except now you have to be careful and make sure that person is not registered on the Do Not Call list. If they are, you can instead direct them to your Web site, where they can download (or have sent to them) a free "special report" in which they might be interested. If they do so, you know you have a potentially excellent prospect. (See more about this in Chapter 14, "Attraction Marketing.")

Once you obtain their permission to call, or however you originally make contact, continue to be nice, nonpushy, and caring about their needs. Once you've established a rapport, begin doing the things you've learned in this book about networking and cultivating relationships.

Go Door-to-Door, Business-to-Business

Although this method of prospecting is the most time-consuming, it is very effective. Whenever you succeed in making direct contact with the decision maker, you are in the very best position to establish the rapport necessary to open the relationship or to close the sale.

Again, depending on your particular business, your sales might be of the one-call, two-call, or several-or-more-calls variety. Regardless, getting in front of your prospects cuts out all the in-between steps. You can read their body language, gather your facts, and answer objections without their having a quick escape.

The more people you see face-to-face, the more sales you will make and the more lives you will enhance.

A Lesson on How *Not* to Prospect Door-to-Door

The following lesson from Davis Fisher, Founder of MoneyTree Consulting in Evanston, Illinois (www.moneytreeconsulting.com), is excellent advice for anyone giving a sales presentation. Because it was the result of door-to-door prospecting, we'll feature it here.

In a place I used to work, our offices were located in a 10-story building not far from O'Hare International Airport. For some reason, we were in a perfect location for salespeople who made cold calls. One day, there was a unique moment when I was in the office alone. It was around noontime. The receptionist had stepped down the hall and our coworkers were either at lunch, on errands, or out of town.

A knock on the door. "Come in," I said, and in walked a young salesman. He said to me, "Do you have a minute?" and I said, "Sure." And with that he pulled up a chair, sat down at my desk, opened his briefcase, pulled out some brochures, moved a couple things on my desk, and spread the brochures out.

For the next 13½ minutes we went through his brochures. He told me all about what he was selling—computers for the small office. I sat there looking at his brochures, nodding my head, saying "Uh huh," "Ooooh," "That's a big one," "Wow," "Color on that one's neat."

At the end of the 13½ minutes, he picked up his brochures, put them back in his briefcase, set it down next to him, looked around, and said, "Nice office you have here." I said, "Thank you." He looked over my shoulder through a big picture window looking out on the spaghetti bowl intersection of a major expressway and toll road. He said, "Wow, you really have a view of the toll road from here." I said, "Yeah, we do." He looked at me and asked, "What do you folks do here?" I replied, "We teach people how to sell." "No kidding," he replied. "How am I doing?" And I said, "Not very well."

Why not? Because in his 15-minute sales call, this salesperson had spent 13½ minutes telling me how much he knew about what he was selling. He never asked me any questions. Had he asked, he would have discovered that we had bought a computer for our office six months earlier and had no immediate need.

At that point, he might have asked questions such as, "No kidding, what kind did you get? How did you happen to go with them? What's been your experience over the last six months? Who was involved in making that decision? If you were going to make that decision today, what would be different about it? I realize that you are tied into a contract now with those people, Mr. Fisher, but let me leave a brochure describing several of our products, including one here that I think may give you some assistance based on some of the problems you have had.

"Feel free to give me a call over the next three months in the event I may help you out. In fact, if I haven't heard from you, may I call you? Do you have a brochure describing what you do? I always like to know what some of my prospective clients do. Possibly I can refer some business your way. May I have one of your cards? Thanks...I'm curious: do you know of anyone in the area who might be in a similar position to the one you were in six months ago, so I might talk to them and see if I may be of some assistance? Thanks. Bye."

...And then leave, saving himself 13½ minutes on a 15-minute sales call—valuable time he could then use down the hall or across the street, where he might have encountered someone who could indeed become a qualified prospect based on appropriate probing and listening!

Good selling is not telling!

Davis makes an excellent point. The worst thing a salesperson can do is simply walk in, introduce himself, sit down without being invited to do so, and start "machine-gunning" through a presentation. In fact, the same applies even with a planned appointment. If faced with the decision-maker, we must first discover (or create) a need, a want, and a financial capability.

With just a bit of questioning, the salesperson in the above example would have discovered early on that there was no need. With some creative questioning, however, he also could have discovered the prospect's itch cycle, received permission to keep in touch, and maybe even picked up a few referrals along the way.

As professionals, we don't want to waste our prospects' time. We don't want to waste *our* time, either.

Some Thoughts on Effective Prospecting

A friend of mine, Sonia Cooper, is a salesperson and prospector *par excellence.* Her motto is, "Put the needs of your customers/prospects/referral sources first…and your paycheck will follow."

A few years back, Sonia was an account representative for a title insurance company. One day she noticed a real estate agent from the neighboring county stuffing the mailboxes in a real estate office in the county where she worked.

Sonia felt that as a commercial real estate broker, this man must have better things to do than travel office to office (which Sonia did as part of her job), so she offered to pass out his fliers for him since she'd be there anyway. To which title account representative do you think that commercial broker referred his title orders from resulting sales? The answer should be obvious.

A true believer in self-promotion and the principle of "keeping your name and telephone number in front of prospects," Sonia constantly looks for new and creative ways to accomplish this goal.

Once, when she was on a cruise ship, she noticed that each day the crew would pass out word games for the passengers to solve. Each day's game had a different theme. Sonia had the social hostess put together a packet of all 12 games, along with the answers—not knowing exactly how she would use them. Upon returning to work, she came up with the idea of passing out a word quiz to all of her individual prospective agents. Each month, on appropriately colored paper, she would distribute her and her firm's name along with a different word quiz. Answers to the previous month's quiz were on the back.

According to Sonia, it was a huge hit. In a very subtle, nonintrusive way, they would see her name and phone number all month long. This was especially effective during normally slow times. Instead of just sitting around doing nothing and waiting for the phone to ring, her prospects were actively having fun with her word quizzes. Some of the offices actually had internal contests as to which agent could come up with the most correct answers. Says Sonia, "This was one of the most inexpensive and successful prospecting promotions I ever implemented."

Sonia is now an account executive with BellSouth Communications, Inc. in West Palm Beach, Florida. Upon joining the company, she got off to another impressive start, racking up huge sales numbers. Sonia knocks on a lot of business doors and is often faced with having to get past the gatekeeper. She has six methods she uses with great success:

1. *Treat them as if they owned the company.* They are probably the person their boss looks to for protection from the outside world. If you can make them feel good about themselves, they'll help you do the same, by ensuring you get to see the decision maker. (And who knows? Maybe one day they *will* own the company!)
2. *Know them by their first name.* Show them that they are important to you by using their name.
3. *Tell them that you need their help.* The fact is, most people want to help, and to feel that you know they have the power to help.
4. *Include them in the promotional materials you pass out.* Keep them in the loop. Make them a part of the sales process.
5. *Put yourself in their shoes.* How would you like to be treated if you were in the same position? Respect them as people—unlike other salespeople, who treat them as nonentities whose sole purpose in life is to keep the salesperson from achieving her goal of seeing the decision maker.
6. *Be of service to them.* Ask them if there is any way you can help them—maybe drop something off at the post office for them on your way there?

In other words, make them your ally. Smile, be sincere, and appreciate the importance of the job they have to do.

Pat Hance, broker-owner of Pat Hance Real Estate Company in Plantation, Florida, feels it's very important when prospecting to continually have your name out to the public. She operates constantly out of the belief that everyone she meets, anywhere, is either a prospect or an excellent source of referrals.

Pat is also an expert at prospecting other Realtors®. She attends every real estate convention she possibly can, handing out a flyer with her photo on it that says, "Pat Hance wants your referrals!" in huge print. She says consistency is important, keeping the same message year after year after year, making only minor changes to show additional designations and honors she's received.

Says Pat, "This little flyer has been given to every attendee at every real estate convention since 1969. Do they remember me? You bet! When I replace the photo with a more recent one, I get comments like, 'I see you're no longer using your high school photo!' I've received referrals from agents I've never met—agents who received this flyer somehow, somewhere. It's not important that they remember how or where, just that they remember Pat Hance!"

After discovering that a New York ERA real estate office had blown up her picture to poster size and tacked it up on the bulletin board, she arranged a neat cross-promotion with that office's broker. When he visited Florida on vacation, he took a video recorder to Pat's office and taped her saying, "Come on to Florida. Send your buyers! Send your sellers! We want to work for you in sunny, south Florida." This resulted in numerous sales and referrals for Pat.

Pat considers herself the biggest "flesh presser" of them all, meeting people in all walks of life, from the supermarket to her church. Yet wherever and whenever she does this, she always focuses on the *other* person's needs, not her own. She knows that eventually, with the way she is positioned and known in her community, that person will remember her when the time is right for business or referrals. One introduction and handshake, through the twists of fate, resulted in referral fees on approximately 35 transactions over the course of several years.

Key Points

- Never stop prospecting.
- Prospecting is a numbers game. The more things we do right, however, the more sales we will get in less time and after calling on fewer people.
- There is a definite relationship between calls and contacts, contacts and appointments, and appointments and sales. Learn yours and use it to your advantage.
- When using the telephone as a prospecting tool, establishing a relationship with that prospect becomes even more important.
- Knowing how to talk to (and get past) the gatekeeper is vital to teleprospecting success.
- Ask the prospect, "Do you have a real quick minute or have I caught you at a really awful time?"
- Qualify to ensure you are speaking with the decision maker!
- Use your short benefit statement to pique prospects' interest so they'll want to hear more.

- If using the telephone simply to set in-person appointments, be sure to limit your conversation to just that. Give too much information and you might disqualify yourself right then and there.
- Utilize the following tips from Jim Meisenheimer:
  1. Prepare in advance.
  2. Limit your own talking.
  3. Focus. Concentrate on your conversation and the customer's needs.
  4. Put yourself into your prospects' shoes. Understand their needs and concerns by thinking like them. Take their point of view in order to help them solve their problems.
  5. Ask questions.
  6. Don't interrupt.
  7. Listen for the whole idea or complete picture. Words alone are not necessarily conveying what your prospect fears or desires.
  8. Respond (as opposed to react) to the ideas—not to the person. Don't allow yourself to become irritated or insulted.
  9. Listen between the lines. Often, what is not said by the prospect is just as important as what is, or the way it is said.
  10. Use interjections.
- A few final tips for using the telephone effectively:
  1. Use a mirror to check your attitude.
  2. Be careful with the hold button. If you must put a person on hold, do so for as short a time as possible.
  3. Hang up last. No one likes the sound of the "click" in their ear.
- Prospects can be found from both conventional and unconventional sources.
  1. Physically position yourself in front of the right people.
  2. Find the orphans. They are company customers and clients that a departing salesperson left behind when leaving the company. You may adopt them.
  3. What's the itch cycle? Depending upon the product, there is an average time expectancy between purchases. In other words, a time length before one itches to buy again.
  4. Look in local newspapers. Always scour your local newspaper for prospects.
  5. Go door-to-door, business-to-business.
- Follow Sonia Cooper's motto: "Put the needs of your customers/prospects/referral sources first...and your paycheck will follow."

- Follow Sonia Cooper's six tips for winning over the gatekeepers.
  1. Treat them like they own the company. They are both the bodyguard and direct link to their boss.
  2. Know them by their first name.
  3. Tell them that you need their "help."
  4. Include them in the promotional materials you pass out. Keep them in the loop.
  5. Put yourself in their shoes. How would you like to be treated in the same position?
  6. Be of service to them. Ask them if there isn't any way you can help them.
- Listen to Pat Hance's sage advice: "Continually keep your name in front of the public."
- Follow the road map, be creative at times, and most of all, always have the other person's wants and needs in the forefront of your mind.

CHAPTER 8

Using the Internet to Help Build Your Network

As you might imagine, the Internet is a terrific prospecting tool. Has it revolutionized business networking? Transformed it? Radically altered it? No—it has enhanced it, that's all. And that's enough for it to still be of great value.

The moment we start to talk about the Internet and its uses in the world of building your businesses through networking, I always caution people to understand that while it is a powerful tool, it is just that: a tool, not a panacea. It won't do the work for you any more than will any other great tool. You must be its master—not its servant.

This might sound a little dramatic, but the reason I say this is that people often get caught up in this great technology and forget that people don't do business with or refer business to computers. They do business with, and refer business to, *people*—specifically, those people they know, like, and trust!

As long as we keep that foundation intact, the Internet certainly can provide us with yet another excellent vehicle for reaching those we desire to meet, and help accelerate the *know you, like you, trust you* aspect of the relationship.

Many years ago, when I was working as a television news anchor, I asked the news director of another station what he thought of the TelePrompTer, which at that time was still a relatively new technology. (The TelePrompTer is the gizmo that allows news readers to read the words while looking directly into the camera, making it appear that they are not reading, but simply looking at you, relating information they have stored in their heads.)

I thought he would either describe it as the *worst* thing to happen to news broadcasting (i.e., "It's fake, phony, false, etc.") or the *best* thing to happen to the industry since Walter Cronkite (i.e., "It has changed the entire way we can bring news to the viewers"). But his answer surprised me.

What he said was, "Bob, it's just another communication tool. The information still has to be procured, processed, written and conveyed, all with the same effort and high quality. The TelePrompTer just adds a warmer, friendlier way of communicating that same information. I like it."

"Just another tool." To me, that was a good answer, from a man who understood the principles of broadcasting, yet was open enough to those new ideas and technologies that would help both him and the consumer, that is, the end user of his product. The same holds true for those in the world of marketing: Those who understand the principles of successful marketing, networking and prospecting will apply that wisdom in a positive way to this newer tool, the Internet, to help both them and their end users.

The Networking Parallel between the Cyber World and the Real World

In the "bricks-and-mortar" world of networking and prospecting, our intention is to find the right people, meet them, then win them over through effective follow-up and follow-through. The same is true in the virtual world of sales and marketing on the Internet.

According to Patrick Anderson and Michael Henderson, co-owners of AdNet International (www.adnetinternational.com), a cutting-edge Internet design and marketing company that develops custom business applications for their clients specifically for Internet marketing companies, "The Internet is a big world and can be rather confusing at first. However, once the methods of prospecting are understood, you'll be in a position to increase your profits substantially."

Make a Good System Even Better

If, as part of your overall sales and marketing plan, you already utilize referral-based marketing, direct response advertising, outbound calling and telemarketing, introductory sales letters and brochures, and/or any of the principles and methods discussed throughout this book, the Internet will provide a wealth of new prospecting leads, networking contacts, and strategic alliance partners.

From a technical perspective, the Internet is an interrelated network of computers. From a business perspective, it is a way to interact with people who share similar interests. When the principles of this book are applied to the online world, it becomes, according to Anderson and Henderson, "Inter-Net-Working."

"The most important tool for Internet prospecting" according to Anderson and Henderson, "is e-mail. It will often open the door and become your primary follow-up system once you connect in that manner."

They suggest providing full contact information with your e-mail, just as you would with all of your other business correspondence (such as the note card and scratch pad discussed in Chapter 4). This helps validate who you are and builds trust.

Create a short benefit statement, quote or comment that intrigues and informs. Add this tag line (also called a signature file, or simply sig) to the end of every piece of e-mail you send. With most e-mail programs you can do this automatically. Include more than simply your name and contact information. Make it easy for people to understand why they might want to do business with you or refer you to others.

The following is an example of a signature file for my friend, Heidi Miller. Heidi is a professional trade show presenter.

Heidi Miller – Trade Show Presenter & Spokesperson
(847) 942-6732 cell / (708) 763-8103 fax
heidim@heidimillerpresents.com
Get your FREE audio report, "Overcoming the 3 Costliest Mistakes Almost
All Exhibitors Make" by visiting http://www.HeidiMillerPresents.com
Maximizing ROI ... Reducing Headaches!

This is only one example; there are different uses, lengths, etc. depending upon your target and who will be reading your message. If you target different markets, formulate a different signature file for each one. Also, if participating in an online forum or discussion list, you might have to shorten it according to their rules for posting sigs. You might have noticed Heidi's offer of a "free report." The purpose of this phenomenal marketing tool will be explained in Chapter 9.

The Internet Is Global—But You Can Still Go Local

Let's talk about finding prospects in your market area through the Internet, and then developing with them the type of relationships we've discussed.

Once you've met these people, you'll cultivate the relationship the same way as you would offline; however, meeting them online utilizes a different methodology.

Nancy Roebke, president of Profnet, Inc. (www.profnet.org) and author of *Introduction to Networking*, was an expert traditional networker until 1995, when an automobile accident nearly ended her life. When she was told she would never walk again, she decided she'd better find some way of conducting business that was not dependent on physical mobility. This was just when the Internet was beginning to enter mass consciousness, and Nancy became one of its pioneers when it came to building a business this way.

Fortunately, Nancy was able to walk again after all, and is doing fine in that regard. At the same time, she's also doing fine when it comes to business on the Internet, and she agreed to share here some ideas for how you can utilize this medium to your advantage:

> *The Internet is a huge, global marketplace with literally thousands of people going online monthly. The business potential there is astounding, even if your business serves only local clientele. Marketing a "local" business on the Internet takes creative thinking, but the rewards for being creative are well worth the effort. Here are some methods that I use to find clients for a specific city or town:*

> *1. **Use search engines, as many of them to which you can get access.** Go to the search engine, type in the name of the city or town in which you're looking for contacts, and hit enter. Up will pop the sites with that city listed in their URLs (domain name). Often, those sites are Chambers of Commerce, tourism bureaus, or other such sites. Those are great to use for gathering information about the area and perhaps asking for referrals to others with whom you'd like to connect. But equally often, and more importantly, businesses and business organizations from that city will show up in this type of search.*

> *This might be the time to say, "Hi, I live in your town. I visited your Web site." The usual introduction procedure applies here; in other words, make sure you don't Spam the person (i.e., send unsolicited e-mail). But you have something in common with this business: you're in the same town, and perhaps you would like to begin a mutually beneficial business relationship.*

*2. **Consider devoting a page on your Web site to promoting a charity event in your area.** Issue press releases about the page to your local mainstream media. Make sure the charity knows what the site URL is and uses it in* their *promotional literature. Offer to co-sponsor the Web page with other local businesses in your area who also have Web sites. What a great way to support a great cause while building your own business (talk about win-win!)*

*3. **Form a community "webring."** A webring is a way for businesses who share a common bond to link together, one site after another after another. Consider forming a webring for your town. This is also another great press release opportunity.*

*4. **Read people's signature files, or sigs.** And, of course, create your own. I actually met someone who lives two streets over from me by reading sigs. He posted to an international list I belong to, and I read his sig, which included the name of his city. I probably would never have met him otherwise. If you want to find others in your area online—or make it easy for them to be able to find you—be sure to put your city in* your *signature file.*

*5. **Consider an online promotional program for people from your town only.** If they have a mailing address in your town and they use the Internet, they qualify. You'll be surprised at the number of people you meet who live right in your neighborhood, but who you find on the global information superhighway.*

Taking what you've learned thus far of the Endless Referrals System®, you already know how to engage others online in mutually beneficial, give and take, win/win relationships. The same principles apply.

Again, relationships are the key! Please be careful not to get so infatuated with the *virtual* world of the computer and all that it can do that you forget the *actual* ingredient to networking success: building relationships to the point where the other person feels they *know you, like you, and trust you.*

Remember that people don't do business with, and refer business to, computers. They do business with, and refer business to (altogether now!), people they know, like, and trust.

A Great Example

Patrick Anderson once noticed in a local online discussion group that three people seemed to fit the category of Center of Influence. One of these was an artist.

Patrick checked this person's Web site, really enjoyed what he saw, and felt there might be some way he could use his work for his own Web site as well as referring him to others. So he called the artist, whose name is Joe, on the telephone (note that he didn't e-mail him—he *called* him!) to introduce himself. He then related to Joe his thoughts about the artist's work.

Joe was understandably delighted, and right away suggested someone who could use Patrick's Web site design and marketing services as well. Another 250-person or more sphere of influence was now part of Patrick's life, and Joe's as well.

Please notice that although this situation began online, Patrick approached it pretty much exactly the way we've been discussing all along.

Utilizing Links

Speaking of relationships, one excellent opportunity to establish these online is through the use of links. According to Anderson, "Online marketers discovered long ago the incredible power of advertising for other people by promoting them on your Web site—or mentioning their business and saying nice things about it. The fastest, most remarkable way to solidify the goodwill of a relationship is to refer business to someone by pointing people to that person's Web site."

This is called "adding a link" to their Web site from yours. Links are a way for a person to click their mouse and move to a different Web page or site. Anderson believes links are so potentially beneficial to the online relationship-building process that he says they are described by some Internet authorities as "the hidden power of the World Wide Web."

Anderson suggests, "Giving someone a link can be a golden hook that pulls people into your Web site. It gives people a reason to like you and makes them want to refer business to you. Perhaps even put your link on *their* Web site. Once you are to the point with someone where you are trading links, you are set up to benefit each other greatly." He adds, "Trading links is the fundamental spirit of networking on the Internet."

There are two major benefits to exchanging links. One is the immediate increase in traffic to your Web site. This can begin the relationship-building process with a brand new prospect. The second benefit, and most important in our minds, is the ongoing funnel of new, prequalified prospects it brings to your doorstep. From there, you can use the various principles of the Endless Referrals System® to build and cultivate these relationships into sales and/or referrals. It also provides a great opportunity to set up a mutually beneficial cross-promotion (see Chapter 10).

Here's one way you might set up a link exchange with someone you don't yet know. As Nancy Roebke directed earlier, use the major search engines to find the URLs for cities and towns where you want to network. Then locate some Web sites of businesses that sell noncompetitive or complementary products or services to the same prospects you are looking for.

Once you've identified these businesses, send them a short note by e-mail (though if you wanted to, you could call them instead; while "mixing metaphors" is not desirable, mixing media is!). In your note, offer to add a link on your Web site to their Web site. Mention that they provide a product, service or resource that your customers might be interested in knowing about.

Make it very easy for them to come to your site. Let them know to feel free to come by your site any time and to add their link. Inform them that your database marketing research suggests that your customers would be willing buyers of their products. Remind them to say something really nice about themselves when they add their link.

Patrick Anderson takes it a step further: He says a surefire way to make this even more effective is to add a link to their site beforehand! Say something highly complimentary about their site and, of course, if you're familiar with their company and know that they have a good reputation, give them a tremendous endorsement. Mention the reasons that people would want to visit their Web site. Then send a note letting them know that you've added their link. Tell them that you want to be sure you have correct information for copyright notices and contact information.

As Anderson says, "Will that person click immediately on your site? Will they look for their link? Will they beam when they read what you said about them? Will they tell other people about *your* Web site? Will they add a link to their Web page cross-promoting *you*? Will they be open to discussing joint ventures and other cross-marketing and potential opportunities? You bet— to all of the above! In fact, they will most likely do anything you suggest that is easy for them to do."

This is tremendously powerful and can generate a lot of new business.

The beauty of this approach is that everybody wins. Even if they never buy anything from you, directly refer you to others, or even place a reciprocal link on their site, your customers have you to thank for providing such a useful resource!

I met Patrick Anderson and Michael Henderson years ago via the telephone. They called to tell me that after reading the original edition of *Endless Referrals*, they began basing the marketing/referral aspect of their Internet marketing business around the philosophies of my book.

Knowing virtually nothing about the Internet at that time, I recall being fascinated with the way they had systemized the follow-up process. Even more importantly, I was intrigued with their innovative method of sharing links to make people want to see them succeed and *want* to help them find new business. Sounds familiar, doesn't it?

These two entrepreneurs actually developed a marketing program specifically designed to elicit referrals via the Internet community. At the time, what impressed me was the degree to which, regardless of the physical reach of the computer, the actual business being transacted was still based on personal relationships. And what *really* impressed me was that Anderson and Henderson had so clearly recognized and capitalized on that fact.

Blogs and Networking

My friend, Kevin Eikenberry (www.kevineikenberry.com), who consults and trains organizations on team-building, is an expert on the benefits of using blogging as a tool for networking and prospecting.

Kevin suggests that savvy marketers create ways to make this new medium a part of their overall networking and promotion plan. Here's Kevin:

> *While Web logs, better known as blogs, can come in all shapes and sizes, a blog is just a very simple way to publish a journal, record of events, thoughts, ideas, or whatever the author wants to write about. A blog sits on a Web site, whether that site is run by you or managed by another company that will host your blog.*

Blogs started coming into the general public's awareness with a large number of political blogs written during the 2004 U.S. presidential election campaign. Because of this, one might expect blogging to be part journalism and part political commentary, and therefore not of interest to most of us or the advancement of our businesses. But this would be to miss out on a powerful new medium.

Blogs can *be journalism, and they* can *be political commentary. They can also be personal diaries or journals—and they can just as easily be a way for you to show your uniqueness and build a conversation around your business and professional interests. That is how I use mine, and why Bob asked me to share some thoughts in this book!*

Technically Speaking

Because blogs are designed to be easy to update and are already on a Web site (don't worry, you don't need to know anything *about Web sites or Web design to start one), you might find a blog an easy way to supplement or even replace an e-zine (e-mail newsletter). They are easier to do, easier to update, and you don't have to worry about e-mails getting delivered!*

If you already have a Web site, adding a blog can help you get more visitors who are interested in you because you will be writing about your area of expertise. And because the search engines love Web sites that are tightly focused and updated often, your site can move up quickly in the search results for words that matter to you.

There are plenty of places to learn much more about the technical aspects of blogs and blogging. Just do your own search on Google or your favorite search engine to get the latest information.

How You Can Benefit

Let's say you are an insurance agent. You have expertise in life insurance and a specific set of benefits you bring to your clients. A blog gives you a platform to talk about the latest ideas related to life insurance and life planning. You can give clients (and potential clients) tips and checklists. You can give them new ideas. You can relate the latest news to your products and services. The possibilities are endless.

Of course, if you aren't in life insurance, the same would apply to whatever topics are relevant to your line of work; the premise and benefits remain the same. While there are many, here are three specific benefits you will find:

1. **Getting to know you.** *The blog becomes a part of how you brand yourself. If people read it, they should feel like they are getting to know you and getting to know what your beliefs and values are. Imagine your best referral sources sending potential referrals to your blog as a way to help them get to know you deeper and faster. In this way, your blog can be leverage: People are even more qualified if they call you or might already "know" you when you make the referral call.*

2. **Making it easier.** *Do you have clients who love you but have trouble knowing what to say about you? Encourage them to send their friends and colleagues to your blog as a way to make the connection. That way, they don't have to feel they have to say the perfect words about your business in order to give the referral.*

3. **Keeps you on top of your game.** *By writing often about your work and the benefits of your products and services, you will stay current and fresh. This will help in all phases of your business, but it will also help you in networking situations by giving you something fresh and new to talk about when having conversations with possible clients and new referrals. It also gives you new ideas to share with potential clients as you build your relationships with them.*

I started blogging in March of 2004. I have certainly gained the benefits described above and more. Beyond those I've mentioned, I have also made new connections with potential colleagues and collaborators who have found my blog and sent me comments, feedback or questions.

By writing regularly (my goal is four entries or "posts" per week), seldom does a week go by that I don't add someone to my network or use what I am writing to make a new connection with an existing or potential client.

How to Get Started

This is only a tiny sample of ideas as to the potential of blogs and blogging to help you build your network. If you would like to learn more, here are the first four steps I recommend:

1. ***Start reading some blogs.*** *Do a search in Google for "<insert your specialty> blogs." If you are a chiropractor, search on "chiropractic blogs." If you are a graphic designer, search on "graphic design blogs." Read what others are doing and writing about. E-mail them and build your network with them. Chances are they aren't your competitors, and they might be very willing to help you, perhaps even to collaborate with you.*

2. ***Learn About RSS.*** *RSS (Really Simple Syndication) is one way to "publish" your blog to the world. There are many free RSS readers you can use to keep track of the blogs you are starting to read. Pick one (there are many) by searching for "Free RSS Reader" in your favorite search engine.*

3. ***Read Debbie Weil.*** *Debbie is an expert on blogging for business and will be a good connection for you. You can find Debbie and her blog at http://debbieweil.com/.*

4. ***Start one!*** *You can (and will want to) build a strategy and a plan later, but if you see value for you, jump in! Go to http://blogger.com (what I use) and you'll be started in less than five minutes—for free.*

By the way (and this is Bob speaking again), you can read Kevin's blog at: www.kevineikenberry.com/blogs/index.asp.

Prospecting Via Instant Messaging

While typically thought of more as a keep-in-touch tool for friends and loved ones (and those who would perhaps like to eventually be such), instant messaging can also serve as a very profitable prospecting tool when approached correctly.

You can send an instant message to someone anywhere in the world, including a local prospect. According to Internet prospecting authority Max Steingart (www.maxsteingart.com), author of *Make the Internet Your Warm Market*, "Instant messaging is predicted to surpass e-mail as the primary online communication tool in the next few years because it's easy and fun to do. Almost half the online population currently uses instant messaging once a week, and a growing group of 'intense' users have six or more conversations a day. Instant messaging use is increasing, with more than seven billion instant messages being sent every day worldwide."

Max says, "In addition to using instant messaging to contact the people you know, you can also use it to connect with people you don't know. Sending an instant message to someone you don't know can be the beginning of a wonderful friendship and business relationship. Of course, it can also be viewed as an unwelcome intrusion, so you must approach the process correctly. How your instant message is received by a total stranger depends on the contents of your initial message.

"You want your initial instant message to be the start of a friendship, not a slick commercial for your business. In fact, if you're initial contact is a 'pitch,' not only will you most likely never have this person as a prospect, you'll also be guilty of 'Spimming' (the instant message equivalent of e-mail Spamming)."

In other words, just like sending an e-mail to a potential prospect, the dynamics of sending an instant message is much the same as a traditional contact. Just as we wouldn't introduce ourselves to a potential prospect or networking contact by talking about ourselves and our business, the same goes for an instant message.

In Max's book he relates the story of a financial advisor who took a job with a New York brokerage house and wanted to find another way of contacting prospects without having to depend on the telephone (an ever more important matter these days since the Do Not Call laws went into effect). He searched the Internet for people who had graduated from the same university he attended and found that most of the alumni he contacted online were very receptive to hearing from him.

His initial instant message to initiate a conversation with an alumnus was, "Hello, my name is Wayne. I'm a (name of his college) graduate with a degree in economics, working on Wall Street. What did you major in while you were there?"

According to Max, in the first six months of his stockbrokerage career, this young man brought more new clients into his firm than any other new broker—all as a result of his innovative use of instant messaging.

Max also shares a story about a woman who relocated to Orlando, Florida, from Macon, Georgia, and began a career in real estate. Mary used instant messages to communicate with her friends and family back home on a daily basis. She posted a profile to promote her real estate business in the member directory of the instant messaging system she used. One evening she received an instant message from a complete stranger:

> Hello, my husband and I are looking to buy some vacant lots
> in your area as investments. Are you familiar with what
> is available? I noticed your profile in the directory.

Mary responded:

> Hello, yes I am. My husband and I have purchased a few lots ourselves as investments. I'm very familiar with the market and would be happy to point you in the direction of some great buys. My name is Mary. What's yours? By the way, I like your profile.

Mary received an answer:

> Thank you, my name is Jean. My husband's name is Murray. I liked your profile too. That's why I contacted you. We are coming down there in a week. Can you give me a call tomorrow so we can set up some time to look at some property with you?

Mary replied:

> Of course. I'd be happy to. When is the best time to call?

Jean became Mary's best client. Jean and Murray had recently cashed out of the stock market with millions to invest in property. Over the following 60 days, they purchased enough real estate with Mary to make her the top sales person in her company for the entire year.

Max says that Internet-savvy people have learned they can use instant messaging to establish a friendship and/or business relationship in a few seconds. He reminds us, however, that it's only the beginning, and that just as in the noncyber world, it's still up to you to build the relationship correctly.

A Tool, Not a Panacea

Which brings us full circle. As mentioned right at the beginning of this chapter, the Internet is an excellent tool for prospecting, but it is just that—a tool. It's not a panacea, and it certainly cannot replace the full spectrum of your effective marketing strategies, and particularly its most important aspect: relationship-building. Internet marketing can be a welcome and valuable addition to what you are already doing correctly, so long as it's in *addition to* as opposed to a *replacement for*.

Most experts agree that as we wade deeper into the twenty-first century, effectively utilizing the Internet will become more and more important. It certainly allows the so-called "little guy" to play with the major corporations on a more level playing field. However, to take advantage of it effectively, we must continue to learn and look at it as a continuing, long-term situation as opposed to a quick fix.

By the way, we're talking in this chapter about using the Internet for prospecting and networking purposes, but it has other uses, too, including positioning through published articles, which we'll look at in the next chapter, and especially as an excellent tool for what is known as "attraction marketing," which we will look at in a chapter of its own (Chapter 14).

Whether prospecting by telephone, in person or over the Internet, the same basic rules apply. Follow the road map, be creative at times, and most of all, always have the other person's wants and needs in the forefront of your mind.

Key Points

- The Internet is another excellent tool for prospecting but it is just that; a tool, not a panacea.
- When the principles of this book are applied to the online world, it becomes, according to Patrick Anderson and Michael Henderson, "Inter-Net-Working."
- While the Internet is global, you can still use it to prospect locally.
- Marketing a "local" business on the Internet takes creative thinking but, according to Nancy Roebke, "the rewards for being creative are well worth the effort." Here are some methods Nancy uses to find clients for a specific city or town:
  1. Use search engines, as many as you can.
  2. Consider devoting a page on your Web site to promoting a charity event in your area and make it a "media event."
  3. Form a community "webring."
  4. Read people's signature files (SIGs) and create your own.
  5. Consider an online promotional program for people from your town only.
- Utilize links.
- According to Patrick Anderson, "Giving someone a link can be a golden hook that pulls people in to your Web site. He says, "Trading links is the fundamental spirit of networking on the Internet."

- There are two major benefits to trading links.
  1. Immediate increase in traffic to your Web site.
  2. The ongoing funnel of new, prequalified prospects it brings to your doorstep. Also, it provides a great opportunity to set up a mutually beneficial cross promotion
- Blogs are a great way (and especially, an easy-to-update way) to enhance your online presence.
- You can also prospect via instant messaging.
- When all is said and done, however, the Internet is still just a tool. People don't do business with, and refer business to, computers. They do business with, and refer business to, those people they know, like, and trust.

CHAPTER 9

Position Yourself as the Expert (and Only Logical Resource) in Your Field

When I say the word "astronomer," who comes immediately to mind? Most people will not hesitate even a moment before answering "Carl Sagan."

When talking about science fiction, and especially robots, what author's name might jump right out at us? Many would name Isaac Asimov.

What about child psychologists? Benjamin Spock. How about Vulcans? Well…Mr. Spock. Personal development authors and speakers? Zig Ziglar, Dr. Denis Waitley, Brian Tracy, Anthony Robbins, Jim Rohn, and a few others might immediately come to mind.

What about *your* line of work? Who stands out in the public eye as the person your community would immediately think of?

Is that person *you?*

Are you so well positioned in your community or niche market that when people either need the products or services you provide or know someone who does, they think of you—and only you? If they don't at present, they will! That is your goal.

Fellow speaker and author Peter Johnson is a marketing strategist for major corporations and organizations all over the world. A renowned genius in his field, he refers to this concept as "the science of strategic positioning." In his series, *Johnson on Strategic Marketing*, he describes it this way:

> *To definitively establish in precise terms the strategic identity, image and reputation of your specific company, your products and your services, such that in the mind of your targeted marketplace there could be no acceptable alternative available anywhere…regardless of price.*

That definition certainly works for me. When *I* talk about positioning oneself as the "expert" in relation to networking, however, I'm talking on a much smaller scale: I'm talking about establishing yourself on an individual basis.

In this case, we're talking about positioning the individual as well as, and even more than, the product or service itself. People need to make an association in their minds between who you are and what you do for a living. After all, they know, like and trust you. They want to help you succeed and find new business. Utilizing the principles and methods in this chapter will help *get* you into their consciousness and *keep* you there.

Act As If...and You Will Be

In this chapter, I'd like to share with you my ideas on how to attain the position of "expert" and only logical resource in your field.

The first thing you must do, even before beginning to implement any particular tangible strategies, is to put yourself in the mind frame of already being there. Imagine you are the person who has already attained success using the principles and approaches we are about to discuss. People now come to you for information, referrals, and advice. You have already begun to use these methods and techniques for your positioning benefit, and it hasn't cost you a dime.

Positioning through the Media

One excellent way of positioning yourself as the expert is to write articles for local, state and national print media. Writing articles is a very effective way to position yourself with hundreds or even thousands of people. People automatically regard you as an authority.

Let's imagine you're a financial advisor and your benefit statement is that you "help people create and manage wealth." I'm using that profession as an example, but you can adapt this approach toward your own particular field and find a way to make it applicable.

Write a weekly column for your local newspaper and position yourself as the expert in financial advice. It must serve the public interest, so find an angle that will be welcomed by the editor of the newspaper. One possibility is to serve as a consumer advocate. Maybe you can share interesting tidbits the average reader wouldn't know. That way, people will feel they can rely on you, rather than on others in your field.

For instance, what do you know that the public needs or wants to know about? How about the kind of investment products one should consider? What sort of products should one either be wary of or stay away from altogether? How does one protect one's assets and increase one's wealth without taking potentially catastrophic financial risks? Are there certain myths that every financial services consumer should know? There is no limit to the number and variety of ideas you can come up with that will help serve your readership.

Again, this applies regardless of what field you're in; however, using financial advisors as an example reminds me of something I once heard:

> Q: Do you know the biggest difference between the local financial advisor whom nobody knows and the one who makes guest appearances on network television investment programs and is quoted in the *Wall Street Journal?*
>
> A: The first is unknown outside his local area and present clientele—and the other makes guest appearances on network television investment programs and is quoted in the *Wall Street Journal!*

Was that confusing? Please allow me to explain. There probably is actually very little difference, if any at all, between these two financial advisors, in terms of their level of knowledge in their field. The only difference—the *significant* difference—is that one has managed to effectively promote and position herself within the media as an expert—and the other hasn't.

The same goes for the Realtor® who always seems to show up on local radio and television and in the local newspaper, and the one who doesn't. And the computer consultant, architect, health care practitioner, etc.

What if you're in a profession that's not often featured in the media? Then you can find an angle and be the first.

A chiropractor could write a weekly column on health and exercise. An accountant could write a column entitled, "Tax Tip of the Week." An office products salesperson could give out suggestions on how to get the best quality at the lowest price. A computer troubleshooter can provide some simple, do-it-yourself fix-it suggestions. And so on and so on.

There are many, many topics that financial advisors, chiropractors, accountants, office products salespeople, computer troubleshooters and practically every other person selling practically any product or service could use to write articles. You can, too, regardless of your profession! Just put your mind to it, and even brainstorm with your family and those in your network.

When writing this article, please keep in mind, it cannot be written as a personal advertisement. It must be kept strictly public-interest-oriented. What you want is a byline, as well as your picture and some information about you (space permitting). You are not using this column directly as a sales tool; instead, you are using it as a *positioning* tool that will *eventually* turn into a sales tool.

How Easy Is This to Accomplish?

Here is the challenge you might come up against: The editor of the newspaper is likely to say something like, "But we've never done this before!" Well, you have to find a way of selling that person on why he should do it now.

Author and former newspaper editor Dean Shapiro, points out some very legitimate reasons why editors are not readily swayed into agreeing to this type of situation. According to Dean:

Newspaper columns about businesses are not an easy thing for an editor to give away. They are never free, even when the columnist is not getting any money for doing them. Someone is paying for that space, and that's usually the newspaper. If the person writing the column isn't taking out a commensurate amount of paid advertising in the paper, most editors are loathe to give them "free advertising" even when the column isn't a direct appeal for business. Just putting someone's name out there in connection with what they do is a form of advertising for them, and the editor knows that. Newspapers need ads to survive and they hate giving anything away gratis.

Editors also have to guard against setting precedents that can come back to haunt them. Give a column to a Realtor® each week and you leave yourself wide open to a chiropractor calling and saying, "Hey, you're giving Larry Soandso a column. How about giving me one? I serve more people than he does." And then the water purification system saleswoman calls and says, "Hey, you're giving a column to a real estate broker and a chiropractor. How about one for me?" You begin to get the picture.

Dean concludes with the strongest point of all: If a newspaper does give away column space, there has to be a potential tangible gain, such as an increase in paid readership resulting from that column's publication.

So you need to educate the editor on how your column is going to benefit the newspaper, the reader and *the editor.* Remember, people naturally want to create less work for themselves, and editors are no exception. Therefore, if you can provide them with an article every week, at no cost, that will increase readership and help them fill a news hole with a valuable public service, they might jump at it. But be prepared for some resistance. Find a way to accomplish your goal, and you'll find the rewards worth the effort.

Hint: The smaller and more local the newspaper, the greater the odds of acceptance. While your local metropolitan daily might not be accepting of the idea, your town or even neighborhood weekly might very well be. And don't worry about the amount of readership, as we'll see in a moment how to use it as a positioning tool to as many people as you want. The important thing is to get published in something!

Making It Happen

In an earlier chapter I wrote about my friend, author and former Realtor® extraordinaire, Terri Murphy. Terri is now also a much sought-after speaker and consultant on communication skills, and I'd like to describe how she went about utilizing the media as a tremendous positioning tool when still actively working her real estate business.

One of Terri's most powerful positioning tools was her newspaper column, "Murphy on Real Estate." She had to work for it! According to "Murph," it took her six months to persuade the editor of her local newspaper to run her column. She says she encountered *lots* of resistance and really had to be imaginative.

First, she wrote some sample articles. She also offered her column for free until she could prove its worth. Then she pointed out why the paper's use of national, syndicated columns that applied to major cities throughout the United States was not necessarily in the best interests of those living in their small town. Terri suggested that the stories needed a local flavor, and that she was just the one to give it to them.

Through her combination of determination, sales ability and logic, Terri finally had her column accepted. Eventually, "Murphy on Real Estate" went on to become syndicated in 26 newspapers nationwide.

But she didn't stop there. Terri then worked her way in as the host of a weekly radio show. She accomplished this by first sending in someone from her personal network who had connections at the station. She combined the power of her network with the authoritative positioning she already had established as a newspaper columnist.

Yes, she had to work at that one too, but of course, she managed to come through. Terri found a way to succeed. And her sales production consistently continued to soar in a real estate climate that most people viewed as cyclical.

Forget about Exposure—It's the Positioning You're After

Once upon a time, before there was the intense competition we now face, *exposure* was all anyone ever really needed. You remember the days when it was profitable to simply hang out your shingle? People would see your sign, be *exposed* to it, and voilà! Business!

And if you or your business ever somehow managed to get mentioned in the newspaper or on television, that was it! People called you. People came to see you. You got great exposure, and that directly resulted in business.

It's a different ball game nowadays. It almost seems as though there are more direct salespeople, financial advisors, lawyers, Realtors®, accountants, dentists, chiropractors, and others seeking customers, clients, or patients than there are people who can possibly use their services. That's why today it's so important to separate yourself from all the others and position yourself as the expert and "only resource" for whatever it is you do.

Let's get back to our newspaper column. The exposure you achieve from writing that column probably won't bring you enough business to justify the time and effort needed to get and maintain it in the first place. However, you sure can use that column as a very effective positioning tool.

For example, you can regularly send reprints from your column to those in your network. In your personal brochure or sales presentation kit, you can highlight the fact that *you* are the columnist on that subject for your local newspaper.

Why? What's the point? It's tremendous positioning! Aren't you successfully implying, without actually saying, that you are the *expert*? Hey, you *must* be: why else would the local newspaper choose you, above all your competitors, to share your knowledge? That's what Terri did as a local Realtor®, and many others who know the importance of what Terri calls "power positioning" do likewise.

Do you think Terri ever tried to get direct listings or sales from her articles and radio talk shows? Absolutely not. That would be counterproductive. She simply positioned herself as the expert by giving out worthwhile, helpful, sound advice, and it came back to her over and over again.

What If You Still Can't Get a Column?

Sometimes, entering through the front door is so difficult that walking through the back door simply makes more sense. While waiting for the break that will land you the actual column, Dean Shapiro has some smart suggestions.

Aim a bit lower and shoot for monthly or periodic articles. Submit what are known as "filler" copy that can fill a given amount of space in a news hole when the need arises. Make sure the articles are not tied to a specific time frame, because they may run weeks or even months from the time they are submitted.

Dean advises sending a note with your submission saying, "Please run as space permits," or something similar.

Editors, especially at weeklies, pick up on these things, usually in the last few minutes before press run when they have a 13-inch (or whatever size) hole to fill and your column, which fits perfectly, just happens to be close by in the "filler" file. Be sure and submit a number of them at varying lengths, so the editor can have a choice to fill whatever size hole exists in those last-minute press deadline crunches.

Another tactic is to "feed" story ideas to an editor. According to Dean:

Very politely (and not too frequently) call or write the editor to suggest stories in your field, and make certain these story ideas are broad-based enough to have a wide appeal to readers. Naturally you, as the story originator, will be quoted in it as the "authority," and that gives it advantageous positioning strength. Eventually, you could establish yourself as the one (or at least the first) person an editor or reporter calls when a story breaks in that field. That can lead to your being granted column privileges and attaining excellent positioning.

Becoming positioned as the expert through media provides you with a huge advantage. After all, the fact is, most people (including me) don't know a whole lot about a lot of different things. Dave and Janet Jones might know nothing about financial planning, real estate, computers, law, or many other areas. When you consider the number of people who approach them regarding their products and services, it's a scary situation for them. All things being equal, don't you think they want to do business with an *expert?*

The Truth Is *Not* Necessarily What It Appears to Be

Unfortunately, there are many people who don't have enough product knowledge to actually help their customers and clients (and some who don't care to), yet they know how to position themselves well enough to be perceived as the expert in their field. At the same time, some of the most product-knowledgeable and caring salespeople remain "client poor" because they have no idea how to position their expertise.

In his book, *Direct Mail Copy That Sells*, author and renowned copywriting legend Herschell Gordon Lewis refers to the word, "verisimilitude," meaning, "having the appearance of truth." Not necessarily *the truth*, but simply the *appearance* of such. Whether something is actually true or just seems to be so, people buy what they *perceive* to be the truth.

Many will agree with the statement, "The truth is what the truth appears to be." I hope you disagree! The truth is *not* simply what it appears to be. The truth is the truth. Unfortunately, the first sentence in this paragraph *is* accurate. In fact, the reason that con artists can fool so many people is that they are experts at causing others to perceive what they say as being the truth. And, in the short run, they do in fact seem to prosper.

Although it can be frustrating, remember: Good guys (and gals) *do* win in the game of networking. Sometimes it just takes a little longer to get there. (And, sometimes not.) Once there, however, we stay there forever, while others are always looking for new territory. And part of our getting there is learning how to position ourselves correctly to and within our target market.

The point is this: I know that you, the reader, *know* your product. You are extremely honest and trustworthy and will use these principles for the good of the customers and clients you serve. With that in mind, these methods will help you position yourself as the expert, the authority in your field, because in truth, you deserve to be.

State and National Media

Another way you can accomplish this goal is to write for your state and national media. Here's how, again using real estate sales for our example.

Your state Association of Realtors® probably has a magazine you can write for, as do the National Association of Realtors® and other trade magazines within that field. Terri Murphy used these media as well.

You might wonder what good this does, if other Realtors® are the only ones reading it? It's a good point, but here's the value: in your listing and selling presentations, it builds credibility with your prospects or customers if they know that you are a published author. You are perceived by your prospects as an expert (which you are). They know that even those in your profession recognize you as an authority; otherwise your article would not have appeared in their magazine.

As a Realtor®, Terri also positioned herself as the expert to others in her field. Consequently, she received referrals from her peers all over North America in the form of newcomers to her area looking for a place to live.

Now, please bear in mind that you don't have to be in any of the professions mentioned to write a column or individual articles and position yourself as an expert through their publications. Just as there are always ways to create a market for your product or service, there are ways to create a market for your articles. It is great positioning! I've personally had several hundred articles published in trade and professional magazines, and my efforts have paid off many times over.

Often, these articles are picked up and rerun by other magazines, which increases my positioning even further. Several magazines have asked me to contribute additional articles after running my first one. I get paid for some of them, but most of the time I'm only doing it for positioning.

Notice I didn't say "exposure." Exposure and positioning are two different animals. As far as I'm concerned, exposure by itself...plus about $1.50 (at Starbucks®, double that number!)—might buy you a good cup of coffee, and not much more.

Positioning, on the other hand, is situating yourself as the authority, the expert in your field. You don't necessarily need to get direct response from these placements; in fact, you usually won't, although we'll discuss how to do that in the chapter on Attraction Marketing. But you can use that positioning constantly and consistently in your marketing efforts.

How to Get Published

When you decide you want to write an article for a trade magazine, simply call and ask for the editor in charge of outside contributing articles or freelance submissions. Tell her your idea as concisely as possible and see if she thinks it's a match. If she does, she'll ask you to submit something, usually a query letter describing what you plan to cover in the article. Sometimes, editors will request the article itself.

I wouldn't submit anything at that point, however. Instead, ask for a set of author's guidelines and a back issue or two of the magazine. Or, if they have them on their Web site, take a look at them beforehand. You want to see how articles are written, the average length of the articles the journal runs, the slant of the magazine, and what kind of biography you will be given at the conclusion of the article. Then you tailor your article accordingly.

If you aim to be published in many periodicals, you can come up with a couple of generic articles that give good, worthwhile advice and then simply gear them to a specific industry or audience and spell out what you're trying to accomplish in your article. You can consult the *Reader's Guide to Periodical Literature* or other reference books in your local library for the names of prospective magazines, or you can look through the racks at the magazines they order. Reference librarians are usually good sources of information on which publications might suit your needs. Of course, the Internet has much of the same information, so you can try there, as well.

And whenever you are published, send a press release to your local newspaper, letting them know about it. If you're a chiropractor and had an article published in a chiropractic magazine, make sure the editor of your local newspaper knows that. If the local paper prints the release you send or mentions it in some other context, such as a "People" column, it's another trophy you can use in order to position yourself as your community's chiropractic authority. A framed copy of a printed article hanging prominently in a waiting room is certainly an effective positioning device to those who are already patients. They can then know they are referring those in their sphere of influence to a recognized authority in her field.

Become an Information Resource/Cultivate the Relationship

A good way to begin the positioning process with the newspaper as a future columnist is to first become a willing resource for information and quotes. When a story takes place on a national level, the editor will often assign a reporter to cover the local angle. If you've developed a relationship with that reporter, there's a good chance you'll be the one he calls. Even being quoted in the story affords you the ability to be able to reprint it and use it as a positioning tool for your prospects and referral sources.

What's important here is to establish, cultivate, and develop that same *know you, like you, trust you* relationship with the reporter or reporters as you would with any other prospects or referral sources.

David Teten and Scott Allen, coauthors of *The Virtual Handshake*, make an excellent point. They say, "Remember to focus on the journalist's needs, not yours or your business's." They're absolutely right. Realize that until your relationship has been developed over time, that reporter doesn't care about helping you achieve your goals; he only cares how you can add to *his* story, convenience, etc. As the authors advise, "The reporter's primary interest is creating an interesting, helpful and credible story for *his* audience."

Begin the relationship by contacting her with a nice, brief note, telling her how much you enjoy her writing. Briefly—and the word "briefly" is very important here and any time you're dealing with a reporter, editor, or producer who doesn't know you yet—explain how you can be of assistance. Every so often, send one of your note pads (see Chapter 4) so your name, face and contact information will always be in front of them in a useful, nonpushy manner. And, whenever you think of a good story idea, send a brief note (on your personalized note card, also from Chapter 4) with any suggestions that might help them in forming their story. Remember not to focus on you. Eventually, you'll most likely get...*the call*.

Teten and Allen offer sound advice for when this happens. They say:

Of course, when a reporter calls you, you should be courteous and helpful. However, if you don't know the answer to a question, just say you don't know, but will get back to them with an answer or the name of someone else who can assist.

Very true. Nothing will more surely destroy your credibility and growing relationship with this reporter than trying to be something you're not, or providing an answer when you don't really know the answer. On the other hand, connecting him with someone who *does* know and can help only positions you as even more credible and trustworthy in their mind.

The authors have one more piece of advice, which I've personally found to be right on the money:

Reporters very much value a fast response to their requests. Even more so than most other people, a quick response to their e-mails carries a lot of weight, because they're always under deadline.

Heidi Richards (www.heidirichards.com) is one of the most prolific self-marketers I've ever known, and she has mastered the art of positioning herself with the media. A floral shop owner for more than 23 years, Heidi combines incredible networking skills, customer service, a giving, sharing spirit, constant creativity, and a marketing mind that would be hard to surpass.

She's now also an internationally known speaker and author of numerous books, including *The Woman's Career Compass* and *Rose Marketing on a Daisy Budget*. This is aside from her continuing active ownership of Eden Florist & Gift Baskets in Miramar, Florida. Heidi's e-zine, entitled, "Self-Marketing News," is, in my opinion, one of the very best on the Internet on this topic. You can subscribe to it by visiting the Web site URL mentioned above.

Here's an excellent step-by-step method by Heidi, excerpted, with permission, from an article in her e-zine entitled, "Writing for Dollars—How to Get Started."

It begins with one of her most well-known quotes:

When you provide good information from which readers can learn and profit, people are more likely to buy your products and services.

That's so true, whether writing for online or traditional publications. It's also the basis for success in marketing and networking, whether on a mass or personal basis. As Heidi implies, when you provide value to others, you become more desirable to them as a source of the products or services they need. Why? Well, you're building their *know you, like you, trust you* feelings toward you. This constant and consistent *giving of value* is the mindset that begins it all, and that is exactly the basis of the entire Endless Referrals System®.

Whether you write articles for print media or for online publications, says Heidi, follow these 10 guidelines to increase your likelihood of getting them published:

1. *Read the publication. Become familiar with the writing styles and content.*

    Heidi says it took several months before one of her articles was accepted by a certain magazine she'd been pursuing. According to Heidi, "Because I was patient, tenacious and had *developed a relationship with the editor*, I was asked to be the South Florida Profile Editor for that magazine and now write an ongoing series of articles for them." As she points out, developing relationships with the editors is very important. Personally, I often refer other writers that might be of interest to the editor, and that helps to establish me further as a resource. Of course, it also positions me with the authors I refer, and I've often been the beneficiary of their referrals to their editors, as well.

2. *Ask the publication for their editorial calendar, which can often be found on their Web site. An editorial calendar lists the focus or theme of each issue. This is a great tool to use when deciding what to write and submit.*

    Magazines often publish with a monthly theme; by checking this out in advance, you're in a terrific position to write according to *their* wants and needs. Remember, in this case, the magazine is your eventual client, and the editor your current prospect.

3. *Find out the submission requirements or author's guidelines. These will include length of article, format, number of words, do's and don'ts, as well as deadlines for submission. In some cases it will also include writer's compensation, if and when they pay for articles.*

    Instead of having them sent, many magazines now post their author's guidelines right at their Web site.

4. *Write about what you know. It's easier to "sell" and easier to write when you draw upon your own experiences and those of others you know.*

Though this advice may sound self-evident, it is actually a profoundly strategic suggestion. The biggest concerns I hear from people when I suggest that they write articles are, "I don't know how to write," or, "What would I write about?" Here's the answer: If you know your topic and you can speak it, you can write it!

Don't worry about perfect grammar. First, you generally want to write the way you speak. Second, before you send it in, pay someone to edit it for you. Simple as that. As far as the "What do I write about?" question, you simply write about whatever it is you know about—in conjunction with a need or challenge your prospects typically experience. In your article, of course, you will provide the solution for them.

By the way, Heidi strongly suggests that you use real-life, personal examples and stories in your writing. They make for a much better article than does a book-report sort of piece. And because it's a better read and will have much greater impact, this sort of real-life article actually has a much better chance of being published.

5. *Keep it simple: plain text, simple fonts, and 12-point type are generally the most widely accepted format.*

6. *Use short paragraphs. Commercials use sound bites to keep the audience's attention. Short paragraphs have a better chance of keeping the reader interested.*

7. *Don't overpunctuate.*

   By this, Heidi is referring to the use of the exclamation points, ellipses (…), question marks and unnecessary commas. She says overpunctuating will cause your words to have less impact. She's correct. (This is something I have a tendency to do, and it's something I need to continually watch out for!!!!!)

8. *Ask questions. Then answer those questions. This will keep the reader's attention and interest.*

9. *Use bullet points. Bullets can accentuate and clarify your information. Since people read in sound bites, bullets help the reader absorb the information in bite-sized pieces.*

10. *Use creative headlines to sell your message.*

In a written sales piece, the headline is the first thing the reader will notice and it must be strong enough to grab their interest. The exact same principle holds true in a magazine or newspaper article. Also, make sure to use action-oriented subheads.

And Finally: Keep Track and Follow Up

Heidi concludes with the following excellent advice:

> *Keep track of where you submit your articles and follow up with editors to find out if and when they will be used. If editors don't use your work, ask for feedback. This will help you become a better writer. Create a record for yourself of the publication, the web site address and the name and contact information of the person to whom you submitted your article.*
>
> *Never give up! Be patient. As the saying goes, "timing is everything," and editors and publishers, like every other prospect, are busy and have their own agendas. If your content is good (and interesting), eventually someone will notice—and you will get published. Once that happens, capitalize on the momentum and keep going. Make writing a part of your marketing plan, and who knows, several articles later, you could be the talk of the town, and of your industry.*

Meanwhile, since the editors are your prospective and current clients, network with them and add value to their lives in the same way you would for your traditional clients. Remember in Chapter 5 when we discussed being a referral source for others? It applies just as well here.

For example, on one occasion, the editor of a magazine to which I sometimes contribute called and asked me if I knew anybody else who could write articles on specific topics for them. Months earlier, I had suggested he use the talents of a fellow member of the National Speakers Association. He did, and that person wrote an excellent article.

When the editor called to ask for more referrals, I decided this was a good opportunity for a lot of win-win situations and excellent positioning for, and with, my other speaker friends. Not to mention the editor himself, who has a lot of pull within the association represented by his magazine.

So I contacted all the speakers within my personal network who I knew could write good articles and relayed the situation to them. By the time I contacted the editor just a short while later, he had already been deluged with calls. He loved it because his magazine was in need of a bunch of excellent articles.

That is win-win networking all around. I positioned myself with both my network of speakers *and* with the editor's network. In fact, he came right out and said, "Please let me know if there's *anything* I can do for you." This type of positioning is actually quite easy to accomplish. It's easy because you're most likely the only one (or one of a very few) who thinks of doing it.

Position Yourself by Placing Articles on the Internet

The Internet has now become a very effective medium for positioning yourself through published articles. Regardless of whether your market is local or international, you can utilize the Internet as an excellent positioning tool.

These days, people in all different areas of business publish their own online newsletters, typically referred to as "e-zines," and you can contribute articles to those publications (we'll discuss publishing your own e-zine momentarily).

First determine, by searching online and by asking questions of those who publish them, which e-zines will accept your articles *and* be good positioning tools for you. It's so much easier to get an article accepted by an e-zine than it is through traditional media that you might as well start there. Remember, by doing this, you're still a published author and can legitimately position yourself as such.

According to Nancy Roebke, Internet marketing authority and president of Profnet, Inc.:

> *It is a widely accepted premise that writing articles for e-zines increases one's visibility, helps develop credibility, and positions the author as an expert in his field. It is a mutually beneficial situation for the editors of e-zines and the authors of articles.*

A true win-win.

Publish Your Own E-Zine

The next great positioning tool you can use to cultivate your network and position yourself effectively and profitably is to publish your own e-zine.

The term "e-zine" is a contraction of "electronic magazine." Again, it's simply an online newsletter; it's relatively easy to publish one, and your only cost is the time it takes to write it, produce it, and maintain your mailing list. This is so much easier and less expensive than producing and sending a traditional newsletter.

On the other hand, there are now so many e-zines going out through cyberspace that you need to make sure you offer something of high value to the reader; otherwise, they either won't want to be subscribed or simply won't open it when they receive it. (And that sort of defeats the purpose of your writing it!)

Depending on your line of work, you should have some brief how-to information, perhaps a question and answer section, and maybe even something humorous. Including a few testimonials at the end from ecstatic customers or clients is also be a nice touch.

If you have products you can sell right from your e-zine, fine, but you're usually better off with a brief mention of something and providing a link to where they can get more information. We'll discuss the principles involved in selling via your web site in the chapter on Attraction Marketing; for now, just remember that your purpose here is positioning, not selling.

It's also very important to remember that Spam (i.e., unsolicited bulk e-mail) has become a very annoying and negative aspect of the Internet, and people are extremely sensitive to being subscribed to a publication without their permission. So please make sure you have that permission. This is best accomplished by what is known as a "double opt-in."

Without getting too technical (which would be very ironic for me to do since I'm the least technical person on the Internet I know!), a *double opt-in* simply means you have a form people fill out or an address to which they send an e-mail. They then receive a notice that in order to be subscribed, they must either reply to that e-mail in a certain way, or click on a link contained in it. That way, if they choose not to be subscribed (or if someone else subscribed them without their knowing it), they simply don't reply. Of course, if they requested to be subscribed in the first place, they'll gladly send it back. (In other words, they have intentionally, consciously "opted in," and done so twice: hence, *double opt-in.*)

How do you acquire subscribers?

Depending upon your line of work, there are several ways. One is by asking people already in your network if they'd like to be subscribed. Another is to ask within your e-zine for current subscribers to pass along your e-zine to others they know, suggesting they subscribe.

A third idea is to offer to subscribe your current prospects. Of course, they might not be interested in doing so, so it's a good idea to let them know that by subscribing, they'll automatically be sent a "free report" on a topic of interest to them. (Now it's up to you to title it in a way so your prospect will be enticed and want to receive it. See the chapter on Attraction Marketing for good ideas on how to do that). You must say this with posture, so that your prospects know you're doing them the favor and not the other way around, or else they most likely will not be interested.

A fourth idea is to develop a quiz that will give people a scoring assessment after they submit their answers. Let them know that by submitting their answers, they are also subscribing to your e-zine. If you can get complementary Web sites to run your quiz as well, your subscribership will increase even faster.

And another idea: When you submit an article to another e-zine for publication, you can ask them to provide a link to your e-zine; this is pretty much standard practice on the Internet.

Still one more very effective method of bringing in the subscribers you want is by piggy-backing on your "establish yourself as the expert" campaign, and make sure your Web site is listed in your bio or byline in any traditional (i.e., print) publication in which you have an article. It's now standard practice for these short bio lines to list your Web site, if you have one, and you can make sure your Web site is set up so it clearly directs the reader to your e-zine. (If you don't have a Web site, just ask the publication to mention your e-zine and how the reader can subscribe.)

When you appear on television or radio, you can often have your "free e-zine" and Web site plugged—and this brings us to another great avenue for your positioning campaign.

You Can Also Position Yourself through the Electronic Media

Another means of positioning yourself in the community is to appear as a guest expert on local radio and television talk shows. When you call the station, don't ask to speak with the host: ask to speak to the producer. In fact, in a larger market it will probably be a *segment producer*.

Explain to her what might be the advantages of having *you* as a guest on the program. You have to be concise and convincing, because producers often get dozens of similar requests every week. You should be prepared with an angle or a hook that will snag the listeners' or viewers' attention.

If you are a medical doctor, for example, you can point out on a radio or television talk show certain practices by many in the medical profession that aren't necessarily ethical. Or you can describe a procedure that doctors should not be doing, even though many of them are. What does the public have the right to know, that they're not being told?

I'm not saying you should engage in yellow journalism or sensationalism, and I'm not suggesting you need to use those precise examples. What I am saying is that you need to *create a reason* why what you have to say is of interest to the show producers and audiences, and that this reason should be genuinely helpful and enlightening. They want a hook, an "angle," and you want to be prepared to give them a great one.

Remember, the programs on which you appear should match the audience you want to attract or before whom you wish to be positioned. If you're an accountant, then appearing on a program geared toward teenagers isn't going to do you much good. You'll get exposure, but because your target audience is not watching, you won't increase your positioning. The only people you need to have seeing you are those who are prospective customers or clients—or more importantly, sources of referrals.

(On the other hand, if you go on that program to teach young people how to become more fiscally responsible, and leverage that appearance through letters and write-ups from the media, that would be excellent positioning for you!)

Here's another tip that serves a twofold purpose: Write a booklet. You don't need to write an entire book (though if you have the time, inclination, and material to do so, that's great), and you don't have to wait until you've been in business for years. Just write a brief booklet filled with clear, helpful information for the consumer. (We'll look at how to do this in more detail in Chapter 14.)

The first purpose of writing this booklet is, again, simply for the positioning it provides. Being a published author will turbocharge your credibility in the eyes of the producers, so this is a wonderful positioning tool to help get you on the air. It's also a very helpful method for your positioning yourself as an expert within your community, as well.

Second purpose: When you do appear on one of these programs as a guest expert, it's very effective if you can offer to send your booklet to anyone who contacts you afterwards, either by fax, e-mail or traditional mail. Sometimes television interview shows are reluctant to allow you to do this, though they will probably write across the screen how people can contact you (perhaps through your web site, e-mail or regular mail) in order to receive the booklet. On radio interviews, it's *always* fair game. The host will either plug it for you or ask you to do so.

Remember, the interview itself must contain lots of helpful information; they don't want you there just so you can plug your booklet. Speak from your heart, share excellent information, and the host will be happy to give your booklet a great plug. While your booklet should provide excellent, helpful information, it should also include stories that help draw interest to your product or services, lots of testimonials from other ecstatic customers or clients, and a gentle "call to action" at the end.

And even if the people who received your booklet don't take you up on that "call to action," you have their addresses for follow-up. (We'll look at additional ways to utilize this strategy in Chapter 14.)

Even if you don't have an actual booklet (though it's a really good idea to have *at least* that), the idea will work with practically any helpful giveaway. Entrepreneur and marketing authority Sean Woodruff relates the time an estate attorney friend of his told him he was going on a radio talk show soon to answer some questions about estate planning. Sean strongly suggested that he offer something free to callers that they'd find useful.

The attorney offered to send anyone who called his office a list of five areas to consider carefully when deciding on a will or trust. According to Sean, he later received something like 400 phone calls to his office requesting the free information. Of course, with the information, the attorney included a nice note with an offer for a free initial appointment to review the prospect's current situation.

Did this result in any new business? I'd say so. As a result of that one interview, Sean's friend did over 100 wills and 20 trusts! This would not have happened had he not had some type of concise, simple information to give away. And it had to be useful information that the listener would care about. Offering to send a "free brochure" would not have done it. Instead, he offered something of actual "use value"—something that would serve the actual needs of the potential client.

Fellow speaker and author Judith Briles of Denver, Colorado, is one of the National Speakers Association's main authorities on mastering the media. Judith, who speaks mainly on women's issues, has appeared on all the biggies, including *Donahue, Oprah, Sally Jesse Raphael,* and *Geraldo* (yep, some of these are from quite a while back!). She has used the media simply as a vehicle to position herself as an expert to her prospects, and it's worked.

Charles Garcia, a Realtor® based in San Francisco, did a superb job of exploiting the media as a positioning tool. He let the segment producers of the local CBS affiliate know he was available for real estate advice and opinion. They eventually took him up on his kind offer.

Remember the San Francisco earthquake in 1989? A couple of days after that event, a friend asked Charles how he thought this disaster would affect local real estate values. Charles immediately realized that a lot of San Francisco and Bay Area people were wondering the same thing.

He called the station and provided a list of topics relating to the earthquake, its effect on real estate values in different neighborhoods, and projections of what might be expected. He suggested that they wait 7 to 10 days before doing this story, in order to give the market a little time to respond.

Meanwhile, Charles began doing his homework. He canvassed his colleagues in the real estate community, interviewed the managers of the major real estate offices in San Francisco and the Bay Area and talked to consumers. He put together an interesting story on the effects of the earthquake on real estate values in the Bay Area.

In this two-minute segment, he revealed some surprising statistics: very few real estate companies reflected a sharp increase in the number of deals falling out of escrow in the short time after the quake. Most buyers who had been in the process of house hunting before the earthquake were still looking. According to Charles, "Is the home seismically upgraded?" became the question of the day. Charles's status as "real estate expert" was established.

These days, Charles's brochure and mailing pieces feature a wonderful picture of him being interviewed by the two anchors. Doesn't that tell his prospects they have the opportunity to work with an expert? And when he sends this to his current customers and clients, they are proud to refer people in their own sphere of influence to "their real estate expert." Who wouldn't be?

As a footnote to this story, the first time Charles appeared on that news program was because the Realtor® they had been using before stood them up. She simply didn't show. The producers then let Charles know they were looking for a dependable real estate agent with whom they could form and develop a relationship.

The more you understand the media in general and how it works, the greater your chances of being successful in utilizing them as a positioning tool. There are now a number of excellent books on the market that share information on how to market yourself to the media, and what to say and do (and just as important, what *not* to say or do!) once you get there. I've listed a few in the resource section at www.Burg.Resources.html.

Are You an Information Resource for Others?

Let's discuss another aspect of positioning yourself as the expert: being an "information resource" for others. In other words, helping people in your community find products, goods, services, or even jobs.

You want to be that person others call to ask, "Hey, do you know a good printer? Do you know a painless dentist? Do you know who has a good cellular phone and provides excellent service?" Be that person who's almost *brokering* the information. Not for a fee, but for positioning. Whenever you hear of someone needing something, come right out and match her up with someone who can help her. Do this consistently, and in time, people will know that you are the one to approach for this type of service.

Are You a Referral Source for Others?

When it comes to positioning oneself as a referral source, a truly great example is the late John Kuczek. The highly esteemed Mr. Kuczek was president of Kuczek and Associates of Youngstown, Ohio, and a perennial top-producing Life Insurance agent. He discovered early in his career that positioning himself as the Big Person on Campus by way of helping others was a major key to his success.

I included the following story regarding Mr. Kuczek in the first two editions of this book. Although his passing since that time certainly leaves a void, you'll see where the principles he lived by are as vital today as ever.

Addressing members of the Million Dollar Round Table at one of their annual meetings, Mr. Kuczek shared many of his excellent methods with his fellow life insurance sales professionals. Here's one.

> *I help clients set up loans and mortgages, and they feel indebted to me because they usually dislike dealing with bankers and I help them get what they want. I also advise them on how to handle their earnings and divert some money into savings and remind them never to invest money they can't afford to lose.*
>
> *By helping clients structure mortgages and loans, I also build a positive relationship with local banks. When I deal with people growing financially, somebody's always borrowing money. As they pay off loans, new projects come up and they are borrowing money again.*
>
> *Over the years, I have done more and more business with bankers. By learning to use bankers, I created the ideal situation. The bankers would*

come to me instead of me approaching them. In the last year or so, banks have come to me and asked for referrals. I gladly oblige as long as my clients who are banking with them are getting the best service available, and that includes getting preferred interest rates on loans.

Now that my company is comfortably positioned with area bankers, we also ask them for referrals. We ask them to take a look at their customers who have commercial loans and see if they would benefit from our services. Interestingly enough, since we have begun to take this approach, we have actually had situations where banks are now calling us to refer clients. Banks are an indispensable part of my business.

Did you notice the phrase he used? "Comfortably positioned" with bankers. Mr. Kuczek was a man who knew the meaning of long-term business relationships, which is what networking is all about. No wonder Mr. John Kuczek was a qualifying member of the Million Dollar Round Table, Court of the Table, and Top of the Table.

Positioning through the Law of Large Numbers

Even if many of your prospects are currently doing business with your competition, if you feel they are worth your persistence, stay with them. With your excellent, classy follow-up, you'll be ready to step in if your competitor messes up, moves on, or for some other reason loses that person's account and referrals.

In his book, *Swim with the Sharks without Being Eaten Alive*, author Harvey Mackay points out that you should position yourself as the number-two person to every prospect on your list and keep adding to that list. He continues that if your list is long enough, there are going to be number ones that retire or lose their territories for a hundred other reasons and succumb to the Law of Large Numbers.

According to Mackay, "If you're standing second in line, in enough lines, sooner or later you're going to move up to number one." I agree, totally! Especially, if you're doing enough things right, such as using the follow-up methods I've been describing in this book.

If you're the number-two person on enough lists, and you're doing the right things, you'll eventually *have* to move up to number one on many of those prospects' lists. And in the networking sense, of course, that doesn't mean being number one just for that person's direct business, but for her referrals as well.

An excellent analogy has to do with one of my niche markets, the insurance industry. In that profession, actuaries are wizards with numbers who can actually predict, almost to the percentage point, how many people in a given area are going to die as a result of traffic fatalities over a certain holiday weekend. Morbid, but true. The only thing they can't tell you is *who* they will be.

Mr. Mackay points out that the insurance industry has basically been built on the Law of Large Numbers. That's why, as Mackay says, if you position yourself as the number two person on enough lists, then sooner or later you've got to work your way up to number one on many of those lists.

What If They Are Already Someone's Customers?

What if many of your networking prospects are currently doing direct business with someone else? Do you realize that you can still get their referrals? Yes, even if you are number two on their list for direct business, you can be number one for their referrals. And position yourself to eventually get their direct business while you're at it.

You might be wondering, "Why would a person possibly refer business to *me* if they're doing business with someone else?" Numerous reasons. All things being equal, they may be doing business directly with your competitor out of a sense of loyalty to that person or maybe even to somebody else—a friend or family member. How many times have you been told by prospects that they *have* to do business with someone because they are somehow connected or related? It's happened to most of us. Or they may feel they are in a position, at least for right now, where making a direct change would be too costly or inconvenient.

If you've impressed this person enough, however, he'll go out of her way to get you referral business. One networking prospect felt so bad that his wife gave some business to a competitor that he actually went on a hunt to find some referrals for me. He was quite successful in that particular venture. Therefore, so was I.

I had earned his loyalty and his help by going out of my way for him previously, using my network to assist him with information he needed to help some of his clients. What goes around *does* come around.

So are your networking prospects worth your persistence? If so, stay with them. Position yourself as the number-two person on a prospect's direct business list, if that's all the current situation will allow. Position yourself as number one, however, for their referrals. Eventually you may be number one for *both*.

Using the principles, strategies, skills, and techniques described in this chapter, you will become positioned as the expert, and only logical resource, in your field.

A Further Use of the Booklet as a Positioning Tool

When Harry Crosby began selling Long-Term Care Insurance for General Electric Financial Assurance (now Genworth Financial), he became a quick study of the industry and the product. He soon wrote a booklet entitled, *Should I Buy Long Term Care Insurance, or Would I Prefer Crisis Management?*, a 16-page, fact-filled and very helpful publication.

In this booklet, he first provided a general explanation of Long Term Care Insurance and then answered just about every question and objection a prospective client might have. He also included the few reasons for *not* purchasing a policy. It was really an excellent booklet, and Harry would utilize it in two ways.

When he spoke on the telephone, trying to set an appointment with someone who wasn't sure they were interested in speaking with a long term care insurance salesperson, he'd use the booklet as a way to get in the door.

First, he'd obtain permission to send the booklet, calling particular attention to a couple of areas the prospect might find interesting. Then, when he'd follow up with another call a few days later, it was much easier to set the appointment. Why? The simple fact that he was an author provided him with exceptional credibility in his prospect's mind. That was by far the biggest reason, and certainly positioned him above any other salesperson in that field.

Secondly, however, because he noted several places for the person to read, they would usually have taken the time to do so. Because his booklet provided such wonderful information, those who truly needed it most became excited about learning more. In only his second full year in the business, Harry made his company's prestigious President's Club. Shortly after that he became the top producer in the country (out of more than 25,000 agents), setting an industry-wide production record by helping over 405 people apply for long-term care insurance. Small wonder why. Harry eventually wrote a full-length book about the industry, entitled *Long-Term Care Insurance: The Complete Guide*, and is certainly well-positioned as an expert in his field.

Working Your Niche

Similar to putting yourself in front of your prospects physically, you can also put yourself in front of them mentally, through what has come to be known as niche marketing.

Niche marketing is one of the most profitable ways to prospect and network. When approached correctly, working a specific niche market brings with it several inherent benefits, including superb positioning (as the expert), and easier access to those with whom you wish to speak.

C. Richard Weylman (www.richardweylman.com), author of the exceptional book, *Opening Closed Doors*, is perhaps the world's leading authority on this type of marketing. He suggests the following in order to establish a profitable business within your niche.

*1. **Choose Wisely.** Be sure you have something you can offer to the market that will differentiate you. It might be added value, unique service, improved delivery or any myriad number of things.*

*2. **Choose Where You Feel You Fit.** This is a vital step in the process. Be sure you have identified what it is that you have in common with your prospects and future clients in the market. Trying to work with people with whom you aren't connected in either purpose or passion will work to the detriment of all parties.*

*3. **Choose Markets Where People Network and Communicate With One Another.** If they network, you can join and get involved in the organization. If they communicate, it's a lot easier for positive word about you to get around. People network and communicate in unique ways, much differently than in the past. Today, they group together based upon three types of activities:*

- Activities they do for a living: associations, professional societies, unions, etc.
- Activities they do for recreation: clubs, activities, leagues, events, etc.
- Activities of special interest to them, such as charitable or cultural organizations, family interests and activities, or even activities related to religious or ethnic affiliations.

*4. **Choose to Build Your Business from the Top.** Select your top twenty clients and determine which organizations they belong to. Then target these groups and ask your best clients to assist you in understanding and working in that market.*

*5. **Choose to Concentrate on One of Your Best Markets for the Next Year.** Join the organization, get involved, gather referrals, seek and obtain introductions, sponsor events, create buzz, become visible, bring great value, and ask for the opportunity to introduce yourself professionally, one on one, with those you meet. Focus, focus, focus on becoming a dominant force in the market you choose. Be gracious and your good name will precede you. "A good name," said King Solomon, "is better than riches."*

Key Points

- Act as if you are already powerfully positioned.
- Position yourself (for free) through the media.
  1. Write columns and articles for local, state, and national print media. These must be consumer-oriented.
  2. Prove to the editor why your information is important for his readership.
- Exposure alone is no longer a money-maker. Positioning yourself as the expert in your field is the key.
- Verisimilitude is having the appearance of truth.
- Utilize Heidi Richards's 10 steps to getting your article published.
  1. Read the publication. Become familiar with the writing styles and content.
  2. Ask the publication for its editorial calendar, which can often be found on its Web site.

3. Find out the submission requirements, or author's guidelines.
4. Write about what you know.
5. Keep it simple—plain text, simple fonts.
6. Use short paragraphs.
7. Don't overpunctuate.
8. Ask questions. Then answer those questions. This will keep the reader's attention and interest.
9. Use bullet points.
10. Use creative headlines to sell your message.

- Richards also advises to keep track, follow up, and if editors don't use your story, ask for feedback. This will help make you a better writer.
- Make writing a part of your marketing plan.
- Become a resource for your media contacts.
- Position yourself as an expert via articles on the Internet. There are two main ways to do this:
  1. Write articles for other people's e-zines.
  2. Publish your own e-zine.
- Being a guest or resource for television and radio interviews is another excellent positioning tool. You must have a hook or angle that will make you a desirable guest in the producer's mind.
- Authoring a booklet will help you in two ways when it comes to working with the media:
  1. Credibility. It positions you as a published author (i.e., an "expert").
  2. It gives you something to give away on the air as a way of attracting listeners to contact you.
- Be an information resource (jobs, services, etc.) for those in your network.
- Be a referral source for others.
- Position yourself through the Law of Large Numbers.
- Utilize booklets even as a nonmedia positioning tool.
- Choose and work a niche market or markets.

CHAPTER 10

Cross-Promotions: True Win-Win Networking

W hen we think of two people networking with each other, especially as it pertains to referrals, we look at the ideal situation as being, "This person finds business for that person and that person finds business for this person." And that in itself has the makings of a fine, mutually beneficial, give-and-take, win-win relationship.

What if we expanded our horizons a bit, and imagined these two people actually going in on a joint promotional venture: two individuals jointly planning the idea and goal of generating carryover business?

In order to learn how to do this effectively and profitably, I sought the advice of expert marketing strategist and corporate consultant Jeff Slutsky (www.streetfightermarketing.com), author of the best-selling books, *Streetfighting: Low Cost Advertising/Promotions for Your Business, How To Get Clients,* and many others. The following is an excerpt of our interview that was published in the first edition of this book way back in 1994, but you'll see how timeless these principles truly are.

> *BB: One of the great concepts you developed in your business was the cross-promotion. This, to me, is the quintessential example of win-win networking. Before we delve into its uses, can you give us a brief history?*
>
> *JS: Cross-promotions have actually been around for a very long time. The oldest cross-promotion I'm aware of was done by Benjamin Franklin over 200 years ago. He ran a special certificate in Poor Richard's Almanac. He cross-promoted with Paul Revere, who gave a special deal on his pewter ware if the person bought Poor Richard's Almanac. This served to increase*

the value of the magazine, and the consumer could buy the pewter for two cents less.

This cross-promotion worked out well for both gentlemen. It was like the first coupon.

In my own case, when we started cross-promotions with our retail clients, we found out cross-promoting can go beyond retail sales into direct sales or just about anything.

BB: *How does a retail cross-promotion work?*

JS: *A simple cross-promotion could be nothing more than a fast-food place that is trying to gain more customers. It would set up a relationship with any other type of merchant that reaches the same type of customer base. Let's say the goal of the fast-food place is to go after children to promote their kiddie meals. So they could approach a Toys "R" Us, a kiddie shoe store, a kiddie clothing store, or a children's bookstore and set up a win-win, cross-promotion.*

The key is to find a cross-promotion partner that targets the type of people you want.

BB: *Let's take the example of a pizza place and a video store. Something like that would seem to go hand in hand. How would that work?*

JS: *That's a classic cross-promotion: pizza, especially if the store does delivery or carryout, and video, which is home entertainment. Both involve an activity at home, so it makes a lot of sense. If you are the owner of the pizza place, you would approach the video store owner and say, "How would you like to provide your customers with something extra—a way they can get a little bit more for their money when they come in to rent your videos, and a great way for you to personally thank them for being your customer?"*

You might end up offering a certificate (I don't like to use the word coupon) for $2 off a large pizza that the video store would distribute to its customers. The actual offer is irrelevant as long as it has some sort of value, savings or freebie attached to it, so it gives the video store an excuse to handle your advertising for you for free.

Now a person goes in and rents three videos. It costs him six or seven bucks, which seems like a lot of money to them. But he's told, "Thank you for coming in—and here's something special for you. When you order your pizza from Joe's Pizza Parlor, you're going to save $3." The video store owner, in essence, is telling the customer: "You really only spent $4 with us today, not $7." The customer then goes away feeling good about doing business with the video store for having gotten something extra.

This is an example of a one-way cross-promotion. All that's required on your part is to provide the video store with certificates. Keep in mind that it's important to put the name of the cross-promotion partner right on the actual printed piece. A nice added touch is to put the video store owner or manager's name and signature —"Compliments of Dave Johnson"—on it as well. This technique works really well.

A two-way cross-promotion is even easier to set up because it is essentially the ultimate example of networking: "I'll hand out yours and you hand out mine." The difference is, now you have to reciprocate. You have to go that extra mile and actually distribute.

In practice, this is fine to do once in a while, but it is difficult to do regularly. When we set up cross-promotions for our clients, we do it on a weekly basis, so we're doing about 50 a year.

You might just decide you don't want to hand out 50 certificates all the time. But it might be just the right approach for some really big cross-promotions.

A two-way cross-promotion has another advantage: You don't have to put an offer on the piece itself for it to contain value. The very fact that you're doing it for them means they will hand out your advertising, and it could be nothing more than a reinforcement of another campaign or just a regular ad, but it doesn't have to be a coupon or certificate of value.

Reverse cross-promotions are totally different. Back to the example of the pizza store. Let's say the video store customers are coming into my store with the certificates to buy my pizza. You might respond, "Thank you for coming into my store and buying pizza. As a little extra gift, I've contacted five other merchants in *my area: the ice cream shop, the shoe store, the video store, the car wash, and the beauty parlor. I've created a coupon booklet, and if you use all five coupons, you're going to save $20."*

So while the customer may have spent $10, she actually gets $20 back. For my part, I have a premium of great value to give away. After all, many people often pay $20 or $30 for actual coupon books. This one they get for free, just for buying from me. The result is a lot of added value to my business for the mere cost of a little bit of printing.

The other advantage of the reverse cross-promotion is that all 5, 10, 15 or more of the reverse cross-promotion participants owe me a favor, and now I can set up one-way cross-promotions with each of them very easily. Essentially, it's really a two-way in disguise, but I'm taking care of all of my two-way obligations in one effective little booklet or packet.

This technique is also good for doing theme cross-promotions, which might be important for a certain type of salesperson.

Let's say you have a jewelry store. You want to cross-promote with several other companies that cater to weddings, something very specific. Let's say you approach a tuxedo rental place, bridal shop, limousine service, photographer, musical band, etc. These businesses can't always reach the prospects before they make their decisions on who to hire for these services. Where is the first place people go when they get engaged? They go to the jewelry store.

BB: *And all else being equal, you want them buying their wedding rings from you, not from the jewelry store down the street.*

JS: *Exactly! So the reverse cross-promotion is, "If you buy your ring from us, there is a $250 gift packet of great value for your wedding. It has 20 or more certificates, from the wedding cake on up." This not only saves them money, it practically plans their wedding for them. So it's a great closing device for someone to make a decision.*

And again, the promotion is at a very low cost. Reverse cross-promotion becomes targeted by an event or by a specific type of product.

BB: *Now, this was a jewelry store owner or salesperson who set this up. What about the other wedding suppliers who want to get in on the ground floor of the wedding plans?*

JS: *It really doesn't matter which of these businesses you are in. If I was the tuxedo shop, for example, I would go to the jewelry store and try to set up the promotion. I might possibly suggest the idea for the packet, as long as I would be assured of getting the business for my tux shop. The key point is that I would try to set this up with a lot of jewelry stores because that is where I'll get my referrals and my leads.*

As a cross-promoter, you pick out any kind of special event and then figure out what else they have to buy. The neat thing about cross-promotion is this: Not only does it cost nothing, except for a little bit of quick printing, but it is so targeted. Most advertising is untargeted, except for direct mail or maybe telemarketing. With a cross-promotion, I can find my customers, if I know who they are, and target by virtue of the cross-promotion partner I use.

I'll share with you one of the biggest success stories in cross-promotions ever. It has to do with a comic book store in Ohio. I had just completed a whole series of training programs for Marvel Comics, a big client of mine.

Comic book buyers are a very specialized type of audience. Only a very small percentage of the population collects comic books, as compared to mass media. It's not like eating pizza, which appeals to almost everybody, or video rentals, which are fairly broad-based as well. Comic books are still fairly specialized.

When the movie Batman Returns came out, which was a big, big event, the comic book store owner set up a cross-promotion with the manager of the movie theater that carried that movie. This comic book store, of course, carries Batman comic books, as well as Penguin, Cat Woman, and all the other related comic books.

Naturally, anyone attending that movie might be in the market for comic books. But the important thing is, you know that anyone who is into comic books is going to be at that movie. Now you've found your target market, so you set up the cross-promotion.

Here's what happened.

The theater employees handed out to moviegoers about 10,000 certificates for $1 off the higher-end, more expensive Penguin and Cat Woman comic books. The comic book store owner got 150 returns out of 10,000. Although that is not a very high percentage, it doesn't matter. All that matters is the return on investment.

Out of the 150 redemptions—and this is the important part— more then 100 customers became regular customers. An average regular customer, according to the owner, spends $10 a week in his store. An additional 100 regular customers translates into $52,000 in sales the first year alone—all from that one cross-promotion.

Let's take it a step further. Most comic book stores live off referrals from friends. If those 100 new regular customers refer their friends, then that $52,000 figure is just the beginning.

BB: *When we talk about the sphere of influence of the average person being 250 people, if they can refer just five of those people, what a success!*

JS: *You can start with these 100 people just bringing in one friend apiece. Now it goes from $52,000 to $104,000 in extra income.*

That certainly demonstrates the potential power of a cross-promotion when you target the cross-promotional partner appropriately. Not only is a movie theater a good target audience to network with if you have a comic book store, but it was that specific type of movie.

BB: *How would somebody more into direct-contact sales, such as an insurance person, Realtor®, computer salesperson, or copying machine salesperson, use a cross-promotion? And what about professionals, such as accountants, lawyers, or dentists, who need to bring in new business but can't blatantly sell? How do they begin the cross-promotion process?*

JS: *Here's a good example. This woman is a pharmaceutical representative whose job is to get in front of the doctor and present her case for the drugs she represents. That is not necessarily an easy thing to do since there is a lot of competition out there in that particular field.*

She knew that a significant percentage of the doctors that she called on were avid golfers. Not a big surprise. So she asked herself the key question: What other businesses or organizations would also benefit from having access to those same doctors?

One thing that came to mind was one of the big discount golf franchises; in her city, there were four units. Let's say out of all the doctors she called, 40 or 50 were avid golfers. Doctors are usually not poor, so when they spend money on golf, they probably spend a lot of money on clubs and everything else.

I suggested that she approach the franchisee of the four stores in this area and say, "Listen, I call on a number of doctors and other golfers. If you'll give me a gift certificate that entitles them to a free sleeve of Titleist® golf balls (this being a top name brand), I'll make sure to put it directly in their hands."

Keep in mind, we are talking about a retail item that is worth about $7 or $8, so it costs the franchise owner $3 or $4. What would it normally cost that retailer to get a potential customer in that front door? They probably spend $20 or $30 per person on mass media advertising to get them in for the first time. Yet she was offering to go out there and give her people a gift certificate that will cost the franchisee only $4 apiece. She explained that as she handed these out, she would sign her name to authorize them and require that the doctors appear in person with the certificate to redeem it.

She also used this as an incentive to get the doctors to see her. She had to sign the certificate right in front of them and explain that they needed to take this to the golf shop in person, in order to take advantage of the gift.

As far as the golf shop owner was concerned, return on investment was the key. Nobody goes in and just gets the golf balls. Golfers look at the clubs and everything else, and possibly become regular customers. At the very least, the retailer gets that doctor's name on his list.

As far as our salesperson is concerned, she now has the ability to distribute, for free, these sleeves of Titleist® golf balls, which would normally cost her $7 or $8. If she did that 50 times without company reimbursement, it would run into some money. Instead, everybody wins—the ultimate in cross-promoting and the ultimate in networking.

BB: *What is crucial is how she used the incentive to get past the gatekeeper and right in front of the doctor.*

JS: *The doctor had to sign it in her presence to validate it. That was one of the techniques that she used to make sure that she got to see the doctor in person. It had to carry both her signature and the doctor's signature, and it had a tight expiration date. They had to redeem within two weeks.*

BB: *The next step would be to find something else doctors like and set up a cross-promotion with another vendor, right? After a couple of times, the doctors would start to associate her visit with a free gift, and they would see her every time. And in her type of business, frequency is the name of the game.*

JS: *Another example is a life insurance salesperson whose specialty and niche market is helping people build for retirement. For this, you could use the reverse cross-promotion approach. Let's say you find someone who wants to save for retirement. Not only are you going to help her save money, but you're also going to help her save money for those things she needs for her retirement.*

What is it that people need for retirement? Maybe they want membership in a golf club, or money off at a restaurant—an early bird special anytime they want. In other words, benefits that offer special consideration. So you think it through and write down 10 or 15 of these merchants or salespeople together.

You let them know that you are a life insurance salesperson and will be calling on some very wealthy people who spend money on cars, homes, club memberships, food, and so on. You are giving these people an excellent opportunity to position themselves in front of this very lucrative market.

Every time I get new clients or clients who increase their coverage, I provide them with a thank-you. This thank-you is going to be a packet which almost looks like a wedding invitation and contains maybe a dozen nicely printed certificates as a thank-you from me, their agent. It will represent hundreds of dollars of savings. Not only am I helping them save money for retirement, but I'm also helping them save money now. I can even use this as a closing device.

BB: *Could you use this as an opening device as well? Let's face it; Often the toughest part of doing business is getting that first face-to-face appointment with the prospect.*

As an opening tool, you would maybe not have as elaborate a package. It depends on whether you could get a restaurant to do a two-for-one, which could run into some money for them. In some cases, you might get them to do freebies. Or you could offer gift certificates that are worth $25: $5 at this restaurant and $5 at this place. The restaurant owners will do that in a second, just for the introduction to those people.

You can use this to get in front of somebody, or as a closing tool, or as a frequency-gaining tool. And in any case, the cost is low. Of course, there will be some time invested in setting these relationships up. On the other hand, it also gives you an opportunity to sell your products to the other merchants with whom you are cross-promoting. After all, they have to think about retirement as well. It forces you to network.

BB: *What about those fields in which the salesperson or professional can't come right out and publicly cross-promote? How might that situation be handled?*

One example of a really soft cross-promotion is a doctor who provided hypertension screening as a free service on the premises at a grocery store. It was good for the store because they could advertise the fact that the doctor was going to do this free service. Meanwhile, the doctor obtained the actual test kits free from a pharmaceutical company. And it was a great way for this doctor to build up his practice without offending his peers. So it was not blatant advertising, but more like a community involvement project. It was a very effective way of getting him in front of those potential patients.

BB: *What about professionals, such as a doctor and an accountant, cross-promoting with each other in a very low-key way?*

An easy way to do a soft cross-promotion is in your waiting room. Let's say you're an accountant and you want to reach a doctor's patients to sell your accounting services. If you do a newsletter, that could be put in the doctor's waiting room for patients to read. Simple little things such as that are very effective. Of course, the doctor's newsletter could be put in your waiting room, too. The same situation would work with an attorney.

You find ways of subtly infiltrating one another's customer base.

BB: *What about a doctors suggesting that if her patients called her attorney or accountant and used her name, they could get a few minutes of advice without being charged?*

Let's say you are an attorney and you're networking with an accountant with whom you'd like to cross-promote. You offer an arrangement whereby somebody can call the accountant with a quick question for a limited time for a 30-day free trial, and the accountant's clients can call the attorney and ask a quick question. This way, you get each other's clients to actually call. That is your initial lead for converting them to becoming your clients.

BB: *Let's take one more example and pretend we have a person selling a copy machine. The copy machine sales business is very competitive. We must get at least three or four of these salespeople a month in this office. How could they cross-promote in order to successfully get appointments with the decision makers?*

One really effective cross-promotion that comes to mind is actually more of an internal cross-promotion, which was done by a copy machine company in my hometown of Columbus, Ohio. At the same time, it crossed over to another area called community involvement.

They ran a contest. The idea was to get businesses to simply fill out a four-question survey. Every time someone did, the copy machine company would donate $2 to a certain charity. Whichever employee got the most questionnaires filled out would win some sort of prize—but all the lead money, the referral fees, were being donated to charity.

Here's what happened: A company repair person, not a salesperson, was fixing a copy machine upstairs from us. He went around to a bunch of offices, eventually getting to ours. He told us about the contest and said that if we would simply answer these four or five questions, then his company would donate $2 to this charity.

Normally I wouldn't talk to anybody with questions like this, but since this was for charity, I decided to answer the questions. The company had actually managed to get its repair people prospecting for the salespeople. Of course, the questions were basic, designed simply to see if they needed to follow up. Again, most people would answer the few questions because $2 was being donated to charity. As you can see, a cross-promotion with a nonprofit organization is a great idea because everybody wins.

You can also develop relationships with those who are selling noncompetitive items to the same prospects—perhaps computer salespeople, telephone salespeople, and office furniture salespeople. I would develop a networking relationship with salespeople in my territory who were doing that, with the aim that we would share.

Let's say I'm in an office on a cold call. The prospect is not interested in a copy machine because she has a brand new one, but in talking with her, I discover a need for a product or service she could buy from one of my networking buddies, and I ask if she'd like to hear from that person. If it's a situation where I do make the sale, one or two more questions can determine whether the prospect is also in need of one of the other products or services.

If all of us are doing that for each other, we're getting a four-for-one prospecting deal.

Now, what about you? Given how your particular business works, what can *you* work out with somebody or some business that would be a win-win situation? It isn't always easy to come up with a viable idea, and depending on your type of business, it won't necessarily be in the form of a discount certificate.

But brainstorm with those in your network to come up with some strong ideas. Sooner or later you'll hit upon a winner, and as we learned from Jeff Slutsky, the payoff can be substantial.

Key Points

- As explained by Jeff Slutsky, a cross-promotion is a win-win promotion between salespeople, merchants, or professionals who are trying to reach the same customers.
- There are different types of cross-promotions:
    1. *One-way cross-promotions.* You provide certificates to your cross-promotion partner, who hands them out to his customers upon purchase.
    2. *Two-way cross-promotions.* Essentially, "I'll hand out yours and you hand out mine."
    3. *Reverse cross-promotions.* Your cross-promotion partner supplies you with the certificates, which you hand out to your customer upon purchase as an added value for buying from you.
- A huge advantage of the cross-promotion is that it not only costs nothing (except for a little bit of quick printing), but also it is highly targeted to the audience you want to reach.
- With just a bit of creativity, everyone from the direct salesperson to the professional can use cross-promotions to his advantage.
- One advantage cross-promotions give the direct salesperson is that they are an excellent way to get face-to-face with an ordinarily difficult-to-reach decision-maker.
- Cross-promotions are also an excellent closing tool.
- Professionals (doctors, lawyers, accountants, etc.) can often utilize soft cross-promotions as a way of sending prospects to one another.
- Internal cross-promotions get everyone else in the company (nonsalespeople) prospecting for leads.

The Referral Mindset: Turning Appointments into Referrals

In the next two chapters, we're going to target one particular aspect of the referral process: getting referrals as the natural result of giving a sales presentation. This aspect of business is an area of such rich potential, and one that is so commonly not taken advantage of effectively, that it seemed to warrant the type of thorough treatment that simply wouldn't fit into one chapter.

I don't believe there is a sales manager in the world who would doubt the following statement: An unconscionable amount of potential new business is "left on the table" by salespeople who, whether through fear or lack of knowledge, fail to ask for referrals after a successful sales presentation. Addressing this failing and providing the solution is what these two chapters are all about.

Every presentation you make will fall into one of two categories: 1) those that result from a referral, and 2) those that don't. Your goal is eventually to have practically every presentation fall into the first category, but here, let's focus on the second. For the sake of this instruction, let's say you are making a presentation to someone with whom you have no solid relationship, perhaps a company-generated lead, or a brand new prospect you've found through some conventional prospecting method. We're going to start from scratch and build the relationship, resulting in numerous referrals from that person—and geometrically numerous referrals from those to whom you are then referred, and on and on and on.

In our example here, we'll use the scenario of an in-home sale of a somewhat expensive, high-quality product or service that's being presented to a couple, although I'll sometimes speak as though we're addressing just one person. But understand, this could just as easily be a "business to business" presentation or any other sort of sales presentation, and the same basic principles apply, though you might need to adjust them to your own unique selling situation.

By the way, since making the presentation and completing the transaction are not the focus of this book, I'm going to assume you've learned how to do that, either from your company training or from books or other programs specifically on those topics.

When you utilize these principles and methods correctly, you can leave the presentation with a number of good, high-quality, qualified referrals. This means that you can leverage practically every presentation you make into many more presentations. And you can do the same with the referrals from those, and thus experience exponential growth in the number of presentations you can make, similar to that of compound interest.

The Importance and Power of Referrals (Yep, the Benefits)

It's important to understand exactly why referrals are so vital to success. I know, we've been discussing referrals throughout this book, and their importance seems rather obvious, doesn't it? But then again, maybe it's *not* so obvious.

Time after time, when I'm brought into companies to speak—even well-known companies whose profits are based on how many presentations their associates, salespeople, advisors, consultants, or agents can make and complete—I'm told, "We just can't get these people to go after referrals; it's our biggest challenge."

By the way, just so you know how rampant this issue is: Even the highly productive sales leaders of companies and organizations where production is a qualifier just to belong tell me they still need to get over their fear of asking for referrals. Both times I've had the honor of presenting at the prestigious Million Dollar Round Table (MDRT) of Insurance international convention, I've been amazed to hear the highest echelon of production, the "Top of the Table," tell me that asking for and getting referrals is one of their biggest challenges, and an area in which they greatly need to improve.* The good news is how many of them have later said that the Endless Referrals system® has helped them to do so.

---

*It's worth noting that when these top producers say it's "one of their biggest challenges," we need to realize that still, many of them do most of their business via referral! This is typical: Those who are already hugely successful are the very people who are most interested in improving themselves even more. That, of course, is one reason they're so successful. So what they would consider a weakness, most of the rest of us would consider a strength.

I believe that if people truly understood the benefits to their bottom line and lifestyle that an endless amount of continuous referrals would bring, they would do whatever it took to master the art of getting referrals, instead of being content to cold-prospect and accept leads of unknown quality from their company's lead-generation department.

But they don't. Why not? Because most salespeople simply *don't* grasp the true benefits of referrals. In fact, only those who totally understand and grasp the benefits of referrals will make the effort necessary to perfect their skills in this area.

So let's start this chapter by looking at seven major benefits of referrals.

Seven Benefits of Referrals

The first three benefits come from my friend, Bill Cates (www.referralcoach.com), an internationally renowned authority on referrals and author of the terrific book, *Get More Referrals Now!* For anyone interested in learning the art and science of developing a referral-based business, Bill's book is a true must-read.

Bill asks, "What is a referral?" and answers, "Gold. Pure solid gold." Then he provides several reasons why this is so.

1. Referred prospects are easier to set appointments with.

How right that is! As we've discussed numerous times already in this book, the key ingredient in developing referrals is cultivating relationships where people *know you, like you, and trust you.* How does this translate into more easily setting an appointment with someone you don't know? Because you're going in on what prospecting master Rick Hill calls, "borrowed influence."

The referral came from a trusted third party who has experienced directly the benefits of doing business with you and has the best interests of the recipient at heart. And even if she (the third party) hasn't done business with you directly (perhaps she is not in your target market or has no need for your product or service), at least she can vouch for you as a person worthy of trust and respect.

This is also what Dr. Robert Cialdini (www.influenceatwork.com), author of the excellent book *Influence: Science and Practice* (formerly titled *Influence: The Psychology of Persuasion*) refers to as "social proof." The concept of *social proof* refers to the principle that people often unconsciously look toward others, especially those with whom they have certain elements in common, to determine the correct course of action. In this case, social proof suggests that when someone in our social or socioeconomic sphere recommends us, the chances are much better of our offer of an appointment being accepted and even welcomed.

This third-party person, who knows you, likes you, and trusts you enough to connect you or recommend you to her friend, relative, co-worker, or fellow club member, most likely has a *know you, like you, trust you* relationship with *that* person. In other words, that person (the prospect) feels the same way about your referral source as your referral source feels about you. So you get to leverage those relationships and set the appointment with someone you don't know, but with whom you have "borrowed influence."

2. With referred prospects, price is less of an issue.

It's not that price doesn't matter. It's just that now the trust factor comes into play. Because of the "borrowed trust" that got you there in the first place and allowed you to set the appointment, there's a carry-over throughout the presentation.

As you know, when a prospect objects to a price as being too high, what he's really saying is that the value *he perceives* in your product or service is not as valuable as the amount of money he's being asked to give up in exchange. This is fairly likely to be a function of the level of trust—or lack of trust—he has in the salesperson. Trust typically develops over time. By going in on borrowed trust, you automatically accelerate that process, and price therefore becomes less of an issue.

3. Referred prospects are easier to close.

This is simply an extension of the previous point. It all comes down to trust, and going into the presentation with borrowed trust gives you a huge advantage.

The Million Dollar Round Table of Insurance is an organization that knows quite a bit about the value of referrals to their profession. According to one MDRT study, "Research indicates that prospects who are approached through a referral close twice as easily, buy more in the first two years, and stay with a salesperson or company longer than other forms of leads."

What a wonderful testimonial as to the power and value of referrals!

Let's look at some additional benefits of referrals.

4. You are automatically positioned as a referral-based salesperson.

In other words, referred prospects are already "trained"; they understand and are already of the mindset that that's how you do business. That you are worthy of referrals. That this is your modus operandi: You work via referrals. After all, that's how they met you! So giving you referrals at the end of your presentation seems only natural to them. There will be much less hesitation or reluctance on their part (or none!) to refer you.

I believe this may just be the biggest benefit of all from creating a referral-based business.

Many salespeople experience "referral resistance" from new customers or clients even after successfully completing a transaction—when the appointment is not through a referral. Perhaps you've experienced this: Sure, they like you, they even purchase your product or service—but when you ask for referrals, they sort of, with a touch of embarrassment for having to disappoint you, say something like, "Well, I really don't like referring salespeople to my friends."

Why would they say that? Perhaps they provided a referral in the past and the very same salesperson whom they really liked wasn't liked at all by their friend. And then their friends called them and said, "Hey, do me a favor and don't refer salespeople to call me anymore, okay?!" And that took care of that. From that moment on, they were pretty much determined not to make that mistake again.

Who can blame them? And, remember, if they didn't meet you by way of referral, but perhaps by way of a company-generated lead, they don't know how you'll come across when you contact the person they refer you to.

A bit later in the chapter, we'll handle and overcome that objection, but this is one reason I so strongly emphasize the importance of referrals. If instead your new client had met you through the referral of a friend or associate of theirs, it's a lot easier for him to justify referring you to someone else. You're an already-proven referral commodity—and that's just the way you do business. You've proven (to him!) that you can handle it, and that family, friends, neighbors, and associates just naturally refer you to family, friends, neighbors, and associates. Can you see where that makes a huge difference in the way you're positioned in that person's mind?

Let's take the importance of referrals still another step further.

5. Referrals give your prospect the advantage of indirect experience.

In an article by Fergal Byrne entitled, "How to Boost Your Sales Through Referrals," published in *The Director* magazine in the United Kingdom, he writes the following:

"Referrals provide a low-risk way for individuals or businesses to get *indirect experience* of the product or service." What does the author mean by "indirect experience"? Certainly not that the prospect has used it himself. But because someone he knows, likes, and trusts *has* used it and can vouch for it, the prospect now has the benefit of that knowledge and experience.

According to marketing consultant George Silverman, "The single greatest factor holding back a product from greater and faster acceptance is usually a lack of a positive experience." Silverman adds, "Word of mouth can dramatically accelerate the speed of product acceptance and adoption."

In the same article, Steve Crowe, of the Suffolk, England–based management training company Oak Tree Management, says, "We have found with our referrals that we can go from an initial formal meeting to the beginning of the contract in three weeks, where normally it can take between six months and a year—or even longer. And this has had a tremendous impact on our rate of growth. Money is generally less of an issue."

Remember, if the prospect doesn't personally know, like, and trust the salesperson, then some form of borrowed influence or credibility is needed to speed along the process, which goes back to Dr. Cialdini's principle of *social proof.*

6. A referral builds the loyalty of the person who gave *you the referral—and he will continue to do so.*

Now that seems a bit odd, doesn't it? Why would providing you with a referral build a greater sense of loyalty in the person who made the referral? Again, let's cite the wisdom of Dr. Cialdini. He calls this phenomenon, "the law of consistency" or "the consistency principle."

> *Once we make a choice or take a stand, we will encounter personal and interpersonal pressures to behave consistently with that commitment. Those pressures will cause us to respond in ways that justify our earlier decision. We simply convince ourselves that we have made the right choice and, no doubt, feel better about our decision. It is, quite simply, our desire to be (and to appear) consistent with what we have already done.*

I've made quite an informal study of this principle over the past few years and find it to be one of the most powerful principles of human behavior— perhaps even *the* most. Quite simply, once we make the personal, psychological, emotional, and ego investment in a decision, we have a huge personal stake in believing we made the right decision. As such, we will act accordingly and consistently with our decision, even if everything in front of us seems to say we were wrong.

That's not to say we'll never make a new decision, but the proof must be absolutely overwhelming—and even that is no guarantee that we will change our belief. By the way, a person who doesn't buy into this principle of human nature will rarely be able to be persuaded that it's so. And that's okay. Everyone has a right to his opinion. If we recognize this principle in *ourselves*, however, it can keep up from making some huge mistakes in our own lives. As it relates to referrals, it can also help us to understand why once someone is on our side and wants to help us, she will continue to do so.

7. Referrals give you additional time with which to work.

When your business depends on your constantly having to prospect for new business, you're spending the majority of your time taking actions that do not directly result in making money.

First you must determine where you can prospect. That takes time. Then you begin meeting people or getting on the phone and calling people. That takes time. You sort through those who are interested and those who are not. More time. You call to make appointments and, because there is no borrowed influence to help you, it takes you a lot more calls to get some appointments. And because you can't qualify these people through a referring person who knows them, you'll have to go through a lot of people who aren't really interested or qualified. Lots more time wasted. Finally, you get to make your presentation to people who *possibly* need, want, and can afford what you sell—and possibly don't and can't.

You can make a living do this, but you're wasting a lot of time!

A referral-based business constantly puts you in front of qualified prospects who have already passed over what I call the "Marketing Bridge." They *need* your product or service, they *want* it, and they can *afford* it. Having met you through a mutual acquaintance, they are likely the best sources of more referrals. *Now* you are using your time at its optimal effectiveness. You're making more money in a lot less time—and having a lot more fun doing it.

At the End of the Rainbow

I sometimes call this last point the "rainbow analogy." What do you find at the end of a rainbow? A pot of gold, right? That's where you want to invest the majority of your time: around the money. At that pot of gold at the end of the rainbow. In other words, in front of the prospects who can say yes and purchase your products or services—prospects who are ready, willing, and able to buy from you.

Make sense? Of course—but doesn't it seem that most salespeople spend far too much time at the beginning of the rainbow? That's the initial prospecting, calling, qualifying, sending information, and all that this entails.

I'm assuming you want to be around the money—constantly speaking with and presenting to, the people whose "yes" decisions result in your receiving a commission check while you add positively to their lives through helping them own your terrific products or services. If you want that "pot of gold" type of business where you are constantly around the money, getting referrals from those with whom you do business is absolutely key!

According to business consultants Paul and Sarah Edwards, up to 45 percent of most service businesses are chosen by customers based on the recommendation or referral of others.

Far from being a vague or intangible benefit, referrals are a concrete, vital, and profitable asset. Plan on receiving them and expect to receive them—and then make sure you apply the correct principles during your presentation so you do receive them.

Types of Referrals You'll Receive, Their Benefits and Results

Now let's look at several different types of referrals you'll receive and what kind of impact each will have on your business. We'll call these three types A-list referrals, B-list referrals, and C-list referrals.

A-list referrals are just what they sound like: the best type you can get. A-list referrals are those who are pretty much ready to buy when you show up. Typically, they need or want your product or service and have no trouble paying for it; that is, they have unequivocally crossed the "marketing bridge." What's more, they have so much respect for the person who referred you that as long as you don't blow it, you've got yourself a sale.

Obviously, A-list referrals are great, and your ultimate goal is to build a network out of these prospects.

B-list referrals are also good referrals, just not quite as solid as the A-listers. You'll still have to work for the sale, and might have to make some effort when it comes to helping them cross the marketing bridge of need it, want it, and can afford it. Of course, if they genuinely do not need or want it or are genuinely not able to afford it, you shouldn't sell it. What I'm saying here is that a B-list referral might need the help of a qualified salesperson (you) to help him see why it is affordable, because he hasn't realized this on his own. You might face and need to answer some objections. No problem. Again, B-list referrals are good, and you can make a nice living with a consistent supply of them; they're just not as ideal as A-list referrals, nor as profitable.

C-list referrals are those you want to avoid presenting to, as soon as you're in a position to be able to do so. These are good people; it's just that, for whatever reason, they're not your best prospects. If you're at the beginning stage of your business, you still might present to them, and sometimes they are in fact qualified buyers. And they are also good people with whom to practice your presentation. However, as soon as you're at the point where you don't have to work with them, it's best not to. After all, you're a business person and you owe it to yourself, your family, your company, and those prospects whose lives can be improved via your product or service to work with those people who are most likely to buy from you and refer you to others.

You may even get referrals from C-list people, although chances are good they will refer you to other C-list prospects, so even that's not the best way to go.

Using the 80/20 Rule to Your Advantage

This brings up a fascinating point: As a general rule, A-list referred prospects will typically refer you to other A's, as well as some B's and C's. B-list referred prospects will typically refer you to other B's along with some C's. And C-list referred prospects will typically refer you only to other C's. It's a principle of human nature: People will tend to refer you to others at their same self-perceived level and below, but people rarely "refer up."

Because of this, a version of the famous Pareto principle comes into play here. More commonly known as the "80/20 rule," the Pareto principle (named after the late-nineteenth-century economist Vilfredo Pareto) states, "A minority of input (say, 20 percent) produces the majority of results (80 percent)."

A common example of this principle, applied to sales, teaches that 80 percent of your income will come from 20 percent of your customers or clients, what Pareto termed "a predictable imbalance." Another application of the

Pareto principle, well-known to sales managers, is that 80 percent of your sales staff's production will come from 20 percent of your salespeople.

As with any universal principle, this is something you can resist, or you can ignore, but you can't change! However, by understanding it and embracing it, you can utilize it to tremendous advantage.

Let's say you're going to focus on A-list and B-list prospects. Once you get going and the referrals start coming in, you'll probably soon notice that about 80 percent of the referrals you're getting are B-list referrals, and only 20 percent A list. These A's, of course, most likely came as referrals from A-list prospects. A smart strategy is to keep working with as many of the A's as you can, and then work with *their* A-list referrals, so that as you go along, you decrease the number of B-list referrals you are calling.

The ultimate goal is to get to the point where you are presenting only to A-listers and then contacting the A-listers they refer to you. This is what I refer to as, "Survival of the referral fittest." Once you are presenting only to A-listers, as Rick Hill puts it, "you'll still have problems in your life, but one of them will not be money!"

I mentioned earlier that the flow of referrals can be compared to compound interest. Compound interest has often been called the "eighth wonder of the world." It feeds and builds upon itself and, before long, that little bit of money you've invested, reinvested, and allowed to grow has developed into an enormous sum.

Here's how this principle works in building your referral-based business:

Once you begin receiving referrals and become proficient at it, you'll begin to track the average number of referrals you obtain per presentation. I don't know the figures for your particular industry, so let's just use a reasonable figure and say you're now averaging five qualified referrals per appointment, referrals you could classify as either A-list or B-list. (Of course, in those presentations where the prospect is just not interested, there will be fewer, and those where the prospect makes a purchase and/or the rapport is great, there will be more—often many more.) Let's see where this average of five referrals per presentation gets us.

Week one, you do three presentations, and each one results in five referrals. (Remember, we're averaging.) Now you've got 15 referrals. Eighty percent, or 12 or them, are B-list referrals, and 3 are A-list referrals. As you contact them all, you find that 2 of the A's and 6 of the 12 B-list are not interested, leaving 1 A-list and 6 B-list referrals for next week. (Sometimes you can turn a "not-interested" appointment into referrals, but we won't bother with that here.)

Let's say that out of these 7, you're able to set appointments with 5 for next week: one appointment per evening. (Again, we're using an in-home presentation for our example, and evening is commonly the best time for these.) The other two will see you later, perhaps the following week, but we'll leave them out of our calculations, just to keep things relatively simple. (Note, though, that you're already getting even more business than we're accounting for here!)

Out of those five appointments, let's say you are able to complete a transaction (close a sale) with 2 or 3—but you again average 5 referrals per appointment, resulting in 25 new referrals. Applying our 80/20 rule again, we find that 5 of them are A-list referrals and 20 are B-listers.

As you call to set appointments, you find that two of the 5 A-listers are interested, and 10 of the B-listers. You're able to set appointments for the following week with both interested A-listers and 6 of the B-listers. (Again, the others will see you at a date in the near future, but we'll leave them out of the mix.)

Now you have eight appointments scheduled with these prospects. At these appointments, you close several sales and receive 40 referrals (eight appointments times an average of 5 referrals each). Out of those, still following our 80/20 rule, 8 are A-listers and 32 are B-listers. Of those, 5 A-listers are ready to set appointments for next week, as are 12 of the B-listers. However, you are now going to politely put some of the B-listers on hold—because the ones you want to present to are the A-listers. You set, say, 10 appointments for the coming week: 5 with A-listers and 5 with B-listers.

You have just turned 80/20 into 50/50!

Now, you complete transactions with 1 of the A-listers and 1 of the B-listers, but you still average 5 referrals per appointment, so you now have 50 referrals. Apply the 80/20 rule: 10 of these will be A-list referrals, and 40 B-list.

Do you see where this is going?

Do this consistently, and in a very short period of time you'll be able to pick and choose exactly when and where you invest your time. The term "pot of gold at the end of the rainbow" takes on a whole new meaning for you. You will become much more independent and financially successful: wonderful benefits of a business based on Endless Referrals.

Of course, while you're doing this, you're also continuing to fill your pipeline of new prospects and referrals by utilizing what you learned throughout this book.

Now that you understand the kinds of benefits you can expect from getting referrals from your presentations, let's look at how to make it happen.

Planting the Seeds of Referrals in Your Prospects' Minds

Regardless of your business or what products or services you sell, referrals are not a "bonus." They're not a surprise, or at least they shouldn't be. They also don't usually happen without your proactively being the cause of their happening.

In other words, you won't get them spontaneously just because you made a great presentation. You won't get them just because you happen to provide excellent customer service. How do I know that? Because all of us have given great presentations and provided excellent customer service *without* receiving referrals! Great presentations and great service are surely very important aspects of successfully doing business, but they are not, in and of themselves, enough to guarantee that you'll receive referrals.

Referrals are the result of doing the right things in the referral-gathering process.

It's a matter of *following a system* for obtaining referrals, just as we've been discussing in relation to every other aspect of the Endless Referrals System®. It is proceeding consistently according to an accurate, systemized sequence that results in a predictable outcome.

In this section, we'll look at the system for obtaining referrals after presentations.

When discussing what I call the "referral mindset," we'll actually be looking at two mindsets: yours and your prospects.

Yes, the referral mindset *of the prospect*. What does that mean? Simply this: rather than waiting until after the transaction is completed for you to bring up the (in the prospect's mind) brand new idea of his providing you with referrals, I suggest you plant the seeds of referrals throughout the presentation.

Remember, in this scenario, you're presenting a product or service to a husband and wife or a single person, in their home, not as the result of a referral, but through another method, let's say, a company-generated lead. We'll pretend that what you're selling is high-priced enough that it isn't a no-brainer; that there will be questions, perhaps objections, and that it will probably take some time, perhaps between one and two hours.

We'll also make this what's known as a "one-call close," which simply means that the decision to buy or not will be made at the conclusion of your presentation, as opposed to this being a merely information-gathering meeting with a follow-up appointment coming later. (However, this scenario would actually play out similarly if this were the second visit of a two-call close.)

Typically, you'll begin the visit with what is known as the "warm-up," which is the initial, rapport-building phase of the visit. During this portion of the conversation, business is not discussed; you're simply attempting to learn about your prospects and helping them to learn a bit about you. Mainly—and this is key—your goal at this point is to develop a rapport with your prospect or prospects.

When I was in a local business very similar to what we're describing here, the warm-up was an absolute key to the success of the visit. In working with the many clients I have in other industries who either make in-home presentations or sell a high-priced product or service, this invariably proves to be true. Remember, you're going in cold; they don't yet *know you, like you, or trust you.* Now is when the beginnings of such feelings are established. The warm-up is so important that without it, a successful sales call is very unlikely.

The first step is to immediately create rapport. Creating rapport means creating a harmony between you. What's the quickest and most effective way to do this? Find similarities between you, early and often. Despite the popular saying, "opposites attract," the fact is, people are generally much more comfortable with, and attracted to, people they perceive to be like them. They also tend to buy more from people who are like them. As Rick Hill says, "People buy what they are familiar with." This includes not only "things," but also the people who sell them.

What do the two of you have in common that you can quickly discover? Are you both originally from the same city or state, or at least from the same part of the country? Do you share interests in common sports or hobbies? Do you both have children, and if so, do *they* share any common interests?

Rapport can be based on practically any similarity. Don't hesitate to keep discussing the similarities that brought you into harmony until you feel the rapport is solid. Only then are you ready to proceed with your presentation.

By the way, this is an excellent time to ask a couple of the Feel-Good Questions® discussed in Chapter 2. You can ask how they got started in their business, what they enjoy most about it, and any of the other questions you feel would be appropriate. A great idea is to ask the One Key Question: "How can I know if someone I'm speaking to is a good prospect for you?" (How often do you think they've been asked that question by a salesperson presenting his product or service to them? I guarantee you: seldom, and probably never.)

The other three parts of the FORM questions would also work well. Remember that FORM is an acronym for F, their family; O, their occupation; R, their recreation; and M, their message, or what's important to them.

Do this and you'll get a good idea of what they find important, which will help you during your presentation. Mainly, though, it will simply build rapport, quickly and solidly.

But what about planting the referral seeds? Here's how it works, and why.

Even during this rapport-building phase, you might receive a question or two about your product or service. It might be more than just an information-type question, too: it might be an actual objection, a reason in their minds that could keep them from making the decision to buy. If you receive either one, a question or an objection, now is a great time to begin planting the referral seeds.

First, use the *words and concepts* of referrals during your response to their question or objection. For example, let's pretend they ask, "Pat, even before you begin telling us about your solar energy hot water heater, I've got to tell you, I'm concerned that whatever the price turns out to be, I doubt it could ever save us enough money to make that price worthwhile."

This objection is actually an excellent opportunity to begin the referral seed planting process within your response. Before we see why, though, let's pause to look at how to answer any prospect's objections.

Answering Objections

Undoubtedly, at some time or another, whether in a book, an audio program, or in a sales training class, you learned what's known as the "feel, felt, found" technique. This is a very kind, tactful way of demonstrating to your prospect that their objection is unfounded, that there is a satisfactory answer to it.

Traditionally, the feel, felt, found response would go something like this:

Mr. Prospect, I understand how you feel. Many people have felt the same way. What they found was…

And now you go on to provide the reason behind your positive response.

The feel, felt, found response is an excellent principle: It acknowledges the feelings of the prospect; it demonstrates that obviously his question is a good one because "others" have felt the same way; and it offers a reasonable explanation as to why he needs have no fear.

However, there is a challenge with it, too, and this can trip you up, if you're not careful.

The challenge is that it's used so often, and is known by so many prospects, that if you simply use it as I did above, his response (probably to himself) is likely to be, "Oh no, not that old technique." And, if that happens, if the person feels he's been "techniqued," that pretty much does it for any type of rapport and harmony with this person. He will no longer trust that what you're saying is from your heart, but will instead assume that you are merely carrying out a strategic and perhaps manipulative plan to *trick* him into buying whatever it is you are selling.

So while we want to keep the excellent *principles* of the feel, felt, found response when handling objections, so that we can honor the prospect and his feelings while at the same time providing the solution, let's change the wording just a bit so as not to trigger off any unnecessary negative feelings in your prospect. Instead, our response can be something like this:

Mr. Prospect, that's an excellent question.

What you're doing here is simply repositioning his "objection" into a fact-finding "question." Or you might say, "That's a very legitimate question," or use another word that has the same connotation, a word that honors him for asking. Then, to continue:

It's totally understandable you would ask that…

This would be comparable with, "I understand how you feel." You might now say:

In fact, I would imagine that question has been asked by a lot of people who want to make sure they get the best return for their investment.

That statement would be equivalent to, "Others have felt the same way," in the traditional method. Next you might say something along the lines of:

The extensive research that's been done on this topic really shows that…

And now you explain what the research shows. This last is the counterpart to the traditional, "What they found was…"

Let's put that all together, unbroken by explanation:

Mr. Prospect, that's an excellent question. It's totally understandable you would ask that. In fact, I would imagine that question has been asked by a lot of people who want to make sure they get the best return for their investment. The extensive research that's been done on this topic really shows that...

And now you explain what the research shows.

If you put together several different forms of each of these, then you can feel very comfortable utilizing the excellent principles of feel, felt, found, without the fear that you'll mistakenly be looked at as being manipulative or "like every other salesperson."

Back to Planting the Seeds

Now let's add that one extra variable, the words and concepts of referrals, into your response in order to effectively begin planting the seeds of referrals.

After you congratulate your prospect on her question and assure her that her question is merit-filled and very worthwhile, let her know that another person, who had a similar concern (remember, others felt the same way) was someone who was referred to you.

For example,

Ms. Prospect, that's an excellent question, and certainly a very worthwhile one. It's totally understandable you would ask that. Recently, another person; in fact, a very nice gentleman who was referred to me by one of my valued clients, asked me something very similar. He was wondering how we could...

And then go on to complete the question, then your explanation.

The fact that the person who asked the question was a *referred prospect* did not really have anything to do with the question itself, nor with your answer. But it did establish *in your prospect's mind* the fact that at least part of your business is based on referrals.

Now, whether or not she took notice of this on a conscious level, the first referral seed has been planted.

By the way, if you have never actually been asked that question by a referred prospect, you shouldn't fib and say you have. Instead, ask other salespeople on the team or even your sales manager if *they've* ever had that question asked to them by a referred prospect. The chances are excellent that they have. If that's the case, then you can word it that way in your response to your prospect. It might go:

Recently, another person, in fact, a very nice gentleman who was referred to one of my fellow associates, asked something very similar. He was wondering how we could...

And then go on to complete the question, then your explanation.

Within a short while, you'll encounter practically every objection you'll ever hear pertaining to your business, and you yourself *will* receive a similar objection or question from a referred prospect; at that point, you can legitimately use yourself in your response.

Now let's move into the actual presentation you're making.

Sometime during the presentation, while making a specific point, you'll probably receive an objection about that point. Fine, do the same as you did for the previous objection. First, turn it into a "good question." Then go into our version of the "feel, felt, found," adding the fact that this question also came from a referred prospect, so that you've answered the objection *and* planted another referral seed.

Now, plant still another seed, but a bit differently.

This time, while you are between points in your presentation, perhaps just after you have again alluded to a referred customer, actually interrupt yourself and make a statement similar to the following

You know, Mr. and Ms. Prospect, I've got to express my appreciation to all my customers. As you know, at Sunray Solar, we're committed to bringing home energy savings to everyone in this area we possibly can, and it's the referrals we receive from our customers that really make our job easier. It also allows us to focus much more heavily on taking care of our customers, since we don't have to go out looking for new business as much as it comes to us. We all really appreciate it.

Then just move on to your next point.

What you've done here is to reestablish that you operate your business by way of referrals. Even though it's not how you met them, you're still implying that this is how your business is primarily built (which it soon will be, if you're utilizing the Endless Referrals system®).

You're also utilizing positive expectancy and giving them something to live up to. First, that they will also become customers, and second, that, like the other customers, they'll be providing you with referrals. And one more thing: you've also told them that once they are customers, they can expect tremendous customer service. Why? Because you don't have to go out looking for new business, you can invest more of your time making them happy.

Altogether, a powerful statement, combining referral positioning, positive expectancy, and a customer benefit.

The Very Best Time to Ask

You've closed the sale/completed the transaction. Your prospect is now your customer or client. This is a great time—in fact, it's the best time—to ask for and receive referrals. Sure, you can ask for referrals anytime from anyone, at any time, once they *know you, like you, and trust you*. Still, there's no question that the best possible person to ask for referrals is the one who has just made a purchase from you.

Why? For one thing, at this very moment, this client probably feels the best and most excited about you he will ever feel. Not that he won't continue to like you afterwards. He will, especially because of the caring and wonderful customer service you're going to provide. But his positive feelings are especially strong right now because when one makes a buying decision (and especially when a substantial price is involved), it's a very emotional decision.

You've probably learned before that people buy emotionally and back up that emotional decision with logic. We all do this. And when we make that decision our brain releases endorphins, those feel-good chemicals in our brain, and we feel good about ourselves, the transaction, and the cause of that transaction: the salesperson. Not surprisingly, now would be an ideal time for referrals!

A second reason harkens back to Dr. Cialdini's principle of *social proof*, which says that one way we determine what is correct is by finding out what other people think is correct. As Dr. Cialdini puts it, "We view a behavior as more correct in a given situation to the degree that we see others performing it." In other words, human beings have the tendency to see an action as more appropriate when others are doing it.

But wouldn't that more accurately describe why someone would agree to see us when someone in his social group referred us? Absolutely, and that's the application of *social proof* we looked at earlier. But it applies here, too: one way a new customer or client can be assured he made the right decision (in this case, to buy) is by seeing other people in his social group (friends, family, neighbors, associates, etc.) making the same buying decision. Making referrals to you is his way of creating that opportunity.

In essence, your new customer has a vested emotional interest in referring you to his friends and acquaintances, and hoping that they buy as well. He is probably not thinking this consciously, but that doesn't matter. This should provide you with the confidence of knowing that asking for referrals, far from being undesired, is actually quite welcome.

So they've bought. It's time to ask for referrals. This is where the pros stand tall. Amazingly enough, most salespeople at this point will simply not ask for referrals! And that's so unfortunate because you won't get them unless you ask, and ask correctly. Remember, contrary to popular belief, referrals are not necessarily the result of a good presentation. They are not even necessarily the result of excellent customer service. They are the result of doing the right things in the referral-gathering process.

Do the right things in the referral-gathering process and you're practically assured of receiving many referrals and having a highly fun and profitable business.

Key Points

- More money is "left on the table" by salespeople who fail to ask for referrals after a successful sales presentation than in virtually any other phase of business.
- There are seven major benefits of referrals:
  1. Referred prospects are easier to set appointments with.
  2. With referred prospects, price is less of an issue.
  3. Referred prospects are easier to close.
  4. You are automatically positioned as a referral-based salesperson.
  5. Referrals give your prospect the advantage of indirect experience.
  6. A referral builds the loyalty of the person who *gave* you the referral—and he will continue to do so.
  7. Referrals give you additional time with which to work.
- You can divide your referrals into three types: A-list, B-list, and C-list. The ultimate goal is to build your network out of A-list referrals, and avoid presenting to C-list referrals altogether.
- During your presentation and/or when answering objections, you can plant the seeds of referrals, which lays the groundwork for when you later ask for referrals.

CHAPTER 12

Why Most Salespeople Don't Ask for Referrals and How to Overcome It

In the last chapter we began looking at why most salespeople don't ask for referrals; now it's time to explore this question in some detail. Again, this opportunity, when you have just completed a successful presentation, offers such rich potential for gaining new referrals and further building your network—it's such a shame that so many people fail to capitalize on it!

Why is it that most salespeople don't ask for referrals? I believe it comes down to the following reasons:

Reason 1. They Forget

Why do they forget? It could be for any number of reasons. They're not used to asking; it's not an established part of how they operate. When the situation gets tense—filling out paperwork, answering more questions, etc.—it's easy to forget what you're not yet used to doing. In other words, it's not yet part of their consciousness.

After I worked my way up to sales manager of one company, I constantly taught my salespeople about using certain positive terms and avoiding certain negative ones. One example is the term, "sign the contract." What a negative thing to say. Can you imagine a phrase that could possibly trigger a more frightening image of binding commitments, lawyers, and lawsuits? Instead, as I learned from the great sales teacher, Tom Hopkins, it's so much more productive to ask them to "okay the agreement" or "endorse the paperwork." I would encourage my sales team to practice this—not just listen to me saying it and nod their heads, but actually practice it! (As Mr. Hopkins would say, "practice, drill, and rehearse.") Actual firsthand practice is the only way a new idea like this will become a living, breathing, and even remotely automatic part of one's consciousness.

Funny, though: during a sales call (which I often went to observe), when it came down to asking for the prospect to take action and they were feeling the tension of the moment, most of them would—sure enough—ask their prospects to "sign the contract." Why? Because they hadn't internalized the teaching. It wasn't part of their consciousness. They kept it at the theory level instead of moving it to the usage level. Yes, they had the knowledge, but hadn't turned that knowledge into wisdom.

The same holds true in asking for referrals. Even the asking must become part of your consciousness. Otherwise, you might be so relieved just to have the sales process over that you plain forget to ask for referrals.

Another reason salespeople sometimes forget to ask for referrals is that they really don't *want* to. In that case, it's just easier to forget!

Oh, not on a conscious level, but as human beings, we're great at rationalizing to ourselves. The interesting thing is, you can do everything else in the selling process (the warm-up, the presentation, the close) and then completely forget about asking for referrals—without actually losing the sale. If you forgot, so what? You still made the sale, right? Yes, you might be leaving money on the table by not asking for referrals—but you got the sale. And you didn't have to go through the anxiety of asking for those referrals.

We often "forget" to do what we don't really want to do, then rationalize it afterwards. (Remember the meaning of "rationalize"? It's telling yourself "rational lies.") We've all done it. In this case, forgetting is a function of convenience and preference.

Reason 2. They Lack the Confidence

Salespeople often retreat from the opportunity to ask for referrals because they don't have the confidence in themselves to do so. Perhaps the new customer or client will say no, and rejection is never fun. They've already gotten over the hurdle of facing possible rejection once, when they made the sale, why court it again? Hey, maybe the client will get annoyed and actually change his mind about his decision to buy!

Or maybe the salesperson simply doesn't believe she is worthy or deserving of referrals.

If any of this in any way describes you, I congratulate you for having the courage to realize it. And I hope you'll take my suggestion that the best thing you can do is work on yourself, from the inside out. Confidence and success is, first and foremost, an inside job, an internal condition that manifests itself as external benefits, such as business success, personal happiness, physical health, loving relationships, and so forth.

The great news is there are lots of powerful resources to help in this area. There are wonderfully effective books on the topic of personal development, confidence, and self-esteem, as well as audio programs and live seminars that will aid you in improving your self-confidence and clearly realizing your remarkable worth. Here are several titles that I particularly recommend; study them carefully and you are more than likely to see enormous changes in your life, your productivity, and your income.

> *As a Man Thinketh*, by James Allen
> *The Power of Believing*, by Claude Bristol
> *Think and Grow Rich*, by Napoleon Hill
> *Psycho-Cybernetics*, by Dr. Maxwell Maltz
> *Peace Power and Plenty*, by Orison Swett Marden
> *The Magic of Thinking Big*, by Dr. David Schwartz
> *The Science of Getting Rich*, by Wallace D. Wattles

And there are many more. These are books everyone should have in their libraries and read and reread on a steady basis. They are truly life-changing and life-enhancing books.

Reason 3. They Don't Think Their Products Warrant Them

This is a very disturbing reason salespeople sometimes don't ask for referrals. If this the case, you must either learn more about your product or service—enough that you come to fully understand how much it serves your customers and adds to their lives, and thus to the lives of all those to whom they refer you—or find another product or service to represent. I hate to be blunt about it, but if you don't believe enough in what you do that you feel it's worthy of helping everyone in the world own it who *should* own it, then you can't expect to be very successful.

A story comes to mind that illustrates this point.

A defense attorney was arguing a case for his client, who was charged with murder. Despite the fact that the victim's body was never discovered, the circumstantial evidence was overwhelming, and everyone in the courtroom, including the jurors, knew that the defendant was guilty. The clever lawyer decided to go for broke. As he addressed the jury in his closing argument, he pointed toward the courtroom doors and said, "Ladies and gentlemen, in exactly 60 seconds, the so-called corpse, the man you *believe* is dead, is going to come walking into this courtroom—right through those very doors. We can begin counting now."

Immediately, the eyes of all the jurors went to the door.

The time ticked by: 1 second, 2 seconds, 3 seconds, 10 seconds, 20 seconds, 45 seconds, 55 seconds, 56, 57, 58, 59 seconds—and finally, one minute. And at exactly the one-minute mark, wouldn't you know it, but who should come striding in through those doors?

Absolutely no one. Certainly not the victim.

The lawyer now faced the jury again and spoke in a conciliatory, reasoning, almost patronizing tone: "Now, ladies and gentleman, I must apologize. I told you something that clearly did not come true. However, you will have to admit that the mere fact that each and every one of you looked toward those doors as you did, showed me and showed you and showed everyone in this courtroom that *you had some doubt*. And as the judge will instruct you, if there is any doubt in your minds, any doubt at all, you must—*you must*—return a verdict of not guilty and set my client free."

The jury went into the jury room to deliberate, and came back out just five minutes later to render their verdict. The foreman stood up, faced the defendant, and when asked by the judge what their verdict was, said that they declared the defendant—GUILTY!

The defense attorney was enraged. "How could you?!" he stammered. "I saw you all watching those doors."

The foreman glanced at the defense attorney and replied, "Yes, sir, we did. But we were also watching you and your client—and you did *not* watch the door; your client did not watch the door. And that's because neither of you believed for even a moment that anyone was actually going to walking in through there."

The moral of the story?

Don't expect anyone to believe in something you don't believe in yourself.

If you don't believe your product is going to help your prospect (or is helping your present clients), well beyond any shadow of a doubt, then you're not going to make many sales—and you're certainly not going to acquire many referrals.

Reason 4. They Don't Know How

Ah, this is the final reason, and it's the easiest one to address. Often salespeople don't ask for referrals simply because they haven't been taught how to do it properly—in other words, how to do it in a way that they'll *get* them. If you don't how to do something right, they figure, why even bother?

We learned how to do this in Chapter 4, and when you put this into practice for yourself, you'll be amazed at just how much of a difference it will make.

The Bridge Phrase

For many people, the most difficult part of asking for referrals is moving from the present part of the conversation to the actual asking. You and your customer or client have just completed the transaction, and good feelings abound. You know that now is an excellent time to acquire some referrals, but you also have the uneasy sense that there might be an awkwardness in doing so.

How do you switch over from a pleasant, postselling conversation into asking for referrals in a manner that's natural, without sounding abrupt or contrived?

You use what I call the "bridge phrase."

A bridge is a structure that transports a person safely from one piece of land to another. You've crossed them before, by foot and by car. To a musician, a "bridge passage" is a short musical structure that leads safely from one piece of familiar music to another. In home financing, a "bridge loan" is a brief financial structure that gets you safely over to a more long-term loan.

This bridge is no different. It transports you from the part where you were (postsale conversation) to the part where you can ask for referrals, without any feelings of discomfort for either of you.

Here's an example:

Mary, I'm in the process of expanding my referral business, and I find it's helpful for me to partner with my friends and clients such as yourself. Can we take a few quick minutes and run past the names of some people I might also be able to help?

You might add, delete, or change around a few words to make it more you, instead of me, but the principles involved remain the same. Let's discuss why the wording used in this bridge phrase works so effectively.

First, it helps to make a very smooth, comfortable, natural transition to what you now want to discuss. Second, you are letting her know what it is you'd like to do, namely, to discuss receiving referrals in order to expand your referral-based business. But unlike many salespeople, you expressed that in a very professional manner, with a high level of posture. Third, you're letting her know the best way to go about this. Fourth you are including her in your success by using the term "partner."

This last point is particularly powerful. Most people (especially those who really like you and feel good about you) want to feel they are a part of your success. If they now choose to "buy in" to your mission and become your "partner," it makes all the difference in the world. You now have a person who has some commitment to helping make it happen. There is great power in this.

Finally, you're letting her know exactly what the next step will be: sitting down and going over some names, best of all, without taking up too much of her valuable time ("a few quick minutes").

This bridge statement—again, adapted to your style and personality—will make the transition much more comfortable and put you and the other person in a good emotional place for referrals.

Make whatever word changes you want to make so that it better reflects your unique personality while keeping with the basic principle. Bill Cates, author of *Get More Referrals Now!* bridges into asking for referrals simply by saying:

Mr. Customer, I have an important question to ask you.

Or you could say:

Ms. Client, may I ask you something very important?

Again, use whichever way fits more into your personal style. I like a combination of Bill's and mine. First, let them know, or ask if you can ask them, something very important. Then use my bridge phrase, which we just went over. Very effective indeed.

Where does the bridge phrase leave you? On very familiar territory: now you're ready to ask for referrals—and to ask in a way that you'll get them!

This is exactly what we covered in Chapter 6, so I won't spend any more time going over that material here. If you like, you might want to keep your place in this chapter and take a moment to glance back briefly through that section (pp. 79-83) before moving on to the next section.

The Power of Testimonial Endorsement Letters

Ever notice that in any good direct sales piece and on *every* infomercial you've ever watched, there arc lots and lots of testimonials. That's because testimonials are one of the greatest tools, perhaps *the* greatest tool, a salesperson can use for closing a sale.

Guess what? They're great for acquiring referrals, too. Actually, a testimonial letter is excellent for many aspects of the sales process, including answering objections, closing the sale, and obtaining referrals. I'll discuss the first couple briefly, then focus on how testimonials can assist you in getting referrals.

The reason testimonials are so important that practically every successful salesperson carefully accumulates them and constantly displays them, is that plain and simply, what others say about you is much more compelling and believable than what *you* say about you.

People are naturally skeptical; unless they *know you, like you, and trust you* (and sometimes even *if* they do), they might still have some doubts, simply because they know that you stand to benefit by their buying the thing you're selling. (It's fine with them that you benefit; it's just that they want to be sure they benefit, as well.)

Understandably, then, most prospects are skeptical about the claims a salesperson makes. Many salespeople see this as a problem. I disagree. I believe that in this case, as with most challenges or problems, the seed of the solution lies within the problem itself. That solution is to have so many other people bragging about you, your product, or service, the job it does, your incredible customer service, and whatever else is important to them, that your claims are now beyond reproach. Any fears that prospect might have are laid to rest through this third-party validation.

Once again, this goes back to a principle we've discussed several times already: the law of *social proof*. In other words, the more people you have who vouch for you and your product or service (especially people who share something in common with your prospect, such as perceived socioeconomic or geographic background, etc.), the greater are the chances that your prospect will feel safe in taking a similar action.

My friend Alan Proctor, a marketing consultant with a New York title insurance company, says there are only two reasons a person won't buy: too much fear, and lack of perceived value. Testimonial letters can certainly add to the perceived value, and they can also hugely reduce a prospect's fear.

The effect of third-party credibility is powerful. Tell me which will persuade you to buy my widget more effectively: if I tell you how great it is, or if your neighbor, friend, work associate, someone for whose opinion you have a great deal of respect, or even just an ecstatically satisfied customer, tells you how great it is?

Make a point of requesting testimonial letters from every one of those ecstatic customers or clients. Ask them to point out, within the letter, how their initial skepticism (regarding quality, value, delivery date, service after the sale, or whatever else it was they questioned) was overcome and how it delighted them. Try to get so many letters that your collection of testimonial letters answers every objection you ever hear from a prospect during the course of your presentation—and the most common ones are answered by numerous different people. Then, if someone is worried about value, you have a range of letters stressing the wonderful value. If a prospect is worried about fast delivery, you have letters that easily overcome that fear as well.

Imagine that your prospect, during the presentation, says, "Susan, I'm sorry but I've heard too many horror stories in your industry about how after the sale is made, you never hear from the salesperson again and you're left on your own to do battle with the corporate office." You can respond in a very gentle, nondefensive, and effective manner. Simply take a letter (or even better, several) from your presentation book that overcomes that objection. As you position the letter(s) in front of your prospect for her to see, very tactfully say something like:

> *Ms. Prospect, that's an excellent question; its totally understandable that would be a concern for you. The fact is, that has unfortunately taken place at times in this industry and as you know, it's those examples you hear about. If I may, I'd like to share with you just a couple of letters from my clients as to what they've experienced in this case, with me and my company.*

Now you share the letter or letters, and do this with the part that answers the concern highlighted, so it's easier for her to see and read. Let her read it, so she can draw her own conclusion. Be careful not to do this with a triumphant, "See, what did I tell you!" attitude, but with a helpful manner.

If you don't yet have one of those testimonial letters yourself, get one from your sales manager or another team member or associate, and use that. You can phrase your response to your prospect by saying that this is a typical letter regarding how those in your company exceed expectations in this area. Even if you have to adjust the terminology, the principles remain the same.

That's how you answer an objection using testimonial letters. You can close a sale the same way. Once you've isolated the one true objection, you can use the testimonial letter or letters to answer that objection and go right into the close.

Utilizing Testimonial Letters to Overcome Referral Objections

Okay, then, how do we use testimonial letters to get more referrals?

Sometimes, when you ask for referrals, your new client will respond with something like, "Well, Tom, I really appreciate your helping us, and you're a great guy, but I just don't like to refer salespeople to my friends." (This is more likely to happen if this was not a referral-based prospect, but one who resulted from conventional prospecting or a company-generated lead.)

Perhaps he did this once or twice before and got burned. Perhaps the salesperson he referred just didn't handle himself properly. Maybe, when the salesperson called the referred prospect and that prospect wasn't interested, the salesperson was kind of nasty about it and the prospect called his friend to say, "Don't ever refer a salesperson to me again!" (Not that *you* would be that way, but this person doesn't know that. Which is why having met your new customer by way of a referral makes him feel so much more comfortable giving a referral to you: he *does* know the way you handle yourself with a prospect.)

We need a method of making your new client feel comfortable that you will never make him look bad to anyone he refers you to. Here's where the testimonial letter comes in.

Again, you want to have a few testimonial letters that answer this exact objection. If you have some about yourself, great. If not, use one from someone else in your company.

You might answer this concern by saying something like:

Mr. and Ms. Customer, I absolutely understand your feelings. I don't think anyone wants to refer someone to a friend, feeling as though they might be made to look bad by the salesperson behaving inappropriately. Has something like that ever happened to you?

If it has, let them tell you. After they have, you can tell them where that's happened to you, as well (if it truly has), or to someone else you know. Empathize with them. Then say:

Mr. and Ms. Prospect, first, I want to give you my personal assurance that, when calling a referral you give me, I will never—and I mean NEVER— say or do anything to reflect badly on you. That will be my number-one goal. Not just because it's the right way to be, but if I did so, I certainly couldn't expect to be trusted with more referrals, which as you know, is the way I do business: mainly by referrals.

If I may, I'd like to share a couple of letters with you from current customers of mine who at first had the same feelings you have, for which I certainly didn't blame them either, knowing how things can be.

Now share with them the letters that explain how your other customers had those same feelings, how they're always hesitant to refer salespeople, but that you made them look like heroes, handled yourself so professionally, and so forth.

Now you simply promise your new customers that they can be assured that you will handle every referral they entrust to you with the same top professionalism that you did for the people who wrote these letters. And that you hope they'll write similar letters after hearing such positive comments from *their* friends.

Explaining to Them the "Out" or "Back Door"

If there is still some hesitation at this point in the process, you can take this next step: Tell your prospect exactly how you'll approach her referred prospects, including the exact language you'll use.

Here's what I would say, utilizing something I learned years ago from one of my prospecting mentors, Rick Hill. Rick's way of inviting himself to an appointment with a referred prospect is about the best I've ever seen, and it lets you relate to your customer exactly what you're going to say.

Mr. and Ms. Customer, just so you feel totally confident that I'll approach those you refer to me in a courteous and professional manner, let me tell you exactly what I'll say and do. Let's say you refer me to Ted Jones. I'll call Ted and introduce myself by saying, "Hi, Mr. Jones, my name is Bob Burg. We've never met, but I believe you know Ed and Stella Customer.

Ted will probably say, "Yes, of course, how are Ed and Stella?"

I'll say, "They're great! In fact, we were having a conversation just recently and your name came up at the end."

He'll say, "Really, how's that?"

And I'll say, "We were discussing (whatever your product or service is), and they thought you also might find it very helpful, as they did. And by the way, Mr. Jones, Ed and Stella didn't assume you'd be interested, and personally, neither do I. But they thought you might be, and believe enough in this that they suggested I call you and that perhaps we get together to discuss it. Does that sound like something you might enjoy doing?"

Mr. and Ms. Customer, if at this point, Mr. Jones is not interested, I'll simply politely end the conversation and get off the phone and not contact him again. If, however, he is interested in getting together, I'll make an appointment, and do the best I can to help him exactly as I'm helping you. Is that fair enough?

At this point, you shouldn't have any problem getting their agreement.

Of course, it's not going to happen every time. Know when to let go, end it, and move on. Remember, you can always come back during installation or company acceptance, or any time in the future, should you so choose.

By the way, Rick's approach here—that is, the approach to Ted Jones that we're describing to Ed and Stella—is an excellent way to increase the odds of Ted's inviting you to present, regardless of whether you had elected to share it with Ed and Stella.

Returning to the subject of testimonial letters, there's one type that practically trumps all others, and that is the one known as the "affinity testimonial letter."

An affinity testimonial is one written by someone with whom your prospect or new customer has something very much in common. This could be someone in the same line of work, or even someone affiliated with the same sort of social club or organization, such as a Rotary club, Elks Lodge, a BPW (Business and Professional Women's) organization, or others. Even if they've never met, it doesn't matter. There's an affinity, and their testimonial, all else being equal, will receive greater weight than one that has no such affinity.

Talk about the law of *social proof!*

Make it your goal to acquire testimonial letters covering as many different areas of question and objection and from as many different types of people as you can. And encourage everyone else on your team to do the same thing so that you can all copy and share your letters.

Getting the Testimonial Letter

Now let's discuss the actual testimonial letters, how you can increase your chances of getting them, and how to make them as effective as possible.

The first step is to let your new customer or client know that after they've used the product or service (or after they've received confirmation of acceptance, or whatever pertains to your particular product or service), you would love to receive a referral letter from them similar to some of those you showed them earlier.

In fact, I'd even plant this thought back at the point when you were showing them the testimonials, so that they'd already get used to the idea that they'll be asked this soon, and will have imagined themselves doing so.

Still, with most people, you've got to coach them as to exactly what it is you want. As networking authority and Certified Professional Coach Leni Chauvin (www.superstarnetworking.com) of Winnipeg, Manitoba, says, "Often, the client has no idea what you want. You've got to help him or her to help you."

According to Leni, here are just a few of the things you could focus on, depending upon your business:

> *The impact working with you had on their business, life, or family. Their favorite part of working with you. How their situation today is different than it was before they bought your product or service. How you, your product or service helped solve their problem or satisfied a need or desire. How they would rate their experience of working with you overall. What results they have achieved as a result of using your product or service...*

One hint on that last part: Try to get the person to provide actual numbers, such as, "Sales went up 37 percent," or, "Our heating bill decreased by $27 in the first month alone, a savings of 39 percent. Wow, that was even better than we expected!" The more specific the better: 39 percent is better than 40 percent, and 38.8 percent is even better. Specifics say "careful measurement."

Remember how pure Ivory soap is? It's not 100 percent pure, or 99 percent pure—it's 99^{44}/100 percent pure. Now, that just *had* to be measured, didn't it?

The following advice is also from Leni, taken from her special report, "How to Get and Use Extraordinary Testimonials to Grow Your Business":

Good testimonials are always about benefits and results. Most of us would far rather hang onto our money than spend it foolishly. After all, we've worked hard for it, and we want to make sure we're not going to waste it. A good testimonial should therefore:

- *Create a strong desire for the person to want to do business with you;*

- *Be credible;*

- *Be specific;*

- *Tell a before-and-after story that gets people to identify with it;*

- *Tell about the person or company performing the service;*

- *Show the impact your experience with the person and/or service had;*

- *Be verifiable; in other words, include first and last names, city or town, state or province, and as much else as possible that is appropriate.*

In her report, she provides examples of two testimonials to an accountant who had done some work for the client. Notice the difference in the two. The first one:

Howard, you're a great accountant. You've helped me tremendously. Working with you has been a real pleasure.

And, the second one:

Howard, when I walked into your office carrying 10 shoe boxes worth of receipts, I didn't think anyone was going to be able to help me sort through my mess. I'm thrilled that you were able to make sense of what I handed you. The systems you set up are so logical and easy to follow that I now always know how much I'm making and how much I'm spending, and I

*always come out ahead! Thanks to your advice and guidance, I've been able
to put $7500 towards Tommy's college fund this year. I tell everyone I meet
about you.*

Night and day, aren't they? Note how specific the second one is, and all
the vivid benefits and results it cites.

As Leni says, it's very important that testimonial letters are signed with
both first and last names. We've all seen the ones on direct mail pieces that say,
"A.S., Oklahoma." This has very little credibility because, as far as anyone
knows, it's could easily be a made-up letter with made-up initials and state. On
the other hand, "Anthony Stevens, Tulsa, Oklahoma," is highly credible.

Of course, if you can get a very excited customer, one we call a "champion," to include his telephone number and invite people to call, that's awe-
some. Just realize that, again, depending on your business, that person could
be bothered a lot, and might regret her decision to make herself so available.
You might want to be very careful with this and utilize such extreme kind-
ness only as a last resort.

You might be wondering, "How easy is it to get people to actually write
these testimonial letters?"

The answer is, it's not always easy. Not because people won't agree to do
it, but just because people lead busy lives and even when they're well-intentioned, they easily just don't get around to following through.

You have a couple of options here.

One is to wait a few weeks, then call again with a gentle reminder of the
basic points you'd like them to make in their letter. You can even let them
know that, to make it easier for them, you'll e-mail the key points.

A second option is to offer to write the entire letter for them and e-mail
it to them. You'll be amazed at how many people will agree. Let them know
that you're going to be very colorful and not pull any punches, and that if
there's anything they don't feel comfortable including, you want them to
delete it, or rewrite in their own words. Most often people will simply write
it on their own letterhead and send it back, just as you wrote it.

You can also send it to them via regular mail, with—and this is key—a
stamped, self-addressed, return envelope. Your response rate will be much,
much higher if you do this.

Again, while we're using the scenario of an in-home presentation, all the
principles we're covering in this chapter apply equally for business-to-business sales as well.

Make the gathering of testimonial letters a crucial part of your marketing and referrals game plan: whatever time and effort you put into it will pay off in huge dividends.

I'll end this section on the power of testimonial letters with a quote by one of the top copywriters in the field of direct response, Joe Polish:

> *What* others *say about you is infinitely more believable than what* you *say about you...so let others say it.*

Using the Do Not Call Laws to Your Advantage

One of the biggest advantages of having a strong referral-based business these days is that it puts lots of qualified prospects in front of you, instead of your having to find them through cold-calling. And that's a good thing, because cold-calling is not only time-consuming and less productive than ever before, but it's fast becoming illegal, as well!

Personally, I would much prefer to see a free-market approach and resolution to the issue of people getting unwanted sales calls at their homes. (And I find it interesting that the politicians who passed the Do Not Call laws have not included political campaign solicitations as part of those laws.) Nevertheless, the fact is, the law is the law, and if you disobey it, you could be subject to huge fines per infraction. Because we must deal with the Do Not Call laws, instead of letting it be an albatross around our necks, let's use it to our advantage.

One of the most common questions at my live seminars has always been, "Should you ask your customer, who is now giving you all these great referrals, to call the referred prospects first, or just call them yourself?"

Until recently, my answer has always been that it depends on several variables, including your particular product or service, and how easy it is to explain its benefits.

For example, do you deal with a product or service in which a large part of your presentation involves first educating the prospect as to what it does, how it works and why it's so beneficial? If so, I'd generally keep away from wanting your referral source to speak with them first. In fact, I'd discourage it. Remember, in the time it took you to make the sale, you were able to educate your prospect enough that she now had the ability to buy it—but certainly not the ability to teach it and sell it to others.

Other businesses are different. As a convention speaker, I absolutely want the client bragging on me before I ever speak to the prospect, and many other businesses are similar in this regard. There are also some customers and clients who have such a huge amount of credibility that whether or not they can explain your product or service, all they have to do is provide their recommendation, and you're in. In that case, having them speak to the referred prospect first is definitely a plus.

But today, with the emergence of the Do Not Call laws, having your referral source contact the referrals first, in one fashion or another, is becoming imperative. In many cases, you cannot call referred prospects at their homes unless you first have *their* permission! That being the case, you need to recruit your referral source to get permission to call your referred prospect.

Let's look at just a few methods of doing this.

1. Provide the reasoning and explain how to do it.

     YOU: Mr. and Ms. Smith, as you may know, current law is that in
       order for me to call Karen Jones, or anyone else you're kind
       enough to refer me to, I actually first need their permission to
       do so. May I ask you to make a quick call and just let her know
       that you've asked Tom Johnston (that is, you) to call her about a
       product that will save her up to 30 percent on her monthly hot
       water bills (or whatever the major benefit you provide happens
       to be), and that it's okay to expect my call?

     MS. smith: I'll be glad to, Tom.

     YOU: Thank you. I really appreciate that. Now, let me suggest in
       advance; there's a good chance Karen might ask, "What it's
       about?" or "How does he do it?" And it's very reasonable that
       she'd ask that. My suggestion is for you just to say, "Karen,
       while I understand the concept, Tom is really the professional
       and can answer all your questions much better than I can, so I'd
       just as soon he explain it to you. I'll have him call you, okay?"

That's one way to do it, and the chances are it will work if your referral source follows through. (Don't hesitate to write out this little script for her. In fact, I'd strongly suggest it. You can even prepare and type it up neatly in advance).

Let's provide a more specific scenario here. Let's pretend you're a financial advisor and you have just helped a couple create a wonderful financial plan. They have given you a referral, and you have asked them to call and explained how to do it. However, because you know that referred prospects typically ask specific questions that clients are not qualified to answer, you need to make sure this potential pitfall is covered. This brings us to the next point:

2. Provide your referral source with the exact language to deflect objections and elicit permission.

Actually, the right language will be imperative in each of these solutions, but here it's even more important that they know exactly what to say and how to say it. Remember, you don't want them saying too much because they'll explain themselves right out of your permission to call. On the other hand, they have to say enough for the referred prospect to feel it's in his or her best interest to grant permission for you to call. The biggest concern is your referral source answering questions. For example:

> C/RS (Client/Referral Source): I'd like to have Brenda Martin call you. She helped Mary and me design a financial program yesterday that's going to ensure we have more than enough money for our retirement, while being protected in the event of any emergencies along the way. Can I have her call you?
>
> P (Prospect): How exactly did she set it up for you?
>
> C/RS: Well, er...uh, it's something called an Asset Allocation Plan, where we have to take $125 out per month and put it towards...
>
> P: (interrupting)...Whoa! I can tell already, that's too rich for our blood at this time.
>
> C/RS: Oh, you don't understand. She's shown us how to do it so that we take advantage of matching payments on our 401k plan at work and deferring...
>
> P: (interrupting again)...Trust me; it's not something I could even consider right now.

Now let's look at how your referral source might handle it a bit differently:

> C/RS: I'd like to have Brenda Martin call you. She helped Mary and me design a financial policy yesterday that's going to ensure we have more than enough money for our retirement, while being protected in the event of any emergencies along the way. Can I have her call you?

> P: How exactly did she set it up for you?

> C/RS: Actually, what I liked about her so much is that she showed us how to do it in a way that fit our individual needs. The best thing for you to do is meet with her and ask her directly those exact type of questions. She'll see if she can help you or not. If she can, great. If she doesn't think she can, she'll tell you that, as well. I'll have her call you.

That should get you your permission to call. Every time? No. Much of the time. If not that time, you can always follow up with a letter to the prospect asking a few simple yet interest-eliciting questions (building on insights which your referral source can hopefully provide). If the prospect responds, you now have permission to call.

3. Gain permission through e-mail.

This one is fairly simple: Just ask your client/referral source to e-mail the person and ask for permission for you to call. Provide your referral source with the exact language already written out. It might read:

> *Hi, Louise, this is Joe. I'm going to have Pat Ryan call you regarding a great plan for being able to send your children to college. Pat is an expert in this field, and Mary and I really appreciate what he showed us. E-mail me back and let me know you're expecting his call, okay?*

Again, while it won't work every time, it will work much of the time. And, if it doesn't work this time, again, you can always follow up a short time later with the type of letter we discussed above.

4. Use a booklet or special report.

This is not only a powerful way to receive permission, it is also a terrific way to qualify a potentially great prospect. In Chapter 9, we looked at the power of booklets. In Chapter 14, we'll look at them again, in yet another context. Here is how you would utilize this tool in order to obtain permission to contact your referred prospect.

> YOU: Mr. and Ms. Smith, as you may know, current law is that
> in order for me to call Karen Jones, or anyone else you're
> kind enough to refer me to, I actually first need their
> permission to do so. May I ask you to make a quick call or
> send a quick e-mail and let her know about me and how
> much you feel my working with you has helped you? And,
> here's the really neat thing; you can even let her know that I
> have a booklet (or special report) that she can either have sent
> directly to her, or she can download it right on the Internet
> to get more information. I can even show you how to put a
> link right to it on an e-mail you send her so that all she has
> to do is click on it and it will take her right to it.

You might first want to go the traditional route of seeing if your referral source can simply obtain the prospect's permission directly via phone or e-mail.

Also, since you have published a booklet, you might suggest to your referral source that he tell the prospect that he's asked you, *a published author on this topic*, to call her about a plan to ensure [your powerful benefit statement here]—is it okay to expect your call? Publishing a booklet, a special report, or even just an article provides you with a great deal more credibility than you would have without it.

You can also mention your booklet to help your referral source be prepared for an objection. For example, after you've asked her to refer to you as a published author, your referral source might say:

> MS. SMITH: I'll be glad to, Tom. What if she asks what it's about?

> YOU: That's a great question. I'd just use the words, "Karen, I
> understand the concept, but Tom is the professional; he even
> had a booklet published on this topic. He's a very credible,
> professional person, so I'd just as soon he explain it to you.
> I'll have him call you, okay?"

That will probably be enough. Will it work every time? No, but it will work much of the time. The best-case scenario, of course, is if the referral invites you to call *and* goes to the Web site and calls you. Anyone who does this is most likely an excellent prospect.

What If They Don't Buy?

Is it possible, at the end of a presentation, to get referrals from those who didn't buy?

Sure, it just depends on the particular situation, and on whether you represent a product or service such that if the referring prospect doesn't buy, that doesn't detract from your credibility with the referred prospect.

If you sell a widget that doesn't depend on set variables, such as house size or type of business or something similar, but is simply a matter of someone's personal preferences and willingness to pay for it, it's more difficult to get referrals from someone who didn't buy than if you sell something that genuinely didn't fit that person's unique situation.

For example, if the big objection was price, meaning your prospect didn't see the value for what you were charging, they'll be less likely to refer you to others. And would you want that kind of referral anyway? I mean, when your referred prospect asks why Steve didn't buy it, what are you going to say? "Well, he didn't think it was worth it...but *you* might." No, in this case, the law of social proof will come back to bite you.

On the other hand, if your original prospect didn't buy because his home wasn't shaped correctly for the installation, or for some other, similar reason, and it broke his heart that this couldn't be overcome, that's a different story. Now you can answer your prospect's question about why Steve didn't buy and add, "And you know, it broke his heart that it wasn't a fit, but he still wanted his friends to be able to enjoy the benefits."

If you do want to attempt referrals from a prospect who doesn't buy from you, here's one way to go about it. You might say:

> Steve, Joanne, I know this widget isn't for you right now, but do you
> feel that it might be right for someone else?

They might say yes, but that doesn't prove they mean it; perhaps just don't want to hurt your feelings. You might continue:

Let me ask you this question, and if there's one thing I've discovered about you in our time together this evening, it's that you might not agree with something, but you are honest. In order for me to ask you to refer people to me, I've got to know your true feelings about this widget. On a scale of 1–10, 1 being no belief at all, and 10 being, "I absolutely think it's fantastic," what are your feelings about the value of this widget for someone who would be interested?

If they respond, "Oh, somewhere around a two," then I'd politely finish up the visit and leave. Of course, you have the option of trying to discover why and answer objections; it's just a matter of how valuable you think that will be.

If they say, "A 10, no question!" then go for the referrals. Here's a great approach, paraphrased from the book, *You Can't Teach a Kid to Ride a Bicycle in a Seminar*, by the late David Sandler, founder of the Sandler Sales Institute®: If they respond with a seven or eight, ask, "What would I need to do (or, what would need to happen) to bring it up to a 10?" Their answer will also be the answer to their main objection. In that case, not only can you get referrals, but you also still might be able to make the transaction happen and help them own your terrific product or service.

So yes, if a person doesn't buy and it's for a legitimate reason, you can still obtain referrals. But in this case, you must be sure he truly believes your product or service is viable for others, and that his reason for not buying is a "condition" (meaning something that truly cannot be overcome, such as a structural problem or that they don't qualify), as opposed to an "objection." Or, be sure that *his* objection will most likely not be his referral's objection, too.

More importantly though, build your list of A-list referrals so high that you're not worried about whether or not you get referrals from everyone, and especially from those people who don't buy from you.

Key Points

- There are four principal reasons most salespeople fail to ask for referrals:
  1. Because they "forget" (which is often because they don't really want to).

2. Because they lack confidence.

3. Because they don't think their products warrant them.

4. Because they don't know how.

- Using a "bridge phrase" can move you comfortably from your postsale conversation to the point where you can ask for referrals.

- Testimonial endorsement letters are one of the greatest tools, perhaps *the* greatest tool, a salesperson can use to answer objections and complete the transaction.

- You can also use testimonial letters to gain referrals.

- If your client or customer seems hesitant to offer a referral, you can tell him exactly how you'll approach that referral, including the exact language you'll use.

- A strong testimonial letter should include these ingredients:

  1. Create a strong desire for the person to want to do business with you;

  2. Be credible;

  3. Be specific;

  4. Tell a before-and-after story that gets people to identify with it;

  5. Tell about the person or company performing the service;

  6. Show the impact your experience with the person and/or service had;

  7. Be verifiable; in other words, include first and last names, city or town, state or province, and as much else as possible that is appropriate.

- Since the advent of Do Not Call laws, you often need to have your referral source contact the referral first, to gain permission for you to call. Here are a few methods for doing this:

  1. Provide the reasoning and explain how to do it.

  2. Provide your referral source with the exact language to deflect objections and elicit permission.

  3. Gain permission through e-mail.

  4. Use a booklet or special report.

- If a person doesn't buy for a legitimate reason, you can still obtain referrals.

CHAPTER 13

Six Essential Rules of Networking Etiquette

As with any game, relationship, or business, networking has its rules, procedures, and etiquette. Knowing what to do is important—and knowing what *not* to do can often be just as crucial to your success. There really aren't that many rules when it comes to networking, but the few that do exist need to be adhered to. If you don't, you stand the risk of destroying the wonderful environment you have created through effective networking.

Rule 1: Don't Ask for Immediate Repayment

When you give something to or do something for someone, *do not expect or ask for something back right away*. For that matter, don't expect any kind of repayment within any time frame at all. Throughout this book we've seen how important it is to be a giver. We know that the more we give, the more we will receive. Trust that process; don't make demands on it.

Is there anything more maddening than someone doing something for you, with the unspoken implication (or even sometimes actually spoken question), "Now what are you going to do for me?" That isn't networking: it's trading. It is no more than keeping a running tally of who owes what to whom.

Asking for repayment, or letting people know that you feel they owe you, will only elicit resentment. Imagine giving someone a referral, or some valuable advice, or maybe you helped his son or daughter get an after-school job at a local sandwich shop. If you then turn around and overtly make that person feel indebted to you, the win-win relationship has been sabotaged. It will only serve as a warning sign to that person that you "don't do something for nothing!"

An incident from my direct sales days immediately comes to mind. I was trying to help a prospect find a product he needed and was having trouble. Suddenly, a man I knew rather indirectly gave me some unsolicited advice on how I could find what I was looking for. Yes, his advice was unsolicited—but extremely helpful.

Later that day he called and asked if his advice was of any help. I told him it certainly was, and that I appreciated his assistance very much. He then politely informed me that, should a sale ensue, he expected a referral fee for his help. I told him that if his advice did lead to a sale, I would honor that, and I said nothing more about it.

Actual Result: Bad Feelings!

The truth is, I very much resented what he did. I decided right then and there I would never ask for nor accept his advice again, and I wasn't really anxious to pursue any further networking relationship with him.

Had he not gone out of his way to mention the referral fee, I would have naturally felt inclined, even obligated, to return the favor down the road. Knowing how I feel about give and take, you can be certain that what he had done for me would have come back to him many, many times over.

Let me clarify something: When I advise you not to make people feel they owe you, I should qualify that statement. Of course we want people to feel they owe us—but we want them to *want* to owe us.

When we do something for someone to help her reach her goals or just to show we care, we evoke good feelings. We foster a mutually beneficial, win-win relationship. That person feels good about us, and whether consciously or not, she will work hard to give back in kind, or even more than "in kind."

But when we make someone feel threatened or inferior, as though he *owes* us, we cause anger and resentment. In that case, the person may *say* he wants to help us, but in reality, chances are his true feelings are that he'd be more inclined to actually sabotage our success, at worst, or simply ignore us, at best.

There are times when a person might mention the idea of payback as a segue, or bridge, into asking us for help. As wrong as this feels, we need to be aware that the person may not feel comfortable simply coming out and asking us for something. It's important to exercise compassion here. In such a case, understand that it's more a defense mechanism than anything else.

A fellow speaker was kind enough to send me some information he thought I might find useful. I immediately called to thank him. During our conversation, he discovered that some information I had could be of help to him. Instead of simply asking if I would share it with him, he said, "Listen, since I gave you that other information, would you send this to me?"

Had I not understood his discomfort in making that request, I might have felt resentful. Someone else might actually have been offended and thought, "Oh, so that's why he did that for me." This is the reason we need to be careful in that aspect of networking.

Do something for somebody without the goal being a payback, and you'll usually be paid back anyway. Again and again and again.

Rule 2: Treat a Mentor Like a Mentor

When seeking a mentor, approach modestly, unassumingly, respectfully, and with the intention of giving more than receiving. A mentor is a person, usually already successful, who wants to take us under her wing and help us become a success in our own right. A mentor is the teacher; we are the student.

It's like a good friendship in the way it develops over time. When seeking a mentor, do so with humility and caution. I've actually heard people just starting in business announce out loud for the world to hear, "I am looking for a mentor." They're probably not going to find one with that approach.

But if you approach your objective correctly, you *can* find people out there who are looking to share their knowledge with an eager young beginner or an eager older professional. You might start by taking him to lunch. (Be sure to pick up the check.) Ask him questions and pick his brain, but do it with sincere respect and appreciation. Make him feel good about the knowledge or skills he possesses. But mainly, find out what you can do to help *him*, and then do it!

In many ways, it's similar to what we discussed earlier about cultivating a Center of Influence person to supply you with endless referrals. The same rules apply. You wouldn't walk up to that person and say, "Hi, will you be my unlimited referral source and help me to succeed beyond my wildest dreams?" Of course not. You wouldn't do that in trying to acquire a mentor, either. You want to establish the relationship gradually, based on mutual give and take, and always try to do more for that person than she is doing for you.

Most Mentors *Want* to Be Mentors

Here's the good news: successful people *enjoy* being mentors. They even seek out students. Why? Because it makes an already-made person feel good to share just how he got there, and even to be able to give that student a boost. Mentors want to be remembered fondly by those who follow their advice and go on to be successful themselves.

Ego probably has something to do with it as well. As an established professional speaker, my advice on how to make it in the field of professional speaking is constantly being sought by speakers just starting their careers. And I love to help them. It boosts my ego and at the same time allows me to share and teach, which I love to do. And when they become successful, it gives me great pleasure to know I had a hand in their success.

When I was just beginning in the speaking profession, I was lucky enough to have found the National Speakers Association. Just by joining, I had access to thousands of other professionals. What I found in this benevolent organization was a great bunch of people ready, willing, and able to share their knowledge. You, too, might find it advantageous to join an organization made up of others in your field. It's a good place to find your mentor or mentors. It worked for me.

There isn't any *one* person I would call my mentor, but I can easily think of several whom I called regularly with questions. It was amazing the number of questions they answered and the amount of information they shared. Of course, I did the right things as well. I sent a thank-you note after each and every conversation.

Not only that: Whenever I spoke with a prospective client and didn't get the booking, I always made sure to plug one of my mentors. And they knew it. When I *did* get the engagement, I'd ask the client if she was interested in knowing about other speakers and, while I would always suggest those I felt would best fit what she was looking for, I would be sure to mention those who were providing so much value in my life and career. The same applied when submitting an article to a magazine for publication. And even though they weren't helping me with the expectation of getting something in return, you can bet that when they saw it happening, it made them feel even better about taking their valuable time in order to help me.

I can genuinely say that much of my quick success as a professional speaker was due to these wonderful people who mentored me, without qualification or reserve. I'm glad I could give something back to them, and I continue to do so today.

One of the nicest compliments I've ever received came once after I had addressed the National Speakers Association at one of our national conventions. During my presentation, I hit hard on the importance of finding a mentor (as well as other networking partners) and establishing give-and-take, win/win, and value-added relationships.

Afterward, numerous members of the audience came up and told me that people who were sitting near, or next to them, had commented out loud, "Burg practices what he preaches. He's referred plenty of business to me."

This is something I've done in practically every business or sales position in which I've been involved, and I've found it always shortens my learning curve and accelerates my success. Not surprisingly, you'll hear most other successful networkers say the same thing.

Rule 3: Keep an Eye on the Clock

When networking with anyone, especially if we are asking for advice or information, it's extremely important that we respect the other person's time. If I'm calling that person on the phone, here is the first thing I will always ask:

> *Do you have a real quick minute to answer a question (give me some advice, refer me to someone in the widget industry, etc.), or is this a lousy time?*

If it turns out it is in fact a "lousy time," I'll find out when might be a better time. Remember, we want the person to feel good about being a part of our network. Wasting her time and not being sensitive to her needs will obviously not help us accomplish that goal.

Respecting others' time is especially important when contacting people who don't know us personally.

For example, let's say we are considering a direct-mail campaign for our product or service, and we realize that before jumping right in, it would be wise to hear some thoughts from someone who's already been there. So we ask someone in our network to connect us with a person he knows in the direct-response industry. She gives us a name.

Now, let's suppose that we call this person, and immediately after introducing ourselves, we started machine-gunning him with question after question after question. How would he feel? Here we are, imposing on his time and expertise, without showing the slightest sensitivity as to his needs—among which is the time he requires to conduct his own business. Every minute he spends answering our questions is a minute away from getting his own job done.

Clearly, if we call this person, introduce ourselves, and then right away say, "Do you have a quick minute...?" we're immediately off on a much better foot.

Enough Is Enough

Sandi, a schoolteacher friend of mine, has amassed a small fortune buying and selling real estate. She went to a lot of seminars, read a lot of books and suffered numerous setbacks before becoming successful in this venture. People who hear about Sandi will often call her and say that a friend suggested they call and talk to her about investing in real estate.

Knowing Sandi as I do, that is fine with her. She's a giver and likes to help. Unfortunately, she tells me, most people take advantage of that trait. Too many times, people will keep her on the telephone for a long time, trying to extract as much information as possible. And they'll call back time and time again. Eventually, Sandi has to tell them that if they want a *seminar* from her, they'll have to pay.

Imagine someone doing that—how obnoxious! And the truth is, it needn't be that way. Most people love to help and are glad to share what they know—and interestingly enough, that's especially true of most *successful* people. However, we need to be completely respectful of their time and let them know how much we appreciate it. A little consideration goes a long way.

Rule 4: Follow Through on Promises

One of the more deadly sins of networking is not following through on what we promise to do. Keeping your promises is generally a good character trait to develop for anyone. For a networker, it's the oxygen you breathe.

Have you ever been exchanging ideas or referrals with a fellow networker who has said, "I'll send you that information right away," and then had the information not arrive for days? It's awkward: You don't really want to call and remind him because you don't want to appear pushy.

Now a week has gone by, and you still haven't received the information, or even a call. On a scale of 1–10, how does that make you feel about that person? How do you rate him for dependability? How much do you trust his word? And on that same scale of 1–10, how effective a networker do you feel he probably is?

Now let's look at a different scenario. Suppose you sell printing, and during a conversation with a fellow networker who's in the business of leasing office space, you learn that a new company will be moving into one of their larger spaces very soon. You recognize the type of business and know they'd be a huge purchaser of printing services.

The person with whom you are networking mentions that she'll get you some information on the company and who's who within the organization.

Two days later you receive an envelope with the letterhead of this leasing agent. You open the envelope, pull out its contents, and notice that the information now in your hands includes the following: the date the company will be moving in, its purchaser's name and telephone number, and a bunch of other valuable data that will surely give you the definitive edge over your competition.

Going back to that 1–10 scale, how would you answer those very same questions regarding *this* person. After giving her a solid 10 all around, ask yourself this: Isn't she the kind of person you will absolutely go out of your way to help? I know I would, because networkers like that are hard to come by.

And the more of those types you know and associate with, the more successful *you* are going to be, because we become like the people with whom we associate.

Rule 5: Be Extra Careful Not to Annoy a Referred Prospect

Let me paint you a picture of a very ticklish situation. One of your fellow networkers, Dave Smith, calls you and excitedly says, "I've got someone for you to contact. Our regional manager's name is Carol Davis, and she would be the person with the authority to purchase more of your widgets than you ever thought you could sell to any one company. Just mention my name and she'll take your call."

You like that! In fact, it makes your day—you think. So you eagerly and confidently pick up that ordinarily intimidating instrument known as the telephone and begin dialing. As the secretary begins the screening process, you nonchalantly say, "Just tell her that Dave Smith suggested I call."

The secretary asks you, "And who is Dave Smith?" and you feel a slight pull in your stomach. Something doesn't seem right. Nevertheless, you do not retreat. You say, "Dave is with the Centerville branch of your company." Unimpressed, she puts you on hold and you now find yourself listening to the Muzak rendition of "Danke Schoen" over the telephone system. Finally, after about four minutes, you are greeted by a somewhat irritated voice. The conversation goes as follows:

> CAROL DAVIS: This is Carol Davis.
>
> YOU: Hi, Ms. Davis, this is Joe Taylor calling from Widgets Unlimited.
>
> CAROL DAVIS: (silence)
>
> YOU: Uh, Dave Smith referred me to you.
>
> CAROL DAVIS: (silence)
>
> YOU: Uh, Dave said you would be the person to speak to regarding the purchasing of widgets for your company.
>
> CAROL DAVIS: We don't need any right now. Just send me some information and we'll call you when we're interested.

Obviously, this was not a good referral. At this point, I might ask one or two qualifying questions, but if there's any resistance in her voice, I will politely end the conversation. Although it might be tempting to tell this person to take a long walk off a short pier, it isn't the right thing to do. Such a comment merely serves to lower you to that person's level. Also, there's a good chance your return rudeness would get back to Dave, who had given you the referral in the first place.

"So what?" you may be wondering. "It was a terrible, unqualified referral that did me no good at all!" True, but at least he was thinking of you and, with a little coaching on your part, his future referrals could be all-stars.

Coach Him on How to Help

This goes back to something discussed earlier in the book: how to "train" those who network for us. As far as I'm concerned, anyone who refers us once certainly thinks enough of us to give referrals again in the future. However, if your friend Dave gets a nasty call from Carol Davis's office or a letter asking him to keep his nose out of corporate headquarters' business, he won't ask you about how rude Carol was—he'll assume *you* came on too strong, and he probably won't risk making any further introductions for you.

Here's a way to tactfully handle this situation.

First, call Dave and thank him very much for thinking of you. Let him know that friends such as him make your job so much easier. Assure him you look forward to referring even more business to him, as well. Then tell him that, as a friend, you feel you should relate to him the circumstances of your contact with Ms. Davis. Let him know that you're telling him this simply for his knowledge, in the event that he may be thinking of referring someone else to Ms. Davis.

In a very matter-of-fact, unemotional manner, review with him your unpleasant conversation with Ms. Davis. Be careful, though. You don't want to embarrass him. Remember, he felt like a big-shot when he gave you the referral ("Just tell her that Dave Smith suggested I call"), so it's imperative you *don't* make him regret that. In this case, I wouldn't repeat the conversation word for word, but just give him the general picture, which is that Ms. Davis was less than receptive, gave you a brisk, perfunctory dismissal, and that was that.

Let him know that a similar situation has happened to you, so you can understand, and that you certainly still appreciate his thinking of you. Then explain that, in future situations, it would probably be helpful to make sure either that the prospect is expecting your call or that his relationship with the prospect is solid.

Again, it isn't *what* you say but *how* you say it. Using the above as a guideline and spoken with tact (tact—the language of strength), you'll defuse any resentment and turn that lemon into future lemonade.

Rule 6: Say (and Write) Thank You

By this time, this should go without saying, but it bears repeating anyway. Regardless of whether the referral turns into a huge sale or a bomb like the one in the example above, let that person know how much his or her thoughts are appreciated.

Another good reason for saying or writing a "thank you" is that this lets the referrer know that something happened.

Once I had to turn down an engagement to speak because I was already booked for that day. However, I gave the person who called the name of another speaker who deals with a similar topic. After a week, I realized I had not heard from that other speaker. It wasn't the "thank you" itself I was after; I just wanted to know for sure whether or not a connection had ever been made. I eventually found out from the client, not from the speaker, that it had.

Between you and me, I'd have liked the thank you as well. We all like to feel appreciated.

Thanking your referrer is one of those automatics. It never gets tiresome to receive a thank-you note. I have people who consistently refer business to me, and they've made it a point to tell me they *always* appreciate my thank-you notes. I'm convinced it's a major factor in why they continue to refer business my way.

Key Points

- In order to maintain and build our network, we must adhere to certain rules of networking etiquette.
- When you give something to or do something for someone, do not ask for (or expect) an immediate repayment.
- When seeking a mentor, approach modestly, unassumingly, respectfully, and with the intention of giving more than receiving.
- Keep an eye on the clock; don't abuse people's time.
- Follow through on promises.
- Be extra careful not to annoy a referred prospect.
- Say (and write) thank you.

CHAPTER 14

Attraction Marketing: Featuring the ProfitFunnel System®

Utilizing the Endless Referrals System® we've been discussing thus far is a very effective way to elicit interest in your products or services, but there are other avenues for doing this, as well. And it's always good to "keep the funnel filled" by using a variety of methods.

Being in a position where you can afford to actually turn business down is certainly far more comfortable than having to scramble to find more. And it's not only more comfortable—it's also better for your business! This goes right back to posture (when you care...but not that much!). Remember, the amount of posture you have and the amount of posture you display is directly proportional to how many quality names you have on your prospect list.

The method we'll look at in this chapter has been around for a fairly short time, yet more and more sales professionals are utilizing it, and with terrific results. It's called "Attraction Marketing," or "Jump through Hoops Marketing."

I first learned this from the great authority on direct response, Dan S. Kennedy (www.dankennedy.com). Dan's premise is that it's much easier and more time-efficient to sell your products or services to or begin a *know you*, *like you*, *trust you* relationship with someone who raises his hand, so to speak, and identifies himself as a prospect.

It's comprised of three basic steps:

1. Advertising (paid or free) in a particular medium.
2. A telephone number (usually toll-free) with a recorded message or Web address where people can receive free information, which could be a report, white paper, CD, or DVD.
3. A "call to action" within the report, which will typically be a number

or Web site the respondent can contact to set an appointment or request the product or service you sell.

As an adjunct to Step 3 (call this 3a), if you don't receive a contact from someone who has received your *free* information, you can then follow up with a call or series of letters or e-mails in order to further pursue.

Dan, who developed the term "Magnetic Marketing," also refers to this type of marketing system as "Jump through Hoops" because in order to identify himself as qualified, the prospect is the one who does the actual work: first responding to the advertisement, then going through the information, and finally either contacting you for more information or purchasing. Your respondents need to "jump through hoops" in order to qualify for your time and prove to you that they're interested.

At first glance, one might think, "Wait a minute, aren't I losing a lot of good prospects who won't take the time to do this?" The answer is, "Yes and no"—with a very slight "yes" followed by a resounding "no!"

Using this approach, you might not reach as many lukewarm, high-main-tenance clients who need to be constantly resold on why they are doing business with you, and who will almost surely end up buying much less from you. (That's the slight "yes.")

However, those who really, really want to do business with you will identify themselves, and these are exactly the sort of excited, on-fire clients that are key to maximizing your referral business. (That's the resounding "no!")

This only makes sense: it will be much easier to develop win-win relationships with people who have already jumped through hoops to say to you, "Hey, please develop a relationship with me!" I think you can see the advantage this gives you in your prospecting efforts.

Again, while I don't believe this *replaces* the type of networking we've been discussing throughout this book, it can certainly *complement* it, and it adds a very productive and even fun element to it.

Here's the fun part: It becomes a machine that you can literally turn on and off. Once you have this system set up, you then do very little work: it's totally systemized and automated.

Building Your Attraction Marketing "Machine"

Consultant Thom Scott, a former direct marketing creative director and Fortune 1000 corporate marketing executive, utilizes an Attraction Marketing system when helping new clients to quickly jump-start or turbocharge their businesses. Of course, he also uses such a system to market his own products and services, too. For a *free* special report by Thom entitled "30 Days to Predictable Profits: Building a Sales Machine to Make More Money, In Less Time, During ANY Economic Climate," go to www.ProfitFunnelSystem.com, where you can download the report.

Thom utilizes seven basic steps for creating a ProfitFunnel System® for any industry or marketplace. He calls the process he uses to create these profit funnels, Marketing from the Heart®; here is his stated goal:

> *To connect emotion and purpose to your marketing, making it more meaningful, compelling and financially successful.*

Of course, that's a good goal for *anyone* in business: to have purpose and meaning in one's work, which by its very nature usually goes a lot further towards making money as well. I really appreciate the way Thom makes the point of utilizing this philosophy as part of his company's mission. It also exemplifies the type of person I know Thom to be.

In short, the seven steps are:

1. Determine your market(s).
2. Craft your market-focused message.
3. Select your market's media outlets.
4. Launch your multihoop marketing system.
5. Measure your results.
6. Maximize the outcome.
7. Maintain your new sales machine.

Now let's look at the seven steps in a bit more detail, along with a few examples of people who are using some form of Attraction Marketing in their businesses with tremendous results.

1. Determine Your Market(s)

This is where you get to know your intended audience and their wants, needs, fear, hopes, and desires. Look for connections with how your products or services meet these emotional hot buttons. Is there a way your product/service fulfills their desires, satisfies their needs or quells their fears?

Thom advises that you use this information to craft a very brief mission statement for your market. Unlike the benefit statements we discussed in

Chapter 6, this mission statement is for your own use in crystallizing your project mission, and not for your prospects. While mission statements can be very complex, the most effective ones are often very simple. In this case, simply use the formula:

I help _____ *(who) to* _____ *(what) by*
_____ *(how).*

For a Realtor®, this might be:

I help homeowners to quickly and profitably sell their homes by aggressively utilizing proven marketing strategies.

In many cases, you probably serve more than one marketplace. That's fine. You can very effectively market to and serve several different markets. However, you'll find your efforts are most fruitful if your missions are tailored to each market individually. This will help them identify with *what you can do for them*, and this is infinitely more important—*to them*—than simply *what you do*.

For instance, let's say you are a financial advisor. If you haven't focused on your specific market, your mission would typically default to referencing features you normally offer through your service. An example would be, "I offer complete financial planning and investment services. I help you determine your needs, and will service you with whatever would be the most appropriate product to help you reach your goals."

Now, see how much more effective it would be, in working with a particular segment or niche market, to have the mission:

I help middle-aged people make a successful transition to their twilight years so that they can take more time for the things they really love to do and rest easy knowing that they can comfortably retire.

The same financial advisor working with another market segment might adjust his mission to say:

I help new graduates get on track to save for their first home and build a financial fortress that will give them any option they want for their life.

The key here is that you are segmenting each market in your mind, and therefore treating each according to the individual wants and needs of that specific market.

While these missions are sometimes stated directly to a prospect, the purpose here is to make certain that all the messages you create for your target markets will be focused on their needs.

Applying this to your business will keep you from falling into the "try to be all things to all people" trap. You will find easier sales and happier customers as they more readily identify with how you are there to serve them—uniquely.

2. Message: Crafting Your "Report"

Once you've created specific missions by examining each of your specific markets, now you can craft specific messages tailored to each one. Each of these messages will be a *free* information product that you will be supplying to prospective clients, in order for them to *qualify themselves* for your attention. In most cases, Thom advises a separate *free* information product for each of the markets you have identified.

One of the most common and practical forms for your message is a booklet. Relatively simple and inexpensive to produce, it packs you with credibility and "expert status" and serves as a valuable door opener. As discussed in Chapter 9 ("Position Yourself as the Expert"), being "published" gives you a step up in all sorts of ways. It also serves as an excellent *free* giveaway for this step of the ProfitFunnel® system; in fact, I know many people who use it as a giveaway on all occasions.

Harry Crosby (whom you met in Chapter 9), now a sales manager with Genworth Financial, rose to number one producer in the Long-Term Care Insurance industry very early in his career. Harry wrote an excellent booklet entitled, "Should I Buy Long-Term Care Insurance, or Would I Prefer Crisis Management?" The booklet's 16 pages were fact-filled and very helpful. While he used it as part of his approach to setting appointments (in an "outbound" way), it could just as easily have served as the second step in an Attraction Marketing system.

Harry knew it wasn't necessary to wait until he'd been in the business for years to create a great credibility and response tool. The information was already there; he simply sought it out, studied it, assembled it, and published it. You can do that, too! And you might recall the results Harry experienced. In a short time, he shattered the industry record for production.

Your *free* information can be in the form of a report, white paper, CD, cassette, videotape, DVD, or even online audio or video file. Whichever approach you choose as most appropriate for your markets, it needs to contain two key elements.

First, this item should provide excellent information that helps to solve their problem or gain a desired benefit.

Second, this free information needs to subtly persuade the reader as to why you offer the best product or service to solve his problem or gain a desired benefit.

The title and subtitle are very important: They are what will draw the potential prospect to the item. Typically, the title should be short and punchy, with a longer and more descriptive subtitle. Do this in such a way that those you wish to target will be responsive to it. If you're a chiropractor, then a good title/subtitle combination might be, "No More Pain: 7 Secrets to Ridding Your Body of Discomfort Once and For All"—providing, of course, that you can back up the title with the correct information.

A financial advisor might use the title, "Safe Wealth," followed by the subtitle, "10 Secrets to Nearly Risk-Free Investing Most People Will Never Know," or something along those lines. Do you see how the title attracts and the subtitle explains, while telling them just enough to elicit their wanting to know more?

Titles or subtitles that have numbers in them followed by "Secrets" are often effective, such as "Seven Secrets to a Firmer, Leaner Body." Another intriguing term is the word "Mistakes," followed by the solution; for example, "Four Mistakes Most People Make When Buying a Car, and How to Avoid Them." Of course, in place of "Car," you insert the word for whatever it is you sell: refrigerator, or heating system, home, etc. Still another intriguing term is "Myths," as in, "10 Myths Most People Believe about Buying a Widget That You Should Know." You could even add, "And How they Could Be Costing You a Fortune."

You might be wondering, "How do I go about thinking up a compelling report title?" Thom points out that the rules that apply to writing great headlines also apply to writing truly motivating report titles.

The *Free* Report title has three primary functions:

a. It identifies the audience you are speaking to. Ideally, the title should be written so that the person reading it could say, "This is for me!"
b. It delivers the message, "You have a problem (or desire) and I have your solution."
c. It compels the audience to read the booklet in order to solve their problem (or satisfy their desire).

Thom outlines two different booklet title formats that can be easily adapted to any situation.

The "How To" Title

The "How To" title offers the reader the promise of a *solution*. If you sell automobiles, an example might be:

How to Get the Best Deal on a Car and Still Get All the Features You Want

This type of title is also strengthened by adding *numbered steps*. Applying this step to the example above, we might create this compelling title:

8 Steps to Getting the Best Deal on a Car While Still Getting All the Features You Want

One more thing that can make your title even more effective is the use of *emotional words and phrases*. Identifying that your information is "secret" or relatively unknown also makes the title more compelling. It might at first feel uncomfortable adding these elements because we've all been hoodwinked into thinking that being "professional" means being "starched" and emotionless. But the reality is, stoic, grammatically correct language is *not* how people really speak, professional or not. So when someone actually reads titles that are intended to be "professional," they often command about as much attention as C-Span when you're channel-flipping for something interesting.

Here is that same report title after undergoing a bit of Thom's "emotional steroid" therapy:

Make Your Car Dealer Cry: 8 Insider Secrets for Buying Your Dream Car at Such an Incredible Price Your Spouse Will Think You Stole It

A little over the top? Perhaps—but wouldn't you want to read it? The important thing here is to make sure that the promise of the information is never greater than the information itself. However, you may be surprised just how valuable your specialized knowledge is to someone who isn't in your industry.

Imagine offering information with this title to potential customers. Wouldn't they want to read it and learn from you, an industry insider, how to get the best deal on their new vehicle? And wouldn't they most likely want to buy from you, the person who was willing to share these ideas with them? Absolutely!

Sometimes when I teach this, people ask, "But Bob, why would I want to give them this 'insider information'?" You probably already know the answer to that one: When you're coming from a true networker's win/win mindset, what you naturally want to do is teach your prospects how to get a great deal for themselves while you still make a healthy profit for yourself (and your business).

The "Reasons Why" Title

Another title format that can be very effective is the "Reasons Why" title. For example:

6 Reasons Why You Should Review Your Life Insurance Policy Today

While it is nearly not as compelling and effective as the emotionally packed title we wrote for the car buyers' booklet, it can certainly be used to raise doubts or concerns that would cause a reader to want to know more. The "Reasons Why" title is also very easy for even the novice self-marketer to create.

In the end, when it comes to writing compelling booklet titles, nothing takes the place of good old-fashioned hard work. Take the time to sit down and write a bunch of possibilities; Thom suggests you write at least 50. After examining the list you've just created, pick your best 3 and see if there is any way they can be combined or improved.

If you are planning to invest a significant amount of money on your initial advertising for the booklet, here's a quick and inexpensive marketing research procedure Thom uses:

Go to a free or low-cost classified advertising site on the Internet. Place ads for each of your three favorite booklet titles, and see which one gets the best response.

If your product or service is not for the consumer marketplace, you might want to simply ask an existing customer or client which they would be most interested in reading.

The important thing is to not get lazy with this vital ingredient. It is less expensive to spend the extra hour or two writing a better booklet title than to go with a hastily conceived title, place ads. and get only half the response you could be receiving!

Thom also suggests visiting a bookstore or going online to check out titles you find intriguing, titles that make you want to know more, and emulate them. Adapt them to your topic.

In the resource section at www.Burg.com/Resources.html, I'm including several books on direct response marketing that offer a world of valuable information on response-generating headlines and titles.

In addition to the excellent and helpful information in your *free* item, you'll also need to include what's known as a "call to action" near the end. This is the part that lets your readers know of your services and tells them how they can contact you to set up an appointment, or whatever the next step is in your particular business.

Make sure you also include several powerful testimonials from some of your most ecstatic clients, either throughout the copy or at the very least, in the call to action. The more testimonials, the better. Remember Joe Polish's words:

> *What someone else says about you is infinitely more believable than what you say about you. So let them say it.*

3. Select Your Markets' Media Outlets

Now that you've determined your markets and crafted your messages, it's time to determine where to advertise your *free* report.

Sean Woodruff, whom we met in Chapter 5, is vice president and co-owner of a small manufacturing company specializing in trailer hitches—obviously a very "niche" industry. His particular product is of high quality and significantly above the average price. Here's why this has not proven to be a problem for Sean.

He began using the Attraction Marketing concept while involved in other products and services earlier in his career, and simply transferred the same principles into his new business. He says he has always used Attraction Marketing as the basis of successfully growing a business, and that it will work in any business, when done correctly. Says Sean:

> *I think the first thing that any small business or independent professional has to realize is that the marketing budget isn't as flush as it would be if you worked for a large corporation. Large corporations such as Coca Cola® can be farther removed from the results of their marketing. They have the cushion to do that. Small businesses and independent profession-als need their marketing to pay off quickly by returning sales, so that they can start the cycle again. This is just a fact. Therefore, I have always used a system that generates sales leads, people contacting my company for more*

information. My current rate is about 25,000 people per year who contact my company and initiate a relationship.

Here's his basic approach to determining where to advertise:

Advertise where your prospects will already be. Location is not necessarily physical. It can also be in the magazines they read, in their homes via traditional mail, and on the Internet sites they frequent.

In Sean's case, most of the advertising he uses for his particular product works best in trade publications and with various targeted Internet sources. As he says,

The only purpose of my advertising is to get the prospect to call a toll-free number or to visit my Web site for an offer of free information.

Sean then utilizes both voice mail and a live person to collect names to send either a *free* report or a *free* video. (Sean has an excellent blog where he discusses all sorts of marketing ideas: www.woodruffdirect.com/index.php/site/blog/.)

Note that it's only after determining who your audience is that you can make wise choices as to where they already are: what they read, what clubs they frequent, etc. Rank the options by the potential return on investment; in other words, the greatest number of quality exposures with the lowest cost per exposure. And whenever possible, choose media options that allow you to test small, then roll big once it's proven itself to be a winner.

In many cases, it is also very effective to put an ad for your *free* report on the back of your business cards. Many who regularly network at Chamber meetings and clubs have found this to be a great way to generate solid prospects from their activities. (If you're going to carry business cards anyway, you might as well leverage them to the max.)

If you speak before any type of business or service clubs and organizations as a way to promote your business, offering your booklet or Free Report to anyone who would like it is very effective, as well. Be careful, though, in the way you offer it. Often, if you just offer to give it to whomever wants it, two negatives can happen: One, people will take it, not because they value it, but simply because it's free; the price they paid will be the value they perceive it to have, which is not a good thing. Two, fewer of the people you really desire to have it will take it because it might be positioned as something *you want* them to have, rather than something valuable that *they should want to have*.

Robert Middleton (www.actionplan.com), author of *Action Plan Marketing*, has some excellent wording for getting attendees at presentations to want your free information. At the conclusion of his presentation he announces:

> *I have a detailed article on what I've spoken about today. I'll be happy to send you one either by mail or e-mail. Just take your cards out and write "e-mail" or "mail" on the back (make sure your information is correct), and I'll get it right out to you.*

Robert reports that this approach generally results in 50 to 75 percent of participants giving him their cards.

4. Launch Your Multihoop Marketing System

Remember, the key to Attraction Marketing is that you are building a system that will attract and qualify those who are interested in the *benefits* of what you offer, not necessarily your product or service itself. In other words, no one likes buying life insurance per se, but they might like the financial benefits, or the way it makes them feel, knowing they're taking care of their family.

That said, remember that as we now start to advertise, we're not doing a one-step ad intended to sell our product or service. We're doing a multi-step ad intended to attract respondents who are interested in the *benefits*.

This might take the form of a small classified ad with the title of your report, along with the phone number. Or it could be a postcard mailer you send to your local Chamber members. It could even be a full-page ad in a trade journal. The important thing is that you are *not* selling your product or service here: You are offering *free* information. And since the information is indeed valuable and not just a sales pitch, if space allows, your ad should stress the benefits of receiving your *free* Report.

With a good title and subtitle along with a media placement (either free or paid) where your prospects are already looking, you have the beginnings of a good Attraction Marketing campaign.

In most situations, the title will be the only part of your advertisement that will cause the potential prospect to make a favorable decision. (And remember, this is a *potential* prospect, not yet an *actual* prospect; they only become actual prospects once they respond to the offer to call, write, or send for your booklet.) But that's all right, because the title is enough.

Back in the 1920s, an entrepreneur named E. Haldeman-Julius sold over 100 million of what were known as his "Little Blue Books." You should see the catalog; it's truly incredible. Just listings of title after title after title—that's it! No descriptions, no selling points. Just the title. If people liked one of Haldeman-Julius's titles, they'd send for the book—and if they like yours, they'll ask for yours, too!

In your advertisement, while you won't have a lot of space, you can at least include a tiny build-up along with your contact information. If you have enough room for a subtitle, all the better. But with a booklet, it's the title that counts.

You will also need a way for prospects to contact you in order to request the report. While some would have those calls come in directly to their office, Thom usually recommends a toll-free voice mail line. The reasons he gives are simple:

> *First, it is most convenient for your prospects to request information when they are available, not when you are available. Second, by putting "24-hour voice mail" on your advertisement next to the phone number, you will get greater response. This is because it is not threatening to a prospect. They know they will not get on the phone with a high-pressured salesperson who will try to take their request for information and turn it into an instant sale. The final reason for the voice mail is that it's inexpensive and easy to set up, so you can have multiple lines or extensions with each one coming in from a different advertisement. This way, you can easily measure your response.*

One service that offers inexpensive voice mail lines is www.800link.com. You can set it up online and have your new toll-free line in minutes.

You may also offer your prospects the option of requesting your report through your Web site or an e-mail. In either case, you can set up an autoresponder to immediately send them their report and notify you of their contact information. If done with an e-mail, you can also use different autoresponder e-mail addresses:

(e.g., info1@greatideas.com, info2@greatideas.com, etc.) for different reports and keyed to different advertisements for the purpose of measuring results.

If the person contacts you after reading your booklet, the chances are excellent you have a new customer or client. After all, she first had to respond to the advertisement (and we saw how you can do this without cost in Chapter 9,

"Position Yourself as the Expert"). Then she had to contact you, either directly, through a toll-free recorded message or through the Internet, to receive the booklet or Special Report. She then read through it and took the action to call you. She is now what's known as a highly qualified prospect!

Remember, though, even when respondents don't call you, you still have their address and hopefully telephone number and/or e-mail, so you can (and should) put each of your respondents in a database and follow up with additional offers of information to help them make the decision to begin using your product or services.

While prospects who receive the information but don't call you are not quite as qualified as those one who do call, that's okay. They are infinitely more qualified than the ones who didn't even respond to the offer of free information. You have successfully created a fishing pool of individuals who may not yet be sold on you or your product, but are still interested in the benefits you deliver.

By repeatedly following up with this audience over time, you'll turn a good portion of these people into customers and clients as well. From there, after you service them properly and help them obtain the results they want, they will now become huge referral sources for you. For that matter, this might happen even before they become customers or clients—as soon as you develop a relationship where they *know you, like you, and trust you.*

5. Measure Your Results

You can't systematically improve what you don't measure. Therefore, you need to *always* include a feedback loop in your marketing process to measure results and eliminate as much waste as possible.

At the beginning of this chapter I mentioned Dan Kennedy, who along with Jay Abraham is one of today's best-known direct response authorities, and is the person from whom I first learned about Attraction Marketing (or as Dan calls it, "Magnetic Marketing"). Actually, the chances are very good that you either know of Dan or have at some point been influenced to buy something from him.

An exceptionally knowledgeable and in-demand marketing consultant and president of several companies in Phoenix, Arizona, Dan has been a behind-the-scenes force in many direct marketing campaigns and has served as a major consultant for Guthy-Renker Corporation, one of the most successful infomercial/direct response companies in the world. (In fact, if you've bought just about anything from a television infomercial, including Guthy-Renker products like Vanna White's Perfect Smile tooth whitening system, Pro-Active acne treatment, or any DirectTalk™ product, you've been persuaded to purchase at least in part by Dan.)

Dan is also an internationally known speaker who has shared the platform with former U.S. presidents, hundreds of celebrities such as Bill Cosby and Larry King, major speaking legends such as Zig Ziglar and Tom Hopkins (and, I'm proud to say, lesser-known speakers such as yours truly), and he is the author of numerous books on free enterprise, entrepreneurship, and of course, direct response marketing.

Dan repeatedly stresses that a key element in the Attraction Marketing process is *testing*. All the mail order greats, people such as Ted Nicholas, Gary Halbert, Melvin Powers, Dan Kennedy, Jay Abraham, stress this constantly in their writings and teachings. Test! Test! Test!

One of the challenges in traditional advertising is trying to accurately measure the results you're getting. There is an old advertising axiom: "50 percent of my advertising works perfectly—the only trouble is, I don't know which 50 percent!" One of the great benefits of direct response marketing (which is what you are doing here) is that unlike with traditional advertising, direct response results are totally measurable.

One way to do this is by what is known as *coding*. Let's say you're running an ad in two magazines read by the same niche market readership—chiropractic physicians. One of your magazines is *Chiropractic Today* and the other is *Healers*. Wouldn't you like to know which magazine pulled a better response? Absolutely. So you use coding.

To code your ad, simply add a letter or department after your address. For instance, 3456 Maple Way, Dept. C. The "Dept. C" on the incoming envelope tells you that this response came from the ad in the first magazine; "Dept. H" would signify the other. If you're asking them to call for a free report, you might use a particular extension number as a code. We already mentioned additional options for coding via separate 800 numbers or autoresponder e-mail addresses.

This is only a basic explanation. As you study the masters in this field, you'll learn more and more ways to measure your responses for lots of different elements of your advertisements and letters. There are all sorts of variables you can test. Among the most important, perhaps *the* most important, is the headline. According to Thom Scott:

Research, including that by the great copywriting legend John Caples, has proven that a simple change in headline can increase response by as much as 1800 percent.

6. Maximize the Outcome

Now that you've run your advertisement and tracked the results, this becomes what direct marketing experts call the "control." Just as with any scientific experiment, this gives you the power to increase the profitability of your Attraction Marketing campaign by testing other ads or ad campaigns against this control.

These tests can include a change of headline, trying a new publication, using a voice mail line versus having prospects contact your office, etc. As Thom Scott advises:

The important thing is to change only one *thing with each test, so that the effect of that one thing can be measured.*

By adopting a mindset of continual testing to constantly improve your results, you will ensure that you will continue to get the strongest responses you can, and not waste money in the process.

7. Maintain Your New Sales Machine

This is where the benefit of having a system really shines. Because you've put all this hard work into developing an Attraction Marketing *system*, perhaps a specific one such as Thom Scott's ProfitFunnel System®, you don't have to spend time each month reinventing the wheel. You don't have to spend endless hours chasing leads who aren't even interested enough in your benefits to request *free* information.

Put your new profitable system on your calendar. Make it regular and scheduled. Check your results on a monthly basis to make sure your ads are still working. Challenge yourself to maximize your results by testing at least twice a year.

Doing this will keep your system low-maintenance, while at the same ensuring that it stays effective.

An Example for All Types of Financial Advisors, Even in Light of Today's Strict Company Compliance Issues

So often, people in business who are used to doing things in "certain ways" encounter an idea such as what we are discussing and see it as being, "a good idea…but it wouldn't work in *my* business." In other words, they determine why it "couldn't work" or "wouldn't work," instead of *why it could* and *how it would!* The following is an excellent example of how this potential challenge might pertain to a financial advisor, but as you read this, see how it could apply to you, as well.

One challenge financial advisors sometimes face is knowing what they can and can't publish, in light of the very strict standards of company compliance departments and policies. Often, they feel restricted by these well-intentioned rules and have a difficult time understanding how to work within them in order to produce information they can use. This could add, if not a roadblock, then certainly a detour to setting up such a profitable and helpful mechanism as we've been discussing (profitable and helpful to both advisor and prospect). Let's look at how two industry experts are doing this so that everyone is happy: Compliance, the advisor, and the prospect.

Howard Jacobson , Ph.D., president of howieConnect (www.howieconnect.com), is author of *Leads Into Gold*, a system for replacing cold-calling with lead generation. Bob Cobb (www.ultimatefinancialadvisor.com), president of Ultimate Financial Advisor, is author of *Building the Ultimate Bank Advisor* and *In the Mind of the Client: The Ultimate Guide to Persuasion in the Only Place It Really Matters.* They both are well-known authorities on Attraction Marketing with a heavy focus on financial services. The following is from an article of theirs published by Horsesmouth (www.horsesmouth.com), an online service that helps financial advisors build their businesses:

Lead Generation Magnets

"If you want to get, give first."

It's one of the core principles of successful marketing: Offer prospects something of value, and they will be much more inclined to trust you and give you their business. One way to give—and get qualified prospects to identify themselves in the process—is to offer what we call a *lead-generation magnet.*

A lead-generation magnet is a purely educational piece of information that you offer to prospects in exchange for their contact information. The best lead-generation magnets help prospects solve a problem—for instance, how to save more for retirement or college. At the same time, the piece establishes your credibility by demonstrating that you have real expertise to share.

There's just one wrinkle: Compliance concerns can make it difficult to get original pieces of writing approved. No advisor wants to invest 10 or 20 hours writing an article, white paper or booklet, only to find that Compliance won't let it out the door. And because they're convinced they'll get shut down before they can get started, we've found that many advisors don't even consider generating leads this way.

But even if you're not allowed to create your own marketing materials, this strategy can be extremely powerful. Because the fact of the matter is, many advisors are sitting on top of a veritable mountain of pre-approved info-products perfect to use as lead-generation magnets. Here's how to find them and make them work for you.

Use What's Already Been Approved

Remember, firms have marketing departments, and they're turning out materials all the time that Compliance has already seen and approved. These professional-looking, four-color pieces are perfectly designed to get prospects to raise their hands and say, "I'm interested in that." If you work in a medium to large firm, chances are you've seen lots of them. Some firms mail them to their advisors in a monthly package or send out an alert when new pieces are available. Some are even available on the firm intranet.

Unfortunately, advisors often ignore these marketing pieces. They look at something like "8 Tips That Can Help You Reduce This Year's Taxes" and say to themselves, "That's not going to help me close a sale today."

That's true, it won't—but a booklet or brochure on that topic would be perfect for use as a lead-generation magnet. In fact, the marketing department may even have created a pre-approved ad in conjunction with the piece. It's like they've done all the preparation for you—all you have to do is use these resources intelligently. Start looking at the materials from your firm's marketing department with a fresh eye. With each piece, ask yourself, "Is this something that I can use to create new prospecting opportunities today?"

You may be wondering, "How can I use some generic marketing piece that is available to every other advisor in my firm? Won't I just look just like everybody else?" That's a good question, and here's the answer: a generic piece becomes unique when you deploy it in an innovative way.

Remember, most advisors fail to use these marketing pieces at all. When they do, it's usually as a handout at a seminar or a trade show. Every once in a while, they'll do a mailing to some clients and say, "Hey, we've got this great piece, and I thought you might have an interest in it."

Advisors do not generally use the firm's marketing pieces for lead generation—as a way to offer something of value to prospects, inspiring them to raise their hands and identify their interest. This savvy strategy will set you apart from the vast majority of other advisors out there.

Choosing and Using the Right Material

Even though the home office may have created the perfect lead generation magnet for you, you still have to locate it among all the other marketing pieces they offer, and you need to promote it effectively. That means you've got to focus your efforts on a clear target market.

Analyze Your Market

Just as if you were going to create your own piece, you must develop a good understanding of your target market before proceeding any further. Who are your target prospects? Where are their watering holes? What is their pain, their need; what is critically important to them?

1) Choose an engaging topic that pre-qualifies prospects.

Once you've done your homework, you can look at the list of available marketing pieces and choose those aimed at your target prospects. You're looking for something you can use to "begin a conversation." One type of title that is effective and that

marketing departments seem to produce in abundance is the
"X Ways to Y" piece, such as:
- 12 Easy Ways to Educate Your Kids About Money
- 8 Tax-Saving Steps You Need to Take Before Year-End
- 5 Things You Should Know About Small-Business Retirement
  Plans

Choosing the right magnet will help you pre-qualify your
prospects. For example, presumably only small-business
owners will care about small-business retirement plans. So if
you're aiming at SBOs, you'd go with that topic; similarly, you
may find pieces oriented to retirees, women, or other groups.

2) Use pre-approved ads to promote your info-product.
   With any luck, your marketing department will have some
   Compliance-approved ads that will fit your target market. If
   you're in a larger firm, you may even have an icon or tab on
   your system that lets you view all of the sales and marketing
   material that is available for download.

3) Ask for help.
   Remember, the folks in the marketing department are not
   turning out all this information for their health. This is their
   career. Often, you can go to someone in marketing and say,
   "Here is what I am looking to do. This is who I am trying to
   market to; this is what I am trying to accomplish. Here are
   the steps that I am looking at and what I'd like to run with,"
   and they will be happy to give you lots of help in getting
   Compliance to approve it, getting the artwork done, and
   getting you camera-ready copy that you can actually send to a
   newspaper.

4) Use ghostwritten articles.
   Almost every firm today has some pre-written articles—
   you can submit them under your name to local newspapers.
   The newspaper will give you a little space at the bottom for
   a paragraph that says, "Howard Jacobson is a financial
   advisor with XYZ. Call him at 555-8383 to receive a free
   copy of *8 Tips That Can Help You Reduce This Year's Taxes.*"

5) Get leads from existing clients.

When you are talking with your clients, be sure to inquire who they know who might be interested in receiving your info-product. It's much easier to ask, "Do you have a friend or colleague who might be interested in a free booklet outlining twelve easy ways to educate kids about money?" than to ask, "Who do you know that might want to work with me?"

6) Put on your Compliance hat.

A little homework goes a long way when it comes to Compliance. If you decide to create your own materials, look at the marketing pieces, ads and ghostwritten articles that are already getting approved. You will quickly get a good feel for what Compliance likes and doesn't like. Demonstrating that you understand the hot buttons will only help strengthen your credibility.

7) Reuse and recycle.

The good news is, once a generic ad is done, it's done. You don't have to go back every month and get it redone. Use it for three or four months. Once it stops pulling, put it on the shelf and run something else. Later on, say in a year, you'll still have your lead-generation magnet system in place, and you can plug your old ad back in again without worry: it will still be pre-approved.

Remember, if you're at a medium- or large-size firm, that material that's just sitting around on your desktop is an untapped goldmine for generating leads. Use it in a way that no one else around you is doing, and with just a little time and effort, you can give yourself a tremendous advantage in the marketplace.

Final Note

I want to express my thanks to Thom Scott, who provided me with a good deal of the background information for this chapter and has helped me steer a significant portion of my own business to the ProfitFunnel System® he developed. I also thank and appreciate Sean Woodruff, Howard Jacobson,

Bob Cobb, Robert Middleton, and Dan S. Kennedy, all of whose wisdom was shared in this chapter. This method of attracting prospects that you've just learned can quickly accelerate your business in a way you might never have previously thought possible.

In every type of business, you'll find a few forward-thinking people are refusing to believe that "it won't work in my business" and instead, go ahead and do it—with spectacular results! I challenge you to be one of those people and put an Attraction Marketing system together for your business!

Again, for a free special report by Thom Scott, entitled "30 Days To Predictable Profits: Building A Sales Machine to Make More Money, In Less Time, During ANY Economic Climate," go to www.ProfitFunnelSystem.com and download the report. Just by studying Thom's setup and report, you'll learn how he applies all the principles you've learned throughout this chapter so that you can more easily duplicate them.

Key Points

- The purpose of Attraction Marketing is to have potential prospects "raise their hands" and identify themselves as qualified prospects.
- The Attraction Marketing process consists of three steps:
  1. Advertising (paid or free) in a particular medium.
  2. A telephone number (usually toll-free) or Web address where people can receive *free* information.
  3. A "call to action" within that information, typically a number or Web site the respondent can contact to set an appointment or request the product or service. If you don't receive a contact, you can follow up with a call or series of letters or e-mails
- Thom Scott's ProfitFunnel System® uses seven steps:
  1. Determine your market(s).
  2. Craft your market-focused message.
  3. Select your market's media outlets.
  4. Launch your multihoop marketing system.
  5. Measure your results.
  6. Maximize the outcome.
  7. Maintain your new sales machine.

CHAPTER 15

Begin Your Own Profitable Networking Group (Or Join Another's)

H ere is a concept that will make you a lot of money over the long run: begin, run, and maintain your own organized networking group, club, or organization. You'll have to work at it. You'll have to cultivate it. But the results will truly pay off many times over.

This is an extremely valuable way to network your way to endless referrals. What it entails, essentially, is involving a diverse group of people (one in each job classification) who are either business owners or salespeople representing a certain business.

You may be familiar with the concept and may possibly even have participated in a similar organization yourself. Unfortunately, however, sometimes these groups are run incorrectly and do not live up to their full potential. Perhaps you felt it was a waste of your time, energy, and money. If this was the case, let me assure you: when it's run well, such a group can be hugely valuable.

Or perhaps you've participated in one that was run quite well, and you benefited from it greatly, only you've since relocated and you realize how important such an organization is to your business success. In either of these scenarios, perhaps you feel it is time to begin and run your own.

On the other hand, there are superbly well-run referral organizations you can join, such as BNI (Business Network International), founded by Dr. Ivan Misner, which is international in scope; NPI (Network Professionals), founded by Eve Peterson, which covers a five-state region; and many others. I'll refer to them again later in this section. There are sure to be some already where you live. If you'd rather go that route, instead of beginning your own, simply research these types of organizations and join whichever one you feel would be most beneficial to you.

Whether you participate in one run by others or begin your own, the information in this chapter can be very profitable for you. Work this correctly and you'll become immersed in leads and many qualified referrals.

By the way, why do I say "leads" *and* "referrals"? Aren't they the same thing? Although the two terms are often used interchangeably (and for the sake of convenience, we'll use them both freely in this chapter), there is actually a significant difference between the two. For instance, while a referral is always a lead, a lead is not necessarily a referral. Referrals are more personal; they are typically based on a *know you, like you, trust you* relationship between the referrer and that person receiving the referral, as well as a relationship between the referrer and the prospect. Leads, on the other hand, are often—though not always—little more than information being passed along.

My mentor in the area of developing this type of referral organization is a woman from Sudbury, Massachusetts, named Tanny Mann. Tanny founded and ran an organization called Sales Networks, Inc. (SNI). Over the years, she has run several of these groups and attained tremendous success with them, helping and mentoring many others along the way.

Tanny's organization was the first of this type in which I was involved. An excellent networker, she was a true inspiration when I began my own group, after I moved to Florida several years later. I began selling for a local company, but, having just relocated, I had no sphere of influence to speak of to help me get started.

Tanny organized her group. She taught people how to network within the group, and she genuinely cared for the success of her members. As you can imagine, this type of giving and genuinely caring attitude went a long way toward Tanny's own success. I'd like to share with you the setup and running of an organization such as Tanny's.

This chapter is based on a combination of what Tanny taught me, methods I have learned from others, and those I've cultivated myself. The group I ran resulted in a lot of business for a lot of people, including me. If you follow this advice, the group you begin or with which you become involved will prove to be just as successful and rewarding for you.

One Is the Magic Number

There's a limit of one person for a particular type or category, of business: one printer, one chiropractor, one florist, one Realtor®, one sign-maker, one insurance person, one banker, and so on until you run out of categories. The total membership in this group can grow to be as big as you'd like but should include just one person for each type of business, so there is no competition within the group. The setup alone provides an excellent opportunity for the participant, providing she works it correctly.

In the normal course of business, because there are many others in your field within your own community, you often need to be 10 times better at networking than the next person just to earn the opportunity to cultivate the relationship with a new prospect in the first place. After all, until you've had a chance to meet them, begin the relationship and then cultivate it, what's to keep your prospects from doing their business with—and referring their business to—50 other financial advisors or Realtors® or computer technical consultants or copying machine salespeople or lawyers or whatever you may be?

By being a member of a referral exchange organization, you have that opportunity right in front of you. Yes, you still have to take the correct actions, which we discuss in this chapter, but at least it's yours to begin with.

The intention of this networking organization is to (1) develop and maintain a give-and-take relationship with as many other businesspeople as possible, (2) to train each of these people to know how to prospect for you, and (3) to know how to match you up with their 250-person sphere of influence. The whole point is qualified referrals, referrals, referrals, and *more* referrals.

We already know how important it is in networking to give to others. It is *vitally* important to do this within your new networking organization—in this case, especially, to be able to refer business to others. Within this organization, those who establish themselves as givers early and often typically reap huge rewards.

Let's even provide a special definition of networking as it relates specifically to this type of group. How about this: "The developing of a large and diverse group of people to whom you effectively and pragmatically give, and from whom you get, worthwhile referrals." That's a mouthful, isn't it? It is also the way this group benefits everyone.

Knowing how to sell your products, goods, or services after acquiring these worthwhile leads and referrals is, of course, another very important subject. As mentioned in earlier chapters, there are many excellent books on this topic, and I hope you either have begun or plan to begin your own resource library. What we're talking about here, however, is simply how to obtain these leads and referrals, and what types of leads and referrals to give.

In a group situation such as this, there are three basic types of leads and referrals: (1) general group leads; (2) individual referrals of the "feel free to use my name" type; and (3) individual leads of the "please *don't* use my name" type.

General Group Leads

These are leads given by one member that could possibly benefit several or more members of the group.

For example, an office building is going up along Highway 1 in Tequesta. This lead could be useful to the copier salesperson, the Realtor®, the insurance salesperson, the cleaning person, the sign person, and many others.

Individual Referrals: "Feel Free to Use My Name"

These are referrals given by one member to another. The referred prospect might be a person who could use that particular service. In this case, the referral provider is friendly enough with the prospect that using his name would be a help.

It should be made clear whether or not the prospect expects a call from the person to whom the referral was given. If that is the case, make sure you do call, or else the person who provided the referral will be made to look bad. That, in turn, will result in no additional referrals from that person.

Also, determine whether or not this is simply a lead (i.e., the referrer knows there is a need, but has never spoken with the prospect about it), or a referral (in that it was mentioned to the prospect who agreed to take your call), or a "presold." A presold is the highest level of referral: here, the referral provider (who most likely has a *know you, like you, trust you* relationship with the prospect) has already established your credibility to the *n*th degree; basically, all you need to do is show up.

Individual Leads: "Please *Don't* Use My Name"

These are also leads—possibly excellent ones—given by one member to another. However, they are given with the stipulation that the lead giver's name not be mentioned to the prospect.

Why not? Hard to say, exactly. For whatever reason, it simply might not be appreciated, whether by the prospect, the lead giver, or both.

Perhaps that person is still a prospect for the lead giver, and the lead giver might feel the prospect will resent the idea that her name is being given out to others.

Or maybe the prospect is someone who doesn't especially like the lead giver. That isn't to say that the person is not still a good prospect. The lead giver might say, "Joe Sprazinski, I know he needs a new fax machine. Unfortunately, he and I don't exactly hit it off, so I wouldn't suggest you use my name." Okay: so find another reason to get in there and see Mr. Sprazinski.

Important point: When lead givers don't want their names revealed to the prospect, their wishes *must be respected*. Otherwise, you'll never get a lead or referral from that person again—or from anyone else in the group who hears that you went ahead and used the lead giver's name despite a request not to do so.

A Definite Agenda

Now let's turn to the procedure for these meetings.

Lasting about an hour, this is a very structured setup, and that structure needs to be followed to the tee. If not, it will turn into just another group of people getting together and socializing, *thinking* they are networking but not actually accomplishing much. As the leader of the group, you have the responsibility of ensuring that the procedure is carefully adhered to.

These meetings have two distinct segments: the prenetworking and the *formal networking* phases. Encourage members to arrive early in order to business-socialize during the prenetworking period. This helps promote the *know you, like you, trust you* feelings necessary for effective networking. And it should be informal: Get as many group members as possible to know you on a personal basis.

During the formal networking phase, after calling the meeting to order, ask each person to briefly address the group, stating his or her name, company, type of product or service with which he or she is involved and types of leads and referrals desired.

Develop Your "Commercial"

Here's a hint that worked very well for me when I ran my group: For your turn, develop a sort of vignette, profile, or short commercial. Use that every single time you give your introduction, and the message will become implanted in your group members' minds.

In case you're wondering whether or not this might become boring for people, don't let that concern you. You are there to do business, and as group members become more and more familiar with your word-for-word commercial, what you do will become a part of them.

In fact, that is exactly what all successful networkers strive to achieve. (And if it makes you feel any more comfortable, let me assure you: *you'll* become tired of your commercial long before the other group members will!)

Aren't there commercials from years ago that you can identify and still remember? "I can't believe I ate the *whole* thing" (Alka Seltzer)…"You're in good hands with Allstate" and "Get a piece of the rock" (Prudential).

How about this fast-food commercial: "You deserve a break today. So get up and get away." To where? Of course, McDonald's. And you know what? Most of these commercials haven't been around for years! But you remember then anyway, don't you?

Play your commercial over and over again, once a week, at every group meeting. Before long, what you do will be ingrained into your fellow networkers' brains.

Here's an example of a short, effective commercial I might use if I were in real estate:

> *My name is Bob Burg, Realtor® with Ocean Realty. I successfully market homes for people who wish to sell, and help those who want to buy the perfect dream home. If you hear a person mention selling a home or buying a home, that person would be a good referral for me.*

Notice that I provided the feature, the benefit, and my own answer to the One Key Question: how to know who'd be a good prospect for me.

If I were a financial advisor working a general market (as opposed to a niche market or specialized financial product line), my commercial might be:

> *My name is Bob Burg, financial advisor with Keene Financial Services. I help people create and manage wealth. If you learn of a person who makes good money but appears to have no financial plan in place, that would be a good referral for me.*

If I worked with a particular product line, let's say I specialized in college savings, the "how to know" statement at the end might be:

...if you meet anyone with children younger than age 10...

That's all you need to say—that week, next week, and every week in the future. Again, what you want to avoid is talking technical. If you're a Realtor®, you wouldn't want to say, "When I list a home, first I do this, then that, then hold an open house, then this," etc. The financial advisor would not talk about his or her financial planning office software or which mutual funds happen to be his or her favorite. The accountant in the group would absolutely *not* talk about how to prepare a form 1120 U.S. corporation tax return. The copy machine salesperson would not describe the bells and whistles in his product. None of that is important.

You might think, "Well, the others in the group should know as much as possible about my products or service so they can help sell them." Not so! You can sell your products or services much better than they can. You simply want them to *get you the leads and referrals.*

Here's a perfect example:

There was a woman in my group who sold paper products—all kinds of paper products. Every week, she would give her brief vignette or commercial and would conclude by saying:

And remember, when you think of toilet paper, think of me.

Everyone laughed every time she said it. But I'll tell you what: When any of us would happen to meet anyone in any business who might happen to need paper products—any type of paper products, *not* just toilet paper—we thought of this woman. How effective! She is a very successful salesperson. In fact, last time I spoke with her I discovered she had been promoted to sales manager of the entire company.

Your commercial should total no more than 15 or 20 seconds. Following that, thank those who gave you leads or referrals at the previous meeting or during the week. Recognition is very important, and they will appreciate the fact that you recognize them publicly.

A very classy thing to do, and one that will be extremely appreciated, is to send a personalized, handwritten note of thanks—by this time, you know what type I mean—to anyone who gives you a lead or referral. Takes just a bit of extra time, and the results will be well worth it. Behavior that gets rewarded, gets repeated—and giving you referrals is just the type of behavior you want to reward, isn't it?

After thanking those from whom you received leads or referrals, you now give out your leads and referrals to the group and individuals for whom you have them.

Out Loud!

I can't overstate how important it is to state your leads and referrals publicly and enthusiastically. Don't wait until afterward and give them out privately. There were people in my group who feared being thought of as conceited or braggadocio for giving their leads out loud.

Why? That's just what you want to do, isn't it? If the people in the group know you're providing leads and referrals, even to other members, then they know you have the potential to do the same for them. That, of course, will make them work harder to find leads and referrals for you and will result in a "delightful cycle of success" for everyone.

As you recruit members for your group, you need to sell them on the fact that they will not necessarily receive many leads and referrals right away. Success in this group is similar to planting the seeds in an enormous garden. It takes care, commitment, diligence, and most of all, patience. Eventually, all who proceed correctly and consistently will reap plenty.

Teach your fellow networkers these exact principles. Assure them that *if* they are willing to stick with it, they will receive the rewards they desire: lots and lots of qualified leads and referrals and the foundation of a terrific network.

They must *not* miss these meetings, except in an emergency. They must schedule the meeting as a business appointment each and every week. There were people in my group who quit after two sessions because they "didn't get business from the group." That's hardly surprising: they hadn't yet given anyone else a chance to get to *know them, like them, and trust them.* Even then, the timing might not have been quite right. Joining a networking organization such as this won't necessarily result in instant gratification. Some people will not be willing to accept that fact and will, therefore, quit.

But another member named Tom, who sold a fairly high-ticket item, patiently cultivated the group for over a year. He received some leads, but nothing substantial. Then, all of a sudden, a transaction came through in which three different members of the group all participated. It was truly a soap opera situation, with none of them even realizing that the others were involved, and it ended up netting Tom a huge commission. To this day, and for obvious reasons, Tom is a hard-core networker. He applies these principles diligently and is very successful.

Other members, depending on the types of business with which they are involved, will see business come in more quickly and more steadily, especially from fellow members. People in that category would include Florists®, printers, and others with products, goods, or services that are often in demand. Their primary focus should be to cultivate their fellow members and earn the business of their 250-person sphere of influence as well.

Work the Spheres of Influence

Every so often, I'm asked to observe a networking group and critique its operation. Almost without exception, the first thing I suggest is, "Stop having as your primary goal selling your products and services to each other." Instead, you want to make it your main objective to have the group members serve as your Personal Walking Ambassadors to their 250-person spheres of influence.

When recruiting or allowing members to join your group, make sure to have them checked out for honesty and integrity. If possible, recruit them by networking with others, including those in your group. Urge your members to invite prospective members—as long as it's in a business category that is presently vacant. The chances are always better that a newcomer referred by a group member will fit the profile of honesty and integrity. You don't want to give a good lead—or worse, a good referral—to a bad apple. That won't make you or the other members of the group look good.

In order to get the group off the ground, you may have to do some "babysitting." In other words, you need to call the members the night before the meeting to make sure they're coming. Although you're looking for leaders and self-starters, and you don't want to waste time trying to raise the dead, so to speak, it's just something you might have to do at first, and until the benefits of belonging to this organization are understood.

I believe, however, that with much of the publicity these sorts of organizations are now receiving in the mainstream and business press, the benefits of belonging are becoming more and more self-evident, so this shouldn't be as big a challenge today as it was when I was first beginning my organization.

Make sure you hold the meetings early in the morning, before the regular workday begins. Sure, it can be tough getting people to wake up a little earlier one morning per week, but you know what's even tougher? Trying to get people to attend immediately after the regular workday ends. That's a battle royal! People normally are fresher and have clearer heads in the morning.

Besides, if they're motivated enough (which are the type of people you want to network with anyway), they'll get themselves up a little earlier in order to make this very important meeting. And hopefully, when their workday begins, they will find the opportunity to use the leads and referrals they just received from the morning's meeting while those leads and referrals are still fresh in their minds.

To Charge or Not to Charge

People ask if they should charge a fee or dues for belonging to the group. Here's what I've experienced. At first, you won't get a lot of people willing to shell out money—not until they see the value of belonging to the group. In fact, at first, it will cost you some out-of-pocket money in time, stationery, and stamps. Be prepared to absorb those expenses in the beginning. In the long run, you know you're going to come out ahead.

Once you get the group off the ground and it has proven effective, then you can begin charging a token sum. This will pay for any miscellaneous expenses that were initially coming out of your own pocket. I charged a couple of dollars per meeting and had the manager of the host restaurant agree to have a light breakfast served. In fact, he joined our group as the caterer.

I feel it's better to start a group of your own than to join and simply be a member of another one. When it's your group, your baby and brainchild, you have an even higher personal stake in making it successful. You also are positioned much more strongly within the group. The other members will always have you and your products or services on their mind whenever there is a good prospect out there—and, of course, vice versa. I believe these benefits are significant enough to warrant forming and running your own organization as opposed to being a member of another one.

At the same time, being a member in another group is not a bad move either. If you'd rather not put the effort into beginning your own group (and it does take effort), there are plenty of groups already out there you could join. Although the group's specific agenda may be different from what I've described, the basics are still the same. Simply use the methods you've learned throughout the book (and especially in this chapter) in order to cultivate relationships with these people. Most cities and towns now have several of these groups, so ask around and you'll find one. Just hope there is still an opening for your business category.

Tanny Mann, whom I mentioned earlier, has run similar groups in the Massachusetts area; another friend, Eve Peterson, has developed a number of organizations in Pennsylvania and Ohio. There are people like Tanny and Eve spread throughout the country, and indeed, throughout the world. Search for them and you'll find them.

Three of the largest organizations, with presence in cities and towns throughout North America and even internationally, are Ali Lassen's Leads Club (www.leadsclub.com), LeTip International (www.letip.com), and Business Network International (BNI) (www.bni.com), all based in California. BNI was founded by a friend of mine, Dr. Ivan Misner, author of *Business by Referral, Masters of Networking* and other excellent books. Since its inception in 1985, his organization (whose motto is "Givers Gain") has passed more than 3,000,000 leads and referrals, generating more than $1 billion for its participants.

For-profit lead exchange organizations such as these charge good money to belong, but the benefits of membership are well worth it. Believe me, the people there work extremely hard to make it worthwhile for their members.

For most of us, these groups are simply a very effective way to build our network. Without doing it full-time, you and I would probably be hard pressed trying to make the group a profit center in itself. Of course, that's not our objective anyway. We're there to significantly build our core business, while helping the other group members do the same. And it works: if you keep your focus on helping the other people through a constant supply of good leads and referrals, then more leads, referrals, and new business will come to you in abundance.

Types of Categories

Regarding the actual membership, you can probably come up with a diverse group of business classifications by yourself. Here are some suggestions:

> *accountant, advertising representative, appliance dealer, attorney, audio-video production person, automobile dealer, banker, boat salesperson, builder, carpet cleaner, caterer, cellular telephone salesperson, chiropractor, cleaning company, coffee service, computer salesperson, copy machine salesperson, dating service, courier service, dentist, electrician, employment agency, exercise equipment representative, financial planner, Florist®, funeral director, hair stylist, health club owner/manager, hot tub salesperson, hotelier, insurance advisor, interior designer, jeweler, landscaper, limousine service, massage therapist, moving company, nursing service, office supply representative, pager salesperson, painter, paper products person, party planning service, paving company, pest control*

representative, photographer, physician, podiatrist, plumber, printer, Realtor®, restaurateur, restaurant supplier, roofer, satellite dish salesperson, secretarial service, solar energy salesperson, sporting goods store, storm windows salesperson, swimming pool sales representative, telemarketing service, business telephone systems representative, title company, travel agent, uniform supply service, valet service representative, veterinarian, wallpaper store representative, water cooler salesperson, water purification person, waterbed salesperson, wedding supplier, weight loss center, window tinter...

By using your imagination, talking with others, and reading through the Yellow Pages, you'll come up with many more business classifications or categories. The selection above is only about a quarter of the list I made up.

Often, where it seems as though two people would be in competition with one another (which you don't want), you can find a way to make them complementary. For instance, there might be two insurance agents, but on closer inspection, you realize that one sells life, while the other sells property and casualty. This actually happened in the group I ran. And guess what? The two referred so much business to each other, they ended up going into business as partners!

There are other examples of subcategories that really offer no competition. This could include a commercial Realtor® and a residential Realtor®.

Depending on how big and powerful you wish your group to become, you can start small and work your way up to big.

Strategic Alliances

Just as some businesses naturally lend themselves to cross-promotion (discussed in Chapter 10), there will be certain professions within your referral exchange organization that by their very nature lend themselves to easy back-and-forth referrals. This relationship is often referred to as *strategic alliances.* Dr. Ivan Misner (founder of BNI) takes this concept a step further with what he calls "Contact Spheres®." According to Dr. Misner, in his excellent book, *The World's Best Known Marketing Secret: Building Your Business with Word-of-Mouth Marketing,*

This is a group of businesses or professions that can provide you a steady source of referrals. They tend to work in areas that complement, rather

*than compete with, your business. For example, if you were to put a lawyer,
a CPA, a financial planner, and a banker in the same room for an hour,
you couldn't stop them from doing business. Each of them has clients or
customers that could benefit from the services of the others.*

Dr. Misner says, "It's okay if Contact Spheres overlap a little—the process still works." As examples, he sights the following:

- Business services: printers, graphic artists, specialty advertising agents, marketing consultants
- Real estate services: residential and commercial agents, escrow companies, title companies, mortgage brokers
- Contractors: painters, carpenters, plumbers, landscapers, electricians
- Health care services: chiropractors, physical therapists, acupuncturists, nutritionists
- Professional services: lawyers, CPAs, financial planners, bankers
- Business equipment vendors: telecommunications, computers, photocopiers
- Special-occasion services: photographers, caterers, travel agents, Florists®

While those within each grouping, or contact sphere, have more of a natural inclination to refer back and forth because they often work within different aspects of the same client's needs, Dr. Misner points out that referrals can also flow naturally and easily *between* Contact Spheres.

*The Florist's® wedding clients may be in need of the services of a printer
(for wedding invitations), a financial planner, or a residential real estate
agent. Each of these professionals may, in turn, gratefully refer other
clients to the Florist® who sent them good business prospects.*

Depending on your line of work, look for strategic alliances or Contact Spheres® and encourage others to do the same.

What about Those Who Have Trouble Speaking in Public?

If you or someone in your group has a fear of standing up in front of the group and speaking, realize that he or she is not alone. Public speaking is considered by many to be near or at the top of the list of most significant fears. That's understandable—and it's also another very good reason to use the same commercial every time. You'll certainly begin to feel comfortable with it, and thus better able to speak before a large gathering.

Another excellent strategy is to visit (as a guest) and then enroll in an organization called Toastmasters International (www.toastmasters.org). There are local chapters all over the world. Toastmasters is an organization of people dedicated to helping you become a better speaker. You, in turn, will eventually do the same for them. It's a very comfortable, win-win situation, and lots of fun.

I have to confess that, although I speak for a living and am a former radio and television news anchor, I still get that lousy, nervous feeling every time before I present to an audience. Believe me, you're not alone.

Other Important Points

It's a very good idea to sit next to different people at every meeting. Even in this formal setting, you will still have the opportunity to exchange positive words and ideas with someone new, as well as establish rapport. This is key. Remember, you want these people to *know you, like you, and trust you.*

Although you'll be seeing the same people every week, the little things still count. Send them articles of interest and extend the extra courtesies you offer your other networking prospects. You can and most definitely should mail them personalized thank-you note cards for any leads and referrals they provide you.

Everyone likes to be recognized, and they will continue to work hard for you if they know they can expect that recognition from you. Their next referral might be a great one. Don't be afraid to toot your own horn. Always give your leads and referrals publicly. Make sure everyone knows you are working hard to help *their* businesses grow. That way, they will want to help *your* business grow. And everyone comes out a winner!

Key Points

- When organizing your own networking group or organization, there's a limit of one person for a particular type or category of business. Thus, there is no competition within the group.

- Meetings are held one morning per week, every week without fail.
- The intent of the group is qualified referrals, referrals, referrals, and *more* referrals.
- There are three types of leads and referrals.
  1. General group leads.
  2. Individual referrals: "Feel free to use my name."
  3. Individual leads: "Don't use my name."
- There is a specific structured setup for the meetings.
  1. *Prenetworking.* Members arrive early to business-socialize.
  2. *Formal networking.* Each member individually stands up to address the group. Develop a vignette, or short commercial, and use it every time.
- State leads, referrals and thanks-yous out loud.
- Look for strategic alliances.
- Concentrate not on getting these people's direct business, but that of their 250-person spheres of influence. Cultivate them as you would anyone else in your network (thank-you notes, etc.).

CHAPTER 16

Networking for a New Job

Whether it's called downsizing, rightsizing, capsizing, or even supersizing, there's simply nothing pleasant about being laid off or fired. And even if you haven't been fired, perhaps you feel it's time to move on, and you simply no longer want to work with your present outfit or company.

Today's job market is extremely volatile. Many high-level executives and midmanagers have been laid off already and others feel the axe about to land. How do these people, many of whom have been with the same company for 10 to 20 years, all of a sudden go out and find a new job where the salary and benefits are anywhere near equal to what they've had for all this time?

If you are in this situation, how do you land the job and position you want in the quickest, most effective way possible? How do you develop the contacts to help you do this, and how do you position yourself as different from and more desirable than the other candidates going for this same spot?

First things first. "Dig your well before you're thirsty" is not only the title of a great book by Harvey Mackay, it's also a very worthwhile saying that's been around for a long time. (Actually, the way I'd always heard it said was, "Dig your well before you need the water.") And that saying is nowhere more appropriate than when it comes to finding your new job.

Let's rate your job-seeking situation, from best-case to worst-case scenario, and see just how this idea applies:

1. You already have another job offered to you or all lined up when you are let go or decide to terminate your employment on your own.

2. You are so well-connected and respected within and without the industry in which you seek employment that it should be no time at all before you land something you want.

3. You begin from scratch.

Which scenario looks better? Hmm, not exactly brain surgery here, is it? Unfortunately, because most people seem to handle their personal and career networking much the same as they handle saving money for the future, they commonly wind up in two uncomfortable positions: no job and little money to live on while they find that job!

The first conclusion we can draw from the above is this: If you currently have a job, it's a good idea to start building your job-referral network right now. This is your best insurance for avoiding the possibility of finding yourself in situation number three. It will also provide you with the *posture* to take any action you feel is best and necessary from a position of strength, rather than from fear and weakness.

And of course, simply by the fact that you are utilizing the principles discussed throughout this book to build your prospect list and referral business, you are already well on your way.

The Hidden Job Market

In your job search, the higher the level of sales, management, or executive position you desire, the more important is what is known as the "hidden job market." Here's what this term means to you: Even as throngs of people are out there searching the newspaper and the Internet, the job you want is already out there, unadvertised to all but those already in the know.

Ready for an amazing figure? Career placements from print media—and this could include everything from newspaper advertisements and company postings to alumni directories and industry-specific magazines—account for no more than *5 percent* of all new executive jobs!

And here's another: Retainer search firms (not contingency firms) account for *another five percent* of executive job placements.

On the other hand, the "hidden job market" accounts for 90 percent of executive job placements. That's right: *90 percent!*

Effectively working the hidden job market is a matter of utilizing your natural sphere of influence, together with the one you are creating through the networking skills we've been discussing, so that you will be referred to those who can help you find the job you desire.

Through these referrals, you'll meet those who can:

1. Provide you with helpful information;

2. Refer you to the person who will hire you for the position you desire;

3. Hire you for the position you desire.

The rest of this chapter will take you through 10 basic steps for running an effective job-search campaign.

Of course, a significant part of this process is to first determine what it is you want to do, but for our discussion, I'll assume you know that already.

(In fact, this is not always as obvious as it sounds; the days of choosing one career for life are long gone. Identifying a new area in which to work may be an important step here; there are excellent books in the marketplace on that topic.)

1. Understand that this is a full-out campaign.

Accept the following: You own a company, and that company is called, *You, Inc.* You are now assuming the most important position in You, Inc.: Director of Marketing. That's right—you must take full responsibility in this area of your company.

This doesn't mean you won't solicit help from those who have skills you might lack, such as a resume-writer, job-search coach, etc. Or that you won't read and study books on the topic of how to find the job you want and any other ancillary topics you might find helpful to your cause. Of course, you'll do some or all of that. But you are the boss and the one upon whose shoulders the entire campaign rests.

Master the Endless Referrals System® so you'll have the people skills and knowledge regarding how to leverage your relationships and the quality contacts you make, until finally, one of your Personal Walking Ambassadors connects you with the person who either has the right position for you or can lead you to someone else who has.

2. Take the initiative.

According to Nancy Noonan Geffner, former Executive Vice President and a founding director of Right Associates, the world's largest publicly held career transition consulting firm in the world, "It's a mistake to believe that your sphere of influence is such that all your contacts will quickly call you and offer new positions. A focused, active, appropriately aggressive approach is needed. Many people report that their biggest shock was the loss of power once they left the company. In other words, the same people who would quickly take their calls when they were in their former position would no longer even return them."

3. Group the people in your growing job-referral network into A's, B's and C's.

The A's are the people you both already know (and who *know, like, and trust* you) and the people you'll continue to meet (and with whom you'll develop those same kinds of relationships) using the Endless Referrals System®.

The B's are the people to whom you'll be referred, and are the people from whom you're looking to simply receive information, suggestions, ideas, and help.

C's are those who are in a position to hire you.

Typically, A's will introduce you to B's and B's will lead you to C's. A's can also lead you to and/or introduce you to C's.

4. Act with posture.

In letting your A's know what you're looking to accomplish, maintain your posture ("when you care...but not *that* much"). While it's okay to make known your current status and desire to find a job, and even to remind them every so often, bringing it up every time you see them will only cause them to start avoiding you and staying away in droves!

5. Make your requests reasonable.

Let your A's know that, while it would be great if it happened, you are in no way *expecting* them to introduce you to a future employer, but only hoping they might introduce you to people (the B's) who might be able to provide advice.

For example, if you'd like to become involved with medical sales, you might approach those in your current sphere of influence (your A's) and let them know you are interested in this field; then ask, do they know anyone either currently involved in the field or with connections to the field who could perhaps provide you with some advice?

6. Remember thank-you notes!

When you receive a referral from an A to a B, such as in the above example, be sure to immediately send a personalized thank-you note (see Chapter 4) to your A. Remember, everyone likes to feel appreciated; what's more, "Behavior that gets rewarded, gets repeated." Get that letter off to her immediately.

It's also a great idea to send another personalized thank-you note to the A person *after* you meet with the B to thank her once again for the great referral and let her know how kind, receptive, and helpful to you the B truly was.

Incidentally, just because you're not an employee of a particular company doesn't mean you can't have a personal note card. The basic setup remains the same, only it's all personal information instead of company information.

7. Handle these people with care!

Meet your B and handle with class. This might be a person who simply knows the industry, or it might be someone who might one day be a potential employer. Regardless, do not ask this person for any favors, least of all a job. These actions are two of the biggest mistakes you can possibly make in this situation.

According to Nancy Noonan-Geffner, the exact opposite is best. Here's what Nancy says:

Either on the telephone, while setting the appointment, or at the beginning of your face-to-face, say, "Ms. Henderson, thank you so much for agreeing to meet with me. I just want you to know and be assured that I'm not here for, nor do I in any way expect, a job, a position, or a favor of any kind. I learned that you know a lot about the industry and job market and are willing to provide some helpful information. And I appreciate that very much."

As you already know, not only is that simply the "right" approach; it's also the one most likely to actually get you their direct assistance.

And remember, after your meeting, immediately send this person a handwritten note of thanks on your personalized note card. If and when she does refer you to anyone for a job opportunity or more information, be sure to follow up with another handwritten thank-you note. Keep the goodwill and good feelings about you flowing.

8. Know your benefits.

When you are finally introduced to a potential employer, be sure you are prepared to state, *in terms of benefits*, why you would be the right person for the job. In Chapter 6, we learned that a benefit statement lets the other person know the benefit(s) *he* would derive by doing business with you. The same thing applies here. Your potential employer cares not a bit (or, even if he does, it won't matter) that you're running out of savings, feeling bad about yourself for not being employed, or any other reason *you* might want the job. He wants to know how hiring you will benefit *him*. And, that makes sense, doesn't it?

Jeffrey J. Fox (www.foxandcompany.com), author of the magnificent book, *Don't Send A Resume: And Other Contrarian Rules to Help Land a Great Job*, says, "You must create more value than your cost." The former corporate CEO and now multi-best-selling author speaks in terms of "dollarizing," i.e., calculating in dollars and cents what you are worth to your "customer," in this case the company for which you might be hired. Fox explains:

If you can increase sales by $600,000, you are worth some of the profit on that $600,000. If you can reduce scrap and waste by $95,000, you are worth some of the $95,000. If you can reduce bank loan interest by 0.5 percent, you are worth some of that interest savings. The more dollarized value the hiring company sees in you, the higher the probability you will be hired...[your potential] value is created by increasing revenues, reducing costs and innovating new products and services.

Again, as Fox advises, "you must create more value than your cost." And, he warns "...the hiring people are always trying to evaluate each job candidate's potential to create value."

Of course, this is where you will really shine, assuming you have done your homework and carefully prepared. This should be so obvious I haven't actually listed it as a separate step, but it bears pointing out here: Proper preparation for your interview is a valuable skill in and of itself, and Mr. Fox does an expert job of teaching this aspect of the process in his book.

Back to your benefits: You should already know in advance exactly what you bring to the table that will be of benefit to your would-be employer. What can you do for his company, and how will that add value? If you haven't got this clearly articulated in your own mind, you start out with a huge disadvantage, and despite all the wonderful networking you've done in order to earn the interview, you most likely will not get the job.

On the other hand, if you're fully prepared with this information, you're well on your way to landing the position you want.

A final word from Mr. Fox:

Every job can be dollarized. Every job has value. You must carefully consider how the job you want creates value. In your interviews, ask questions and answer questions in such a way that your dollarized value becomes evident...There is only one reason people hire someone, and that reason is to solve a problem. You must uncover that problem, calculate the cost to the organization of not solving the problem, and demonstrate that you are the solution.

And you must be able to communicate this clearly.

Nancy Noonan-Geffner says that not clearly understanding or being able to state exactly what it is you can do that will benefit the company is one of the major reasons a job applicant comes away empty-handed. She often faced this situation, she adds, with the displaced executives she worked with for more than 20 years in New York, and she offers an excellent example of this from a 2001 article in the *New York Post* entitled, "Gore Went West After Strikeout on Street."

The answer to the riddle of why Al Gore joined an obscure California fund is that Wall Street wouldn't hire him. The man who would be President sought in earnest all year to land a top spot with one of the major city firms because he wanted to be in the Big Apple, sources say. But none of Gore's prospective employers, including the big buyout firms and major investment banks, would take him on.

Once source explained that, "Gore couldn't provide a good answer to their question, 'What can you do for us?' " The former V.P. apparently learned a lesson from his strikeout on Wall Street, and approached the California fund with a pitch that would diffuse his lack of business experience."

The lesson here for anyone seeking the position they desire: "Job objectives and goals must be focused, clearly communicated, and—more than anything—of benefit to your would-be employer."

According to Ms. Noonan-Geffner, "The former Vice President could have told his potential employers on Wall Street that he could introduce them to the King of Spain or anyone else they wanted to meet." The big lesson is, relate your experience and skills to the prospective employer's needs. Show how you are a walking solution to their problem.

9. Follow up with all those with whom you interview.

Assuming you want the position, send a personalized thank-you note right away. Continue to follow up as you would with any new prospect, whether a direct prospect or potential referrals source.

Look for information that might be of interest to them. It might be a book on a topic of their interest, or a newspaper or magazine article on same. How would you know this? You may have found out their interests during the interview. Perhaps via an Internet search. Or you asked the person who referred you, or even a secretary during your brief conversation.

And, every so often, send a personalized note card and make an occasional telephone call just to check back.

10. Continue to meet new A's and B's and interview with C's.

You must keep marketing yourself and targeting potential employers. Do not diminish your efforts to let others know of your availability, even though a hot job prospect you may now be in discussion with might look as if it might move to an offer stage. Take nothing for granted until the position is yours.

Remember always the basic premise of this book, the Golden Rule of networking:

All things being equal, people will do business with, and refer business to, those people they know, like, and trust.

In this case, they'll lead you to the right person and the right person will hire you.

It's been proven again and again that the greater your skills are in this area, the shorter the time it will take you to secure the new position you want. Positions are secured by effectively building a referral network that can provide introductions to decision-makers.

Simple, but not necessarily easy—especially without a system. As usual, my suggestion is to not try to shortcut the system—because the system *is* the shortcut.

Key Points

- In today's volatile job market, it makes sense to start building your job-referral network right away, so that it's ready in the future when you might need it.
- Ninety percent of executive placement jobs are filled through what is known as the "hidden job market"—jobs that are filled not through advertising but through private referrals.
- Here are 10 steps for running an effective job-search campaign:
  1. Understand that this is a full-out campaign.
  2. Take the initiative.
  3. Group the people in your growing job-referral networking into A's and B's and C's.
  4. Act with posture.
  5. Make your requests reasonable.
  6. Remember thank-you notes!
  7. Handle these people with care!
  8. Know your benefits.
  9. Follow up with all those with whom you interview.
  10. Continue to meet new A's and B's and interview with C's.

CHAPTER 17

The Foundation of Effective Communication

I'd like to begin this chapter by sharing with you an incident. I believe it is the quintessential example of how easy it is to either get along, or not get along, with others. It shows just how much power each of us truly has to add positively or negatively to our network and to our world.

Here's what happened.

My neighbor Carol, a staff supervisor for a local midsized business, called to invite me to a local dinner theater. As a holiday bonus, her company had decided to send the entire staff to the theater for a night of fine food and entertainment, and Carol invited me to come as her guest.

Because the person with the tickets had not yet arrived, the manager would not let us into the main dining area to sit down and begin eating. Instead, he politely asked us to wait at the bar. Nursing a soft drink, I waited with the rest—when I sensed the first sign of trouble.

Carol announced she was not happy with the situation. She wanted us to begin eating right away so that we'd have plenty of time to enjoy our food. As far as Carol was concerned, the manager knew we were simply waiting for the person with the tickets to arrive, "So why couldn't we just go in there now?" I happened to be in total agreement with Carol, but as a guest, I felt it wasn't my place to say so.

Then Carol said the magic words—the words that told me I was absolutely right to sense trouble. "I'm going to raise a fuss about this!" *Oh no*, I thought. This was supposed to be a fun, relaxing evening.

Carol summoned the manager over and began to verbally assault him. He got stubborn and simply repeated, "Ma'am, it's against the rules. As far as I know, the person with the tickets may want to assign the seats." And every time Carol countered with an insult to his intelligence (or lack thereof), he countered with the same excuse.

I came to an executive decision: enough was enough. When Carol finally took a breath between words, I smiled and politely asked the manager, "Sir, aside from the seating arrangements, would there be any other reason why seating us now would be uncomfortable for you?" He replied, "Not at all."

Praying silently that Carol would not interrupt, which is exactly what I could sense she was thinking of doing, I continued, "I understand exactly how you feel, and in a similar situation I might feel the same way. Let me ask, if we were to assume total responsibility for the seating assignments—in fact, if I could get the staff supervisor herself to agree that you would be totally off the hook—would you consider letting us go in now?"

He responded with a smile and said, "That wouldn't be a problem."

I replied, "Great, because being able to eat our meal without having to hurry would certainly add to our enjoyment of the show. And by the way, I appreciate your help and understanding."

How did he respond? "My pleasure!" As a matter of fact, at that point he personally escorted us to our seats, and continued to check in several times throughout the evening to make sure we were comfortable.

Carol was delighted and amazed. "How did you do that? What's your secret?"

"There is no secret," I answered. "It's simply a philosophy. An attitude and a decision to genuinely care about someone else's needs, so that they in turn *want* to care about yours."

Incidents such as this occur quite often in my life. I'm known as a person who can get people to do things for me that they ordinarily wouldn't do for others. In fact, I wrote a book on this very topic, entitled *Winning Without Intimidation: How to Master the Art of Positive Persuasion.* It teaches how to get what you want from others—even from life's "difficult people"—while allowing them to still feel good about themselves.

The objective is a win-win outcome. And isn't that really what networking is all about?

The principles and methods I teach for pulling off what many see (at first) as the seemingly impossible when it comes to difficult people amount to a learned skill, not some mysterious inborn ability. In other words, it is something that you absolutely can learn. Anyone can.

As far as I'm concerned, I had the very best teacher! There are probably only a few people in the history of the universe who have ever had *natural* people skills to the extent of someone like Dale Carnegie. One was Dale Carnegie himself; another is my dad, Mike Burg.

He is one of the world's greatest natural networkers, one of those rare human beings who, despite his humble beginnings, has helped positively change the lives of many others. With everything I've learned and experienced regarding networking in the business sense, what I've learned about networking in the *human* sense has proven many times as valuable.

As we discuss certain philosophies and principles in this chapter, I'll combine some of the thoughts and lessons I've learned from Dad as well as from other "people experts," both modern and ancient.

Make People Feel Good about Themselves

Probably Dad's greatest strength is his ability to make those with whom he comes into contact feel important as human beings. He accomplishes this, not through manipulation or false compliments, but by genuine caring.

We've touched on this before, starting in Chapter 2, when we discussed Feel-Good Questions® that get people talking about themselves. But this philosophy goes much deeper than that. It's realizing that when we look at a person, what we and the rest of the world see is not necessarily the whole truth.

The business Dad founded and ran was a gymnasium school called the Academy of Physical and Social Development. This was a unique, psycho-dynamically oriented gymnasium school that helped countless individuals and families learn to communicate with each other more effectively. It was based on Dad's philosophy that if you could make a person feel good about himself, he would lead a healthy and productive life. Word got around about the success of the Academy, and this eventually resulted in a *Time* magazine feature story.

While I was growing up, I watched all sorts of people come into the Academy. I'd see a family walk in: the man, big and handsome; the woman, pretty and trim, with an air of confidence; the child, attractive and well-dressed, looking like a million bucks. They looked like the all-American family.

But when you got to know them, you realized that this guy with muscles didn't *feel* so strong, this pretty woman didn't *feel* attractive, and the youngster was not happy being their child. You realized that there was more to this than met the eye, and that only when people feel good about themselves do they actually feel as strong and attractive as they might look, and it's only when they are successful and make their parents happy with them that they feel good about being part of the family.

The Academy had a motto I feel is timeless:

To have a body does not make one a man. To have a child does not make one a parent.

What we see is not always what we get, and we need to approach people as individuals whose lives we can somehow make better by making them feel better about themselves.

Can you see how readily this philosophy relates to networking? After all, what comes to mind when we approach Center of Influence types? They might *appear* to have it all together. We might know they are successful in business and always have lots of friends around them, and may therefore appear to be always happy. Yet, below the surface, things may not be so wonderful.

We don't know what is going on with their family. We don't know what their pressures of business might be. We really don't know what's going on inside their heads.

The truth is, they can probably use some good, positive strokes. And if you give them those strokes in a sincere, genuine way, they are going to be very grateful, simply because it makes them feel good.

This is where confidence comes in. The more confident a person feels, the more she is going to appreciate your coming into her life.

Five Questions of Life

Dad's "mentor" was a first-century Talmudic sage by the name of Simeon ben Zoma, whose philosophy dealt with different states of being and appreciation, as expressed through four basic questions. Dad later added a fifth question, which followed along the same lines.

Question 1: Who Is a Wise Person?

Ben Zoma's answer to this first question was, "One who learns from others."

How many famous quotes and sayings run along these same lines? For example, "We have two ears and only one mouth for a reason." Isn't that true?

When we talk, we must be saying something that we already know (or think we know). Only by listening can we become wiser in whatever situation we happen to be involved.

Let's take, for example, a doctor. A patient comes into her office looking sick. Regardless of her numerous years of education and vast amount of knowledge concerning medicine and the human body, the easiest way to get to the root of the patient's problem is for the doctor to first ask about and *listen* to what the patient describes as symptoms. Only then can she intelligently suggest a particular treatment.

In networking, we can relate this question to that person who actively listens to other people. What do they feel? How do they feel? Why do they feel? What's working in their lives or businesses, and what isn't?

As we find their needs, we know what direction to take with them. If a doctor provides a diagnosis and prescription without first knowing the symptoms, that's malpractice. If we, as networkers, assume we know what a person would like from us and how we can best help him, that's malpractice too! And if we, as salespeople, try to sell a product or service to someone without first knowing his true needs, isn't that the same?

Question 2: Who Is a Mighty Person?

"One who can control his emotions and make of an enemy a friend," says ben Zoma.

This simply means having enough self-control and discipline to take a bad situation and make it work for you.

Imagine approaching someone who isn't particularly friendly or open, and having enough strength or being mighty enough to turn that person to your side. Usually, when we can win people over and turn them in our direction, they turn out to be our biggest supporters.

Abraham Lincoln once said, "I don't like that person—I'm going to have to get to know him better." How many friendships do you have right now that began in a less-than-amiable fashion? If you have one, several or many, you know that those are some of your most rewarding relationships. If you have none, then set a goal to try to turn one "enemy" into a friend. Just one at first. Watch what happens. I assure you, the results will be habit-forming.

Question 3: Who Is a Rich Person?

According to ben Zoma, "A truly rich person is one who rejoices in his lot." In other words, somebody who is happy with himself, somebody who really feels good enough about his life and lifestyle that he can be a pretty complete or contented person.

Of course, the standard response to that question from most people is, "Someone who has money." And certainly there's nothing wrong with having money. It's just that money, in and of itself, can only make a person wealthy and open the door to more choices. But it can't make one genuinely rich.

In relation to networking, this would translate into a person who appreciates and enjoys the individuals in her network, even if not yet receiving immediate referrals from those people.

Question 4: Who Is an Honored Person?

Ben Zoma says, "One who honors others." In other words, one who makes others feel good about themselves is himself an honored person.

In networking, this means liking and caring about your networking prospects enough so that they feel it. They will in turn honor you.

Here's a good practice exercise: Next time you are at a social or business function, begin introducing people to each other. Have a one-sentence, complimentary statement about everyone you introduce. As you *honor* everyone you introduce (even by simply taking the time to make the introduction), watch how you become the hit of the function. It works every time.

Question 5: Who Is a Brave Person?

This question is my father's, and so is the answer: "A brave person is one who is smart enough to be afraid and still do their job." According to Dad:

> *I've met a lot of people, both during the war and outside of the service, who were willing to physically fight it out. Although they were willing to go into battle, so to speak, to do things others might not do, they really did not have the sense of appreciation for themselves. They weren't scared because they didn't have a reason to be scared. They didn't know enough to be scared. They didn't have anything to be scared about.*
>
> *While you have to give these people credit for what they do, it's the person who has real feelings about being scared and goes ahead anyway, trying to accomplish what he or she set out to do, who deserves a real pat on the back.*

What does this mean in relation to networking? Simply this: It is the true networker who, though smart enough to recognize potential rejection, still reaches out to give of herself.

Truth, Justice, Peace, and Love

Four ingredients that add to a successful networking recipe are truth, justice, peace, and love. Although my feelings about these four could be argued semantically, you'll see where the philosophies fit into the style of the successful networker we've been looking at throughout this book.

Truth

While "truth" itself is not subjective, one's personal belief of what the truth is in any specific situation is often *very* subjective. What is vital to realize is that knowing what is the truth (or the "correct" way of doing things) in your own mind doesn't necessarily mean that the person you're dealing with sees the truth in the same way. And unless you are transacting with someone who can communicate in a positive way, if you proceed as though your interpretation of the truth *is* the truth, a lack of communication or negative communication will be the result. The hostile feelings or misunderstandings that will come along with this will not work to the benefit of any of the parties concerned.

My friend and fellow speaker Jim Cathcart, author of *Relationship Selling*, explains what he calls the Platinum Rule (which is also the title of a book written by Tony Alessandra). The Golden Rule, of course, is "Do unto others as you would have them do unto you." According to Jim (and Tony), the Platinum Rule is, "Do unto others as *they* want to be done unto."

In other words, just because we see the perfect business relationship being a certain way and following certain rules or procedures, that doesn't mean the other person feels the same way. What is the truth? As far as I'm concerned, if we want a positive business relationship with another person, we must try to see the truth from *that person's* point of view.

This should not be confused with capitulating or necessarily changing our minds, but rather doing our best to understand where they're coming from.

Justice

This is maturity. It's the ability to say, "Hey, I'm wrong. I can do something about it, and I *will* do something about it. I will change." In networking we must be able to admit when we are wrong. So many confrontations occur and continue unresolved because of the parties' inability to admit shortcomings, when admitting those shortcomings would only make the person more of a hero in the other person's eyes.

Peace

Peace comes about when there is comfort and a lack of stress in dealing with people. In a state of peace, you're not afraid to say things to others; you're not under pressure, because if there is any kind of misunderstanding about the truth, you will be able to work it out. People are willing to deal with the justice that accompanies understanding. In networking, peace results from two or more people having a mutual respect.

Love

This means putting the other person ahead of yourself. The other person becomes more important to you than you are. In networking, realistically, we don't love our networking prospects as we love our own families, but we care about them, their families, and their needs, which in turn will influence them to have good feelings about us.

From what I've experienced, putting another person's needs ahead of our own seems to be a struggle few are able to overcome. Too many people approach others with this question foremost in their minds: "How does doing that benefit me?"

I can only say that the successful networkers I know, the ones who receive tons of referrals and feel truly happy about themselves, continually put the other person's needs ahead of their own.

In fact, that is so crucial to the whole message of this book, it bears repeating:

> *The successful networkers I know, the ones who receive tons of referrals and feel truly happy about themselves, continually put the other person's needs ahead of their own.*

Do You Network as a Parent, Adult, or Child?

In the best-selling book *Games People Play*, author Eric Berne, often credited with being the father of transactional analysis, points out three distinct personality states: Adult, Parent, and Child. These are states we each may take on and display in different situations, depending on what we are feeling at that point in time. The following is my paraphrased explanation of these three states and how they relate to networking.

The Child in all of us is the victim. He or she feels like a baby, put down, blamed, punished, controlled. As a result, the person is angry and looking to get even. And usually the Child wants to get even with the person who assumes the Parent role.

The Parent in all of us is usually a victim of our own upbringing, biases, and environment. People in the Parent role mean well; they just don't recognize negative communication. They don't realize that they're putting somebody down. They don't realize that they're making somebody feel bad.

The Adult in all of us, which is the ideal, is the negotiator, the communicator—the respectful, honest, active listener who's trustworthy and just. This is someone you would just love doing business with.

Isn't it a fact that we have all three of these situations in the networking process?

There are people who talk down to us. They are the Parent, and they make us the Child. In this situation, we have to know that it's not something to take personally; we simply have to bring ourselves up to the Adult level. At the same time, we have to make sure we don't come across as the Parent talking down to them as the Child, but as Adult to Adult.

It's also important to keep in mind that you can't expect prospects to act like adults just because *you* know how to. So don't feel put down if they don't respond that way. I realize this is easier said than done. The way to overcome that is to make a game out of it. Be aware, the next time you are in a negative transaction, and see if you can shift the dynamic of the transaction and win the game. Of course, you don't win by emotionally *beating* that person, but by *building* that person to an Adult level, in order to match the level to which you have risen.

Networking Disciplines

Networking discipline says that if you don't abide by networking principles, you won't get all the referrals you are capable of getting. If you do, you will get those referrals—lots and lots of them. Let's number the seven networking disciplines right down the line:

First, get the necessary knowledge needed to effectively network. Review the principles, methods, techniques, and strategies you've learned throughout this book until you really know them, because the more you practice, the better you are going to feel and the more effective you're going to be. The same goes for other books you read and audio programs you listen to.

Second, place yourself in front of potential networking prospects. Understand that you can have fear and anxiety and still be brave enough to do it and be effective. We all have trepidations when going into a room full of people we don't know. And we've all experienced rejection and don't enjoy the feeling. Despite this, we can succeed. Realize that the more you practice, the easier it is to face any new situation. Also know that the more new situations you face, the less intimidating they become.

Third, be wise by learning from others, especially your networking prospects, and learn how you can help *them*.

Fourth, give referrals without any emotional demand. Help the others in your network without expecting any immediate payback. Don't look for a "shake" just because you're being effective and good about your actions.

Fifth, speak with tact. This is so important! Tact is the language of strength. If we could listen on tape to what we say in everyday conversations, we might be amazed at the lack of tact and sensitivity in the way we sometimes relate to others. There's a great deal of truth in the saying, "You can catch more flies with honey than you can with vinegar." Make an agreement with yourself to analyze the way you talk to others for just 21 days. Watch your improvement every day and take pleasure in your improvement.

Sixth, allow yourself to be rewarded with endless referrals after showing persistence. Follow through in gratitude.

And seventh, realize that discipline and networking are nothing more than learning how to benefit from being the "boss of yourself" so you may constructively help and influence others. Only *you* can determine how you are going to handle an individual person or situation. By being the boss of yourself, you control the situation and your own success while adding positively to those whose lives you touch. As Dad says, "We are ideally put on earth to help others." And as we help others, we eventually and invariably help ourselves.

Regardless of what you are used to doing or the way you presently handle conflicts, effective communication is a *skill you can learn.* Speaker and author Anthony Robbins says, "Your past does not equal your future." No matter what your shortcomings in communicating and networking with others have been, you can use the principles and methods presented in this book to begin developing a powerful network of contacts.

The story I began this chapter with, the one about how my neighbor Carol was looking for a fight with the theater manager, contains a valuable lesson for the networker. How can you use that as a guide for turning potential lemons into lemonade—or potential enemies into friends?

Living your life from a perspective of strength is a lot more fun and rewarding. Do we need to continually work at this in order to become ever more effective? Yes! And it's worth it.

Key Points

- Whenever possible, make others feel good about themselves.
- People are not always what they seem to be.
- To have a body does not make one a man. To have a child does not make one a parent.
- These are the five questions of life:
  1. *Who is a wise person?* One who learns from others.
  2. *Who is a mighty person?* One who can control his emotions and make of an enemy a friend.
  3. *Who is a rich person?* One who appreciates his lot.
  4. *Who is an honored person?* One who honors others.
  5. *Who is a brave person?* One who is smart enough to be afraid and still do their job.
- The four key ingredients in a successful networking recipe are truth, justice, peace, and love.
- The successful networkers I know, the ones who receive tons of referrals and feel truly happy about themselves, continually put the other person's needs ahead of their own.
- We each display three personality states:
  1. *The Child:* The Child feels like the victim, like a baby—put down, blamed, punished, controlled.
  2. *The Parent:* The Parent means well but is domineering and controlling.
  3. *The Adult:* The Adult is the ideal—the negotiator, the communicator, win-win–oriented.
- There are seven networking disciplines:
  1. Acquire knowledge.

2. Place yourself in front of potential networking prospects.
3. Be wise by learning from others—especially your networking prospects. Learn how you can help them.
4. Give unrequited referrals. Help others in your network without expecting an immediate payback.
5. Be tactful. Tact is the language of strength.
6. Allow yourself to be rewarded with endless referrals after showing persistence. Follow through in gratitude.
7. Realize that discipline and networking are nothing more than learning how to benefit from being the "boss of yourself" so that you can constructively help and influence others to network. We are ideally put on earth to help others. And of course, as we help others we invariably help ourselves.

CHAPTER 18

Networking: Begin Now

It is one of the most beautiful compensations of life that no one can sincerely try to help another without helping himself. — Ralph Waldo Emerson

Isn't this statement a great summation of what we've been discussing throughout this entire book? Regardless of whether it's working a crowd or networking in a one-on-one situation, positioning yourself through the media, asking questions, having better follow-up than anybody else, running your own organized networking group, or just helping others succeed in their businesses, the more you do for the benefit of others, the more successful you will be.

What never stops fascinating me is the fact that those people who give the most of themselves to others, without demanding anything in return, seem to get back many times over what they give. Truly successful networkers consistently do the little things right, knowing that they will eventually reap the harvest from the seeds they are planting.

But there's one more thing to keep in mind, as well.

Throughout this book you've been exposed to principles, strategies, and methods that can and will account for a dramatic increase in both your personal happiness and financial earnings—but only if you take the information and apply it!

How often has it been noted that "knowledge without action is the same as having no knowledge at all"? To succeed in your quest for endless referrals, you must take the information you have learned (The Endless Referrals System®) and begin applying it to your life right now!

Unfortunately, many people read a book such as this as though it were a novel, skimming through, finding some ideas interesting, maybe even saying to themselves, "One of these days I'm going to use that idea," but they never actually get around to it. These are the "as soon as" people.

You know the type: really nice, well-intentioned people. Unfortunately, they are always in the process of "getting ready." They're "going to" do something based on future, unrelated events that may take place...some day.

For example, "I'm going to learn the 10 Feel-Good Questions® *as soon as* the kids start the school year." Or, "I'll develop a benefit statement *as soon as* the next sales contest starts." (Wouldn't it make more sense to start now, so that the benefit statement is internalized *before* the contest begins?!)

Unfortunately, and all too often, such an attitude is directly reflected in the size of their paycheck.

I can't stress enough how important it is to jump-start your newfound knowledge into action *now*. Go back to the beginning and read this book through again...and again. Use a highlighter. Stop, as you're reading a particular point, and think of examples of what you've just read that might have shown up in your own life. See, hear, and feel yourself picking up new ideas each time through, while strengthening and internalizing others at the same time.

Skip around to different chapters, seeking information for particular projects and needs. Study and internalize the various questions, principles, methods, techniques, and skills. Do you want to focus on working a crowd? Then go to Chapter 3. Looking to position yourself as an expert through the various media? Turn to Chapter 9. Need a review of Attraction Marketing? There's Chapter 14.

I'm so excited for you!

Based on the amount of calls, letters, and e-mails I receive from my seminar attendees all over North America, as well as those who own my CD audio programs and subscribe to my weekly e-zine newsletter, I know that people are applying this system with incredible success. You can do it too! Will the payoff be immediate? Maybe, maybe not. Will you do everything perfectly the first time out? Probably not. I'm still learning myself. (When the day actually arrives that I think I'm doing it all perfectly, I'll *really* begin to worry!)

The point is this: Begin! Begin right away!

And stick with it. If you get knocked down, get back up. If you get knocked down again, get back up again. And by the way, you *will* get knocked down—and will get knocked down again.

The fact is, we all get knocked on our rear ends from time to time. But we don't lose as a result of getting knocked down—only as a result of *staying* down.

The following passage was shared with me from as early as I can remember by my Dad. It was given to him by one of his customers and is excerpted from a poem by Edmund Vance Cooke. I'd like to share it with you:

You are beaten to Earth.
Well, well, what's that?
Come up with a smiling face.
It's nothing against you to fall down flat,
But to lie there, that's disgrace.

The harder you're thrown
Why, the higher you'll wish you bounce;
Be proud of your blackened eye!
It isn't the fact that you're licked that counts;
It's how did you fight…and why?

As long as we keep our *why*, our dream, our reason for doing in mind, we'll overcome anything in our way and proceed until we eventually overcome and conquer. As Dexter Yager, one of the most successful businessmen in the world, is often quoted as saying, "If the dream is big enough, the facts don't count." Do whatever it takes to stay in the race.

Among my favorite self-motivators is a poem authored by a very successful man. I'm sure you've heard it before. It's entitled, "Persistence," and it reads as follows:

Persistence
Nothing in the world can take the place of persistence.
Talent will not; nothing is more common than unsuccessful people with talent.
Genius will not; unrewarded genius is almost a proverb.
Education will not; the world is full of educated derelicts.
The slogan "Press On" has solved and always will solve the problems of the human race.
—Calvin Coolidge

My suggestion is to be persistent. Do the little things right, do them consistently, and realize that selling, networking, and life itself are all simply a numbers game.

Of course, when following proven principles, the numbers seem to get a lot better!

Remember, learn the Endless Referrals System®, apply it immediately, and be persistent, and you *will* network your everyday contacts into sales.

Index

About the Author

Bob Burg, president of Burg Communications, Inc., is a professional speaker and consultant on the topics of communication skills and business networking. A former television news anchor, salesman, and sales manager, he is a much sought after keynote speaker for major corporations, associations, and sales organizations throughout North America. He lives and works in Jupiter, Florida.

Special Bonus

A Resource Section You Can Use Continually in Your Journey for Endless Referrals!

Rather than simply listing many of his favorite books and other resources, Bob wanted to provide you with a dynamic tool that you could use on an ongoing basis.

Please visit **www.Burg.com/Resources.html** to access this comprehensive listing of books, CDs, DVDs, software, web sites and other valuable tools that will greatly assist you in developing your business based on *Endless Referrals*.

Make Sure To Visit Bob's Bonus Online Resource Section